AVODAH

The Penn State Library of Jewish Literature

An Anthology of Ancient Poetry *for* Yom Kippur

Edited and Translated by

Michael D. Swartz & Joseph Yahalom

Library of Congress Cataloging-in-Publication Data

Avodah: ancient poems for Yom Kippur /
edited by Michael D. Swartz and Joseph Yahalom.
　p　cm. – (Penn State library of Jewish literature)
Includes bibliographical references and index.
ISBN 978-0-271-05854-2 (pbk : alk. paper)
1. Avodah piyyutim – Translations into English.
2. Yom Kippur – Liturgy – Texts.
3. Judaism – Liturgy – Texts.
I. Swartz, Micjael D. II. Yahalom, Joseph. III. Series.

BM670.A73S83 2005
296.4'52 – de22
2005002648

Copyright © 2005 The Pennsylvania State University
All rights reserved

Printed in the United States of America
Published by The Pennsylvania State University Press,
University Park, PA 16802-1003

The Pennsylvania State University Press is a member
of the Association of American University Presses.

It is the policy of The Pennsylvania State University
Press to use acid-free paper. This book is printed on
stock that meets the minimum requirements of American
National Standard for Information Sciences—
Permanence of Paper for Printed Library Materials,
ANSI Z39.48–1992.

CONTENTS

PREFACE	IX
INTRODUCTION	1
1. Atah Barata	43
2. Shivʿat Yamim	53
3. Atah Konanta ʿOlam Me-Rosh	69
4. Az be-ʾEn Kol	95
5. Azkir Gevurot Elohah	221
6. Atah Konanta ʿOlam be-Rov Ḥesed	291
7. Emet Mah Nehedar	343
8. En Lanu Kohen Gadol	349
CONCLUSION	367
BIBLIOGRAPHY	373
GLOSSARY	381
SOURCE INDEX	383
SUBJECT INDEX	389

In memory of Aaron Mirsky

איזו היא עבודה שבשמחה ובטוב לבב? הוי אומר זה שירה
(בבלי ערכין יא א)

PREFACE

THIS VOLUME IS the result of our mutual interest in the Avodah piyyutim and our conviction that these compositions are significant not only for the history of Hebrew literature but also for the history of Judaism in late antiquity. In 1996, Joseph Yahalom published the anonymous piyyut *Az be-ʾEn Kol*, an edition of a previously unknown, monumental Avodah composition with an introduction on the history and significance of the genre. During this time, Michael Swartz had begun work on a study of ideas of sacrifice in post-biblical Judaism in which the Avodah piyyutim would play a pivotal role. When we learned of our common research interests, we decided to collaborate on an anthology and translation of early Avodah piyyutim. We decided on a format that would allow readers to understand the intricate network of allusions, biblical phrases, and expressions that characterize this genre. We also decided that the Hebrew texts of the piyyutim should be placed on facing pages with the English translations and that new texts of the piyyutim would be prepared.

We then set about finding a publisher that would be willing to take on the challenge of making this complex volume a reality. We were very fortunate to find enthusiastic advocates of this project at Penn State University Press. Peter Potter, editor-in-chief of the Press, was eager to show us how it could be done and has shepherded the volume to production with intelligence, grace, and extraordinary patience. The editors of the Penn State Library of Jewish Literature, Professors Baruch Halperin and Aminadav Dikman, have also been supportive of this book from the beginning. Special credit also goes to Keith Monley, who as copyeditor contributed immensely by saving us from countless errors and awkward turns of phrase, charging us to be consistent in our discussions and references, and helping us turn this into a readable book. The book was also proofread by M. Novick and Y. Septimus, two Yale University graduate students. Dr. Raphael Posner in Jerusalem, working with Jennifer Norton at Penn State Press, undertook the task of typesetting the Hebrew and English texts and likewise contributed considerably to its accuracy and design. Professors Dick Davis of Ohio State

University, Abraham Holtz of the Jewish Theological Seminary of America, and Norman Bronznick of Rutgers University gave valuable advice on general and specific topics related to this volume, as did Natalie Dohrman at the University of Pennsylvania and Peter Cole in Jerusalem.

This project has also received a great deal of support from institutions and individuals, to whom our gratitude is due. The book was supported by a publication subvention from the Ohio State University College of Humanities as well as research grants from the College of Humanities, the Melton Center for Jewish Studies and the Office of International Studies at the Ohio State University, and a Fulbright-Hays Fellowship for research in Israel.

We dedicate this book to the late Professor Aaron Mirsky, who was a pioneer in the field of piyyut, and who published the Avodah piyyutim of the earliest known liturgical poet, Yose ben Yose. He was one of the first scholars to show how the poetic and mythic dimensions of the Avodah piyyutim could contribute to our knowledge of late antique Judaism.

SIGLA

For the English translations:
[   ]   lacuna in the manuscripts
[xxx]   text restored or emended
(xxx)   text added for clarification
{xxx}   text restored from another manuscripts

For the Hebrew edition:
<…>   lacuna in the manuscripts
<xxx>   text restored or emended
[xxx]   emendation in the manuscript
{xxx}   text struck out in manuscript

INTRODUCTION

EVERY YEAR ON Yom Kippur, the Day of Atonement, in synagogues around the world, congregations recall the biblical sacrifice of purification and expiation that formed the basis for the original Yom Kippur. This recollection takes the form of a service known as the Avodah, designated by the Hebrew term for sacrificial worship. In this service, the prayer leader describes the sacrifice in detail, but not before recounting the history of the world from creation to the erection of the Tabernacle. The text of the service is a long liturgical poem. Within this poem the leader repeats a confession that, according to the ancient rabbis, was recited by the high priest in the sanctuary. When he does this, he and the congregation prostrate themselves to the floor, reciting a doxology that was to be recited on hearing the name of God.

This service, with its unusual prostrations, its detailed discourse on sacrifice, and its historical sweep, is unique in the liturgy of the synagogue. To modern Jews, it has been the subject of attraction and consternation. The great twentieth-century Jewish philosopher Franz Rosenzweig seems to have been so moved by the power of the Yom Kippur liturgy that he revoked his decision to convert to Christianity;[1] yet the Reform movement found any mention of the sacrificial system in the synagogue liturgy deeply disturbing and controversial.[2] Today, messianically oriented sects of Jews pay serious attention to its details, publishing High Holy Day prayer books that emphasize this aspect of the liturgy, illustrated with speculative renderings of the Temple and its service.[3]

The Avodah service goes back to the early days of the synagogue, to the first few centuries after the destruction of the Temple in Jerusalem in 70 C.E. It is an integral part of the lost literature of the ancient

---

1. Nahum N. Glatzer, "Franz Rosenzweig: The Story of a Conversion," *Judaism* 1 (1952): 69–79; see 73.

2. Cf. Abraham Geiger's remarks quoted in Jakob J. Petuchowski, *Prayerbook Reform in Europe: The Liturgy of European Liberal and Reform Judaism* (New York: World Union for Progressive Judaism, 1968), 166–67.

3. *Maḥzor ha-Miqdash* (Jerusalem: Temple Institute, 1995–97).

synagogue known as *piyyut*. This complex and fascinating poetry was once sung in synagogues in Palestine during the classical age of the Talmuds and Midrash, from the fourth and seventh centuries.

Although it was often suppressed by generations of rabbis, its ornamental beauty and its deep exploration of sacred stories ensured its popularity for centuries. This literature, which produced dozens of poets and thousands of compositions before the rise of Islam, was barely known to us until the discovery of the Cairo Genizah, a treasury of discarded medieval Jewish manuscripts, at the end of the nineteenth century. It could be argued that the discovery of this literature is in fact second only in importance among discoveries of Hebrew literary texts to that of the Dead Sea Scrolls for our understanding of ancient Judaism, for it preserves linguistic forms, myths, and ways of thinking that we would not have known from Talmudic literature.

In the Middle Ages, this type of liturgical poetry was not always received with enthusiasm. In the Talmudic academies of Babylonia in the eighth and ninth centuries, the rabbinic authorities Yehudai Gaon and Pirqoi ben Baboi attempted to legislate against the inclusion of piyyut in the liturgy, arguing that it was forbidden to add one word to the statutory service.[4] Their efforts, however, met with limited success, and piyyut continued to flourish even in the Babylonian Jewish liturgy and its Middle Eastern and European successors. In the modern period as well, piyyut was criticized for its length and obscurity, and many piyyutim were expunged from daily services in most Western congregations.[5]

The Avodah poems, a complex genre that includes myth, ritual, and biblical exegesis, can teach us much about the ways ancient Jews understood sacrifice, sacred space, and sin. They are also yield a rich trove of myths and symbols not found in the conventional rabbinic sources such as the Talmuds and Midrash. They contain details about the ancient Temple known to ancient historians such as Josephus and to authors of the biblical Apocrypha but not to the Talmudic authorities. Moreover, they constitute important evidence for the social and cultural diversity of ancient Palestine, while reflecting the concerns of the priesthood in an age dominated by rabbis. They are also valuable as

---

4. For an overview, see Lawrence A. Hoffman, *The Canonization of the Synagogue Service* (Notre Dame, Ind.: Notre Dame University Press, 1979), 66–71.

5. Petuchowski, *Prayerbook Reform*, 122, 155, and elsewhere; cf. note 38 below.

coherent statements in the trajectory of biblical interpretation. Above all, these compositions rise to the level of fine literature. They are the products of great literary effort, continue and extend the tradition of biblical parallelism, and give evidence to the aesthetic sensibilities of the Mediterranean in late antiquity.

The historical importance of this genre lies in one of the central problems in the history of Judaism. In biblical and Hellenistic times the Jerusalem Temple was considered to be the locus for the Potent Presence of God, which was said to descend on the holy of holies when invoked by the high priest at Yom Kippur.[6] It was the attainment of purification and the attraction of this Presence, and not only atonement, that lay at the heart of Yom Kippur. The loss of that Temple therefore meant the absence of that Presence from the world. The rabbis of the first centuries C.E. assured the people that prayer, study of Torah, and performance of the commandments were effective substitutes for Temple sacrifice. But the influence of the Temple and its ritual lived on, in the study of Talmudic tractates relating to sacrificial worship and in poetic evocations of the ancient rites. These were strategies for coping with the loss of the sanctuary in an age when most Greco-Roman communities practiced some form of sacrifice.

The Avodah piyyutim form a central corpus for understanding this problem. These poems, epic in scope, begin with extensive poetic descriptions of the creation of the world and the patriarchs of humanity, and wend their way through Israel's sacred history to the establishment of the sacrificial cult. At that point they describe in lavish detail the process by which the high priest prepares for the sacrifice, dons his ceremonial vestments, and offers up the bull and goat, a sacrifice whose culmination is the triumphant news that Israel has been forgiven.

This volume is an anthology of the Avodah compositions accompanied by a translation. It begins with the simplest, a prose retelling of the rabbinic narration of the sacrifice (*Shiv'at Yamim*) and its poetic preamble, *Atah Barata*, includes several Avodah poems—among them the masterpieces *Az be-'En Kol*, the most comprehensive such composition, and *Azkir Gevurot* by the seminal poet Yose ben Yose—and con-

---

6. On this concept, see Baruch A. Levine, "The Presence of God in Biblical Religion," in *Religions in Antiquity: Essays in Memory of E. R. Goodenough*, ed. Jacob Neusner (Leiden: Brill, 1968), 71–87; idem, *In the Presence of the Lord* (Leiden: Brill, 1974); and idem, *The JPS Torah Commentary: Leviticus* (Philadelphia: Jewish Publication Society, 1989).

cludes with a lament for Israel's lost sanctuary. In our presentation of this material we shall demonstrate why the Avodah held such fascination for generations of ancient Jews.

AFTER THE TEMPLE

According to ancient Israelite religion, in order for the Presence of God to appear in the Temple, the sanctuary had to be rid of all ritual impurity.[7] Yom Kippur, the Day of Atonement, provided the community an opportunity not only to atone for its sins but to cleanse the Temple of physical impurity. On that day only, the high priest, clad in white linen, entered the innermost sanctuary, the holy of holies, with his offer of incense and his prayers on behalf of the nation. It was believed that if the purification and incense rituals were carried out properly and the nation was deserving, the Presence of God would descend on the holy of holies.

In Jewish cultic theology, therefore, the loss of that Temple meant the loss of that Presence to the world. With no sacrifices and no physical sanctuary, the annual appearance of the Divine on earth was no longer to be. That this idea persisted well beyond the first century is attested by a poetic passage in a fifth-century homiletic composition known as Pesiqta de-Rav Kahana describing how the divine presence, the Shekhinah, ascended in ten stages when the Temple was destroyed:

> From the ark cover to the cherub;
> From the cherub to the threshold of the house;
> From the Temple building to the two cherubim;
> From the two cherubim to the roof of the sanctuary;
> …

And so on, finally upward.[8]

The tragedy of that destruction and the crisis it created were thus not simply physical but theological. The Babylonian Talmud paints a portrait of groups of first-century ascetics who abstained from meat and wine in mourning for the Temple.[9] Centuries later, groups known as the

---

7. Levine, *Presence of the Lord*.
8. See Pesiqta de-Rav Kahana 13:11 (ed. Mandelbaum, pp. 234–35) (= Buber 114b); cf. Midrash Ekhah (ed. Buber) Petiḥta 25 (fols. 15a–b); Avot de-Rabbi Natan A (ed. Schechter) ch. 34 (p. 102); b. Rosh Hashanah 31a.
9. B. Baba Batra 60b.

Mourners of Zion developed an ascetic regimen on this basis. The apocryphal Book of Baruch reflects the response of apocalyptic communities that saw the cataclysm as a challenge to their eschatological expectations. The centuries following the destruction of the Temple also saw the rise of the leading rabbis, scholars who needed no priestly pedigree but derived their authority from their mastery of Torah. For the rabbis, the proper substitute for sacrifice was not to be found in the concept of sacred space, but in sacred actions. Yoḥanan ben Zakkai, one of the founders of the rabbinic movement, is said to have declared, "We have another means of atonement, effective as Temple sacrifice. It is deeds of lovingkindness."[10] Other statements assert that the study of sacrificial law, enshrined in the Mishnah and related sources, was equivalent to the performance of those sacrifices.[11] Prayer in the synagogue was also considered to be a form of sacrifice: A famous rabbinic statement declares prayer to be "the sacrifice in the heart" (*Avodah ba-Lev*).[12] According to the Palestinian Talmud, when a prayer leader was called upon to begin the prayer service, the congregation would call, "Perform our sacrifice."[13] A Palestinian midrash interprets Hos 14:3, "instead of bulls we will pay [the offering of] our lips," to refer to prayer.[14]

THE SYNAGOGUE

As it developed over those centuries in Palestine, the synagogue became a major center of culture whose relationship to the vanished Temple was complex. Because, according to ancient Jewish thought, the synagogue was not inhabited by the divine presence, it was never accorded the same status of sacred space as the Temple.[15] At the same time, the synagogue is known in rabbinic literature as the "small sanctuary" (*miqdash meʿat*),

---

10. Avot de-Rabbi Natan A ch. 4 (ed. Schechter, p. 21), B ch. 8 (ibid., p. 22). For a survey of rabbinic statements on sacrifice and the cult, see Naftali Goldstein, "Avodat ha-Qorbanot be-Hagut Ḥazal she-le-Aḥar Ḥurban Bet ha-Miqdash," *Daat* 8 (1982): 29–51; cf. Yakov Genack, "Miṣvat Sukkah ba-Halakhah shel Ḥazal: Ben Bayit le-Miqdash," *Daat* 42 (1999): 283–98.

11. See Goldstein, "Avodat ha-Qorbanot," 31–32, 42–43; Tanḥuma Ṣav 14; b. Megillah 31b; b. Menaḥot 110a.

12. Sifre Deut 41 (ed. Finkelstein, p. 88); y. Berakhot 4:1 (7a); Midrash Tannaim Deut 11:13; b. Taʿanit 2a; Midrash Tehillim 66 (157b).

13. Y. Berakhot 4:4 (8b).

14. Pesiqta de-Rav Kahana pisqa 24 (ed. Mandelbaum, 2:377). Cf. also Rashi to b. Yoma 36b.

15. On the relationship of the synagogue to the Temple, see Steven Fine, *This Holy Place: On the Sanctity of the Synagogue During the Greco-Roman Period* (Notre Dame, Ind.: Notre Dame University Press, 1997); Joan R. Branham, *Sacred Space in Ancient and Early Medieval Architecture* (Cambridge: Cambridge University Press, forthcoming); and idem, "Vicarious Sacrality: Temple Space in

and over several centuries had come to be known as a "holy place" (*atra qadisha*).[16] Furthermore, symbols of the Temple frequently adorned the synagogue's architectural ornaments and mosaic floors. Archaeological sites excavated in Israel in the last century show that the fifth to seventh centuries were a period of great activity in the building of grand synagogues in basilica form and the development of art for them. These sites include magnificent mosaic floors decorated with models of the Holy Ark, menorahs, incense shovels, and other accouterments.

The newly uncovered mosaic from the town of Sepphoris is a particularly rich example of Temple imagery.[17] Its panels depict a wide array of images from Israel's myth and ritual, including the binding of Isaac, the zodiac, and especially the range of offerings in the Temple. Rows three and four of the upper portion of the mosaic apparently depict the ceremony of the consecration of Aaron in Exod 29 and the daily sacrifice as described there and in Num 28. Although most of the figure of Aaron has been destroyed, the remaining fragments show that the mosaic portrayed him decked out in his ritual garments, as described in Exod 29. In fact, we can see the bells and "pomegranates" that adorned the hem of his robe. The panel also shows the laver used in the Temple, the bull sacrificed as a sin offering for the consecration ceremony (Exod 29:10–14),[18] and the first lamb for the daily sacrifice (Exod 29:39).[19] The panel below shows the basket of first fruits as ordained in Deut 26 and described in Mishnah Bikkurim 3:5,[20] the showbread on its table, and the components of the daily sacrifice (Tamid): the oil, the meal, the trumpets blown at the ceremony, and the second sacrificial lamb. All of these

---

Ancient Synagogues," in *Ancient Synagogues: Historical Analysis and Archaeological Discovery*, ed. Dan Urman and Paul V. M. Flesher (Leiden: Brill, 1995), 2:319–45.

16. Fine, *This Holy Place*.

17. On the synagogue and its mosaic, see Ze'ev Weiss and Ehud Netzer, *Promise and Redemption: A Synagogue Mosaic from Sepphoris* (Jerusalem: Israel Museum, 1996), where parallels in rabbinic literature are suggested; for another interpretation of the mosaic and its function in the context of the synagogue, see Steven Fine, "Art and the Liturgical Context of the Sepphoris Synagogue Mosaic," in Eric M. Meyers, *Galilee Through the Centuries: Confluence of Cultures* (Winona Lake, Ind.: Eisenbrauns, 1999), 227–37.

18. Note also that central to Yom Kippur is the sacrifice of a bull as a sin offering; the relationship between the two ceremonies was explored in the Talmuds to chapter 1 of Yoma; cf. also Yisrael Knohl and Shlomo Naeh, "Milu'im ve-Khippurim," *Tarbiz* 62 (1992): 17–44.

19. This and the second lamb in the lower panel are labeled with quotations from this verse and Exod 29:41 in the mosaic.

20. See Weiss and Netzer, *Promise and Redemption*.

images served to remind the worshipers of the historical reality of the Temple.

The synagogue also served as a focus of cultural productivity. In the synagogue, prayer leaders performed a complex liturgy apparently composed of hymns and petitions improvised around legally determined themes and blessings.[21] There too people came to hear sermons, and the liturgical poets practiced their art. The center of rabbinic activity was the academy (*bet midrash*), not the synagogue, although the rabbis were deeply concerned about regulating the synagogue, its physical layout, and its liturgy. Synagogue poetry, then, attests to an identifiable cultural mode, distinct from that reflected in rabbinic literature though intimately related to it.[22]

We have only a rough idea of the social structure of the ancient synagogue. Among the synagogue personnel known to us are the *ḥazan* a functionary whose duties varied over the centuries, ranging from schoolteacher and custodian in the Talmudic period to cantor and composer in the early Middle Ages, and the prayer leader, *shaliaḥ ṣibbur* who represented the community in public worship. In the ancient synagogue there may also have been places of importance reserved for priests, honored guests, and other classes of people, including rabbis. A clue to how the polity of the synagogue developed over time can be found in a remarkable piyyut from a manuscript of the High Holy Day liturgy copied around 900 C.E. The poem is a *reshut*, an introductory composition preceding a key prayer, in which the author asks permission from the congregation to entreat God on their behalf. In this case, the *reshut* precedes an Avodah piyyut, *Eqra be-Garon* ("I Shall Call Out Loudly with My Throat"), by Pineḥas ha-Kohen be-Rabbi Yaʿakov of Kifra, an

---

21. For the liturgy in Talmudic times, see Joseph Heinemann, *Prayer in the Talmud: Forms and Patterns* (Berlin: De Gruyter, 1977); for an overview of the structure of the Jewish liturgy, see Ismar Elbogen, *Jewish Liturgy: A Comprehensive History*, trans. Raymond P. Scheindlin (Philadelphia: Jewish Publication Society; New York: Jewish Theological Seminary of America, 1993), and Jakob J. Petuchowski, "The Liturgy of the Synagogue: History, Structure, and Contents," in *Approaches to Ancient Judaism*, ed. William S. Green (Chico, Calif.: Scholars Press, 1983), 4:1–64.

22. No doubt some synagogues were closer to the rabbinic culture than others; an example is the synagogue at Reḥov, where the mosaics contain direct parallels to rabbinic literature. On this qualification, see Stuart Miller, "The Rabbis and the Non-Existent Monolithic Synagogue," in *Jews, Christians, and Polytheists in the Ancient Synagogue: Cultural Interaction During the Greco-Roman Period*, ed. Steven Fine (London: Routledge, 1999), 57–70. However, even at Reḥov the quotations have to do with cultic matters such as sabbatical law, tithes, and the priestly courses; on the latter, cf. Hanan Eshel, "Shever Ketovet shel K-D Mishmerot ha-Kohanim mi-Naṣrat?" *Tarbiz* 61 (1991): 159–61.

eighth-century poet from Palestine. The passage is notable for its list of classes that make up the congregation:

> I implore the Rock of eternity,
> Who has knowledge of the life[23] of the innocent;
> As I cast my eyes to the heavens,
> I ask permission from the Merciful One.
>
> And so too when I stand before the wise,
> Who hear words from the truthful,
> Who understand words of law:
> I ask permission from the wise.
>
> I look out at the congregation of the noble
> And am fearful of the One who humbles and raises;
> And of those standing behind me and before me as a fence:
> I ask permission from the righteous.
>
> The seed of the faithful,
> Believers, sons of believers,
> Who explore the law and understand:
> I ask permission from priests.
>
> Those who [　　] goodness on my behalf;
> Who are satiated with good teaching and instruction,
> For they attend grace and favor:
> I open my mouth with the permission of Levites.
>
> Those who honor this day and fast,
> and respond, "Holy, holy, holy";
> And teach scripture and Mishnah diligently:
> I open my mouth with permission of *ḥazanim*
>
> Those who are skilled in the subtleties of books,
> Abiding in the shade of the One who dwells in mystery,[24]
> Who sing sweet, pleasant words:
> I open my mouth with permission of scribes.

---

23. Lit., "days."

24. Based on Ps 91:1, interpreted here perhaps as "the Most High dwells in mysteries"; cf. Michael D. Swartz, *Mystical Prayer in Ancient Judaism: An Analysis of Maʿaseh Merkavah* (Tübingen: Mohr, 1992), 150.

Those who eternally elevate the Living One,
Who say prayer before Him,
Who stand before the One who makes mountains:
I open my mouth with permission of those who recite liturgy.

Those who recite the specific and general,[25]
Who sweep behind like water,
Who recite righteousness and justice:
I open my mouth with permission of singers.

Those who lend strong voices in melody,
Let their cry before You be pleasing;
May You consider the melody of my tongue.
I open my mouth with permission of the whole people.

O Almighty, as You forgive treachery;
Listen to my entreaties from above;
Grant me a pure heart that I may speak without fear or
    treachery:
I open my mouth with permission of the entire congregation.[26]

Each two stanzas represent a different category or pair of categories in the synagogue; the first three lines of each describe that category, and the last identifies it explicitly. This poem is also built on a religiously and socially hierarchical structure, with God at the top in the first stanza and the congregation and entire nation in the last two. At the top of the social hierarchy, closest to God, are the sages—the "wise" and "righteous"—who surround the poet like a fence and before whom he trembles. Next come the priests and the Levites, the former being the "believers, sons of believers," in that their office is hereditary. Scribes and *ḥazanim* come next. The *ḥazan* is associated with the scribes and described as one who "teach[es] scripture and Mishnah," two subjects that were taught primarily to children. This is an indication that when

---

25. Referring to the principles by which the Torah is interpreted according to tradition and thus, perhaps, to the midrash embedded in piyyutim.
26. The text appears in facsimile in Joseph Yahalom, *Mahzor Ereṣ Yisrael: Qodeqs ha-Genizah* (Jerusalem: Magnes, 1987), 71–72. The text is edited in Ezra Fleischer, "ʿIyyunim be-Hashpaʿat ha-Yesodot ha-Maqhelatiyim ʿal ʾIṣuvam ve-Hitpathutam shel Suge ha-Piyyuṭ," *Yuval* 3 (1974): 46–47 [Hebrew section]. See also Joseph Yahalom, *Piyyut u-Meṣiʾut ba-Zeman ha-ʿAtiq* (Tel Aviv: Hakibbutz Hameuchad, 1999), 41–42.

this hymn was composed, a significant function of the ḥazan was elementary education.²⁷ Next in the social order comes the payetan himself, who "say[s] prayer," and possibly an accompanying choir of "singers."²⁸ The poet thus places himself in a humble position, close to the people for whom he is a spokesman.

We also have medieval evidence that an author of piyyut (payetan) and performer (*shaliaḥ ṣibbur* or *ḥazan*) could either be one and the same person or two. In letters found in the Cairo Genizah, cantors write to each other of obtaining written copies of particular piyyutim for performance in the synagogue.²⁹ In the thirteenth century, the Spanish poet and musicologist Judah Al-Ḥarizi satirized a cantor whose liturgical poetry suffered from verses that are "broken and contorted, without rhyme or meter," and a choir of "four braying asses who think they are singers."³⁰

After the destruction of the Temple, the main ritual function of the priests was no longer valid. Yet, as we can see from the poem quoted above, they were recognized as a distinct class within the synagogue. What, then, was their status in Palestinian society after 70 C.E.? We know that several rabbis were of priestly descent. Occasionally Talmudic literature, in the course of discussing a matter of cultic law, cites the family memories of individuals whose ancestors served in the Temple.³¹ Rabbinic literature hints at encounters with priestly legislators whose rulings contradicted those of the rabbis.³² More significant, we know of families of priests who migrated to the Galilee and there preserved the clan names and social organization of their preexilic past and claimed the prestige of priestly aristocracy. This fact, as we will see, is significant for understanding the social and cultural context of the Avodah poems.

---

27. On this function of the ḥazan see Hyman I. Sky, *Redevelopment of the Office of Hazzan Through the Talmudic Period* (San Francisco: Mellen Research University Press, 1992), 30-31.

28. See Fleischer, "'Iyyunim." However, according to Yahalom, *Piyyut u-Meṣi'uut*, 41-42, the parallelistic structure of the stanzas, each two standing for one category, makes it less likely that these two stanzas represent separate classes of payetan and chorus.

29. See S. D. Goitein, *Sidre Ḥinukh* (Jerusalem: Hebrew University Press, 1962), 97-103; cf. idem, *A Mediterranean Society: The Jewish Communities of the Arab World as Portrayed in the Documents of the Cairo Geniza* (Berkeley and Los Angeles: University of California Press, 1971), 2:221.

30. Yehudah Al-Ḥarizi, *Taḥkemoni*, ed. Y. Toporowski (Jerusalem: Mossad Harav Kook, 1952), ch. 24, pp. 224-25. See Fleischer, "'Iyyunim," 47.

31. See, for example, y. Yoma 5:6 (42b).

32. See Seth Schwartz, *Josephus and Judaean Politics* (Leiden: Brill, 1990), 96-109, on priests in rabbinic literature; see 106-7 on the possibility of priestly courts.

POETS AND PRIESTS

Late antiquity saw the rise of a new aesthetic, in which ornamentation was prized over classical proportion and lavish description characterized literary value. Michael Roberts, describing this aesthetic in late Latin poetry, calls this the Jeweled Style.[33] Roberts argues that in that period, the goal of the arts was to dazzle the reader or viewer with the interplay of details rather than to express an elegant whole. As he puts it, "Late antique taste did not tolerate the plain and the unadorned; brilliance of effect, the play of contrasting colors, is all."[34] In his view, this aesthetic is not confined to poetry but can be found in the arts and literary criticism. As a result, late Latin poetry abounds in artfully composed lists of distinct parts and what was known as *leptologia*, the lavish description of details in the course of a poem or narrative.

So too, during this period, while synagogues were being adorned with fine mosaic and stonework, the synagogue service itself was being adorned with an increasingly ornamental style of liturgical poetry. This poetry, called *piyyut*, a term derived from the Greek *poiētēs*, sought to impress the listener with its deep knowledge of biblical and midrashic exegesis, its innovative use of language, and its rhythm and assonance.

This genre of poetry began as embellishments to the established liturgical order. The earliest examples stayed relatively close to the themes and language prescribed by the liturgy, lacked rhyme, and used only the simplest rhythm. Neither were the earliest piyyutim characterized by the dense allusiveness, or metonymy, that came to be the hallmark of the genre. In the course of time piyyut developed distinctive forms, each with its own themes and set of structural and prosodic rules. The poems became longer and more complex, eventually adding rhyme and delighting in alliteration, recondite references, and intellectual puzzles. Eventually too the poets began to sign their names to the compositions in acrostics. The first poet known to us by name, Yose ben Yose, is represented in this volume with two important and influential compositions, *Azkir Gevurot Elohah* and *Atah Konanta ʿOlam be-Rov Ḥesed*. The classical period of piyyut was reached in the sixth to eighth centuries, when the poets Yannai, Shimeon bar Megas, Eleazar ben Qallir,

---

33. Michael Roberts, *The Jeweled Style: Poetry and Poetics in Late Antiquity* (Ithaca: Cornell University Press, 1989).
34. Ibid., 118.

and Pineḥas ha-Kohen wrote hundreds of intricate compositions based on the lectionary cycle and for the daily and seasonal liturgies, festive occasions, and times of personal and national mourning.

The most distinctive feature of piyyut, beginning with the age of Yose ben Yose and especially in the classical period, is the use of metonymy, known in Hebrew as *kinnui*. This technique, which may have its roots in biblical parallelism, involves substituting a word or phrase, usually based on scriptures, for a name or thing. Thus in *Az be-ʾEn Kol*, Moses is referred to as the Stutterer in light of Exod 4:10–11, in which Moses professes a speech impediment. Often, these are based on midrashic exegeses and stories known to the poet and audience. Thus in *Az be-ʾEn Kol* the Temple is called "that which is entirely beautiful," based not only on the Psalm's designation of Zion as such (Ps 50:2) but on an exegesis of that verse in the Tosefta (t. Kippurim 2:15) that sees the Temple as the place on which is founded the entire world's beauty.[35] So too the term "gauze," which Yose ben Yose uses for heaven in *Azkir Gevurot*, based on Isa 40:22, is also found in the Babylonian Talmud (b. Shabbat 104a). Sometimes, however, a more direct form of metonymy, not based on scripture, is used. Thus in *Az be-ʾEn Kol* the word "eyelids" stands for "eyes," and the expression "his ankles came early" stands for "his feet hastened."[36]

To modern ears, accustomed to a poetic ideal in which ideas and emotions are expressed through simple eloquence, this technique might seem artificial and forced. Many scholars have noted that a high level of education in biblical and rabbinic literature is required for full comprehension and appreciation of most piyyutim. And indeed, in the Middle Ages, once this technique had developed to a high level of intricacy, the great Spanish Hebrew poets, such as the twelfth-century poet and commentator Abraham ibn Ezra, criticized payetanim such as Eleazar ben Qallir for sacrificing meaning for artifice.[37] In modern times even harsher critiques were made.[38] Yet there is every indication that piyyut was a popular genre in ancient and early medieval synagogues. If this

---

35. For a list of *kinnuim* in the poetry of Yose ben Yose, see Aaron Mirsky, *Piyyute Yose ben Yose*, 2nd ed. (Jerusalem: Mosad Bialik, 1991), 62–71; see also Joseph Yahalom, *Az be-ʾEn Kol: Seder ha-ʿAvodah ha-Ereṣ-Yisreʾeli ha-Qadum le-Yom ha-Kippurim* (Jerusalem: Magnes, 1996), 215–20.

36. *Az be-ʾEn Kol*, lines 760 and 771.

37. See ibn Ezra's commentary to Eccl 5:1.

38. See Yahalom, *Piyyut u-Meṣiʾut*, 10–11, on the attitude of Mendele Mocher Seforim and other modern writers on the language of piyyut.

recondite style was a hallmark of the genre, how could it have been understood by the public?

There is no one definitive answer to this question. S. D. Goitein has suggested that it was the melodies, sung by popular cantors, that attracted the audience.[39] However, it is unlikely that these lengthy, complex compositions survived solely for that reason. We should consider that while most Jews in Palestine in late antiquity were not rabbinic scholars, their level of basic education was not necessarily poor. Elementary education in this period, which was available to some, if not all, might include the extensive memorization of passages from the Bible and some extrabiblical traditions such as the Mishnah. Moreover, people from all walks of life would be familiar with stories about biblical figures and other heroes, told in everyday settings and in sermons delivered by popular preachers. Such stories and exegeses would also be embedded in the translations (Targum) that accompanied the weekly reading of the Torah, which were in Aramaic, the daily language of Palestinian Jews and a close relative of Hebrew. Recently, Shelomit Elitzur, analyzing the compositions of the classical poet Yannai, has argued that these poems were structured in such a way as to telegraph the basic outline (or "plot") by which the poem proceeds while at the same time providing details from the more obscure corners of biblical and rabbinic lore. Thus the educated listener could appreciate the poet's clever allusions and plays on words, while the less-educated listener could follow the basics of the composition and marvel at the poet's erudition and skill. In the case of our Avodah piyyutim, ancient listeners were at an additional advantage. They had already read chapter 16 of Leviticus, which sets out the ritual procedure, and they would know that the poem would begin with the history of the world and Israel's heroes and advance to the description of that ritual. In fact, the description of the ritual itself in most Avodah piyyutim is relatively straightforward in comparison with the poets' treatment of other themes. Moreover, it is in the nature of piyyut to overwhelm the listener with images from Israel's culture; just as the programmatic meaning of a frieze or mosaic need not have been clear to every participant in a Greek temple, Byzantine church, or ancient synagogue, so the subtleties of the payetan's handiwork may not have prevented the ancient Jew from appreciating his craft.

---

39. Goitein, *Mediterranean Society*, 2:159.

If in technique piyyut formed a kind of verbal counterpart to the art of the synagogue, the same could be said of theme, for many of the themes found throughout the mosaics were important to the payetanim as well. Since the zodiac took a central place in synagogue art, it could also be interpreted and elaborated by the poet.[40] Therefore we should not be surprised to find the Temple remembered in major genres of synagogue poetry. The Palestinian payetanim, who seem to have settled mostly in the Galilee, devoted a special place in their piyyutim to the priestly settlements in that region. Sepphoris, for example, was both a center for the rabbinic class and for priestly families.[41] In the fifth century, when the synagogue mosaic in Sepphoris was laid, the priests still held on to at least some of their ancient status. In the Temple, the priests had served according to a strict order of rotation. They were divided into twenty-four "watches" (*mishmarot*), each with its own week. After the destruction of the Temple the priests took up residence in the villages of the Galilee according to these watches. In this fashion they preserved not only the name of the watch but also the exact order of rotation, apparently against the day that the Temple service would be restored. Mention of these watches is found mostly in the congregational prayers for the Ninth of Av, alongside mention of the Temple and grief for the destruction of the city. But poets also wrote piyyutim in memory of the watches for each Sabbath.[42] As late as the eighth century, Pineḥas ha-Kohen, a priest from Kifra, a suburb of Tiberias, was able to write piyyutim for the Sabbath in honor of the priests who would have been making their entrance to the Temple at the end of the Sabbath had the Temple in Jerusalem not been destroyed.[43] Along the same lines, a liturgical poet by the name of Hadutahu saw fit to ornament the Sabbath liturgy of his fifth–sixth century community with highly complex, comprehensive priestly compositions.[44] He, too, was undoubtedly from the Galilee, and probably also a priest. In his piyyutim, Hadutahu expresses

---

40. See Yahalom, *Piyyut u-Meṣiʾut*, 20–24.

41. See Stuart S. Miller, *Studies in the History and Traditions of Sepphoris* (Leiden: Brill, 1984).

42. See Joseph Yahalom, "The Temple and the City in Liturgical Hebrew Poetry," in *The History of Jerusalem: The Early Muslim period, 638–1099*, ed. Joshua Prawer and Haggai Ben-Shammai (Jerusalem: Yad Izhak Ben-Zvi; New York: New York University Press, 1996), 274–75.

43. See Menahem Zulay, *ʾEretz Yisrael u-Fiyuṭeha: Meḥqarim be-Fiyute ha-Genizah* (Jerusalem: Magnes, 1995), 154–63.

44. Paul Kahle, *Masoreten des Westens* (Stuttgart: Kohlhammer, 1927), 1*–66*, 1–23 [Hebrew numbering].

the wish that the priests merit the restoration of the Temple service. So, for example, in regard to the eleventh watch, he says:

> Return those who call out "Restore us" (*tashiv*)
> Those who are called from the community of Elyashiv

Through a wordplay on the Hebrew root for "restore," the poet expresses the desire that the priests of the village of Kfar Kanna, assigned to the Watch of Elyashiv, be returned to Temple service. Another important genre was the lamentations (*qinot*) for the Ninth of Av, the day of remembrance for the destruction of the Temple. Thus Eleazar ben Qallir referred to the priestly orders in his famous *qinot*, which entered the traditional liturgy.[45]

These themes may indicate something about the social position of the poets. We know next to nothing about the lives of the payetanim. Some of them became the focus of legends written down in the early Middle Ages;[46] some reveal small details about their location or lineage. We do know, however, that several of them were members of priestly families. Sometimes this lineage is preserved in their names, which include the term *kohen*, "priest": for example, Shimeon ha-Kohen bar Megas (sixth–seventh centuries); Pineḥas ha-Kohen be-Rabbi Yaʿakov of Kifra, mentioned above (eighth century); and Yoḥanan ha-Kohen be-Rabbi Yehoshua ha-Kohen (eighth century). Others, like Yose ben Yose, are considered by legend and tradition to have been priests.

We therefore have evidence from several sources that piyyut was a literature imbued with priestly piety and that a social relationship existed between the surviving priestly classes of Palestinian Jewry in the Byzantine period and the composers of liturgical poetry. Given this evidence, the Avodah genre has particular significance as a manifestation of Temple piety as it was expressed in the synagogue.

THE AVODAH

The custom of reciting the procedure of the Yom Kippur sacrifice in the

---

45. Daniel Goldschmidt, *Seder ha-Qinot le-Tishʿah be-Av* (Jerusalem: Mossad Harav Kook, 1968).

46. On medieval legends about payetanim, especially the legend related by Ephraim of Bonn that Yannai was the teacher of Eleazar ben Qallir and murdered him out of jealousy, see Yahalom, *Piyyut u-Meṣi'ut*, 240–41.

synagogue service goes back well before the flourishing of piyyut. If the account in the Mishnah, the first rabbinic compilation of law, is correct, the high priest read the biblical passages prescribing the ritual for Yom Kippur at the conclusion of the ceremony.[47]

Moreover, the Mishnah tractate Yoma, which describes Yom Kippur in the Temple, is itself conducive to liturgical recitation. Yoma is not a typical Mishnah tractate. Like a few other tractates, especially those that describe Temple ritual, such as Tamid, Parah, and portions of Pesaḥim, it is distinguished by its narrative style.[48] These tractates form a genre described by Martin Jaffee as "spare descriptive accounts of the most important institutions in ancient Palestinian Jewish society."[49] Each of these tractates follows a key Temple procedure step-by-step, enumerating the ritual and sociopolitical considerations at work in understanding that procedure.

Yoma thus entered the synagogue liturgy soon after its composition. Two sources in the Babylonian Talmud apparently describe a prayer leader who recites his version of the Mishnah before Rava, a fourth-century rabbi, on Yom Kippur.[50] In each of these cases a detail of that recitation causes controversy about the legal opinion it reflects. From that point, the tractate apparently developed a liturgical status. One surviving version of the tractate adapted for the synagogue is represented in this volume. This composition, called *Shivʿat Yamim*,[51] "Seven days," for the opening words of Mishnah Yoma, follows the tractate closely, with a few changes: The dissenting opinions of individual sages are left out, and a confession by the high priest is inserted at three

---

47. According to m. Yoma 7:1, the high priest read Lev 16:1–34 and 23:26–32 from a Torah scroll and recited Num 29:7–11 by heart.

48. On this style, see Martin S. Jaffee, "Writing and Rabbinic Oral Tradition: On Mishnaic Narrative, Lists, and Mnemonics," *Journal of Jewish Thought and Philosophy* 4 (1994): 129–30, and the sources cited there; see in particular J. N. Epstein, *Mevoʾot le-Sifrut ha-Tannaʾim* (Jerusalem: Magnes; Tel Aviv: Devir, 1957), 28–29.

49. Jaffee, "Writing," 129.

50. B. Yoma 36b, 56b. It is unclear whether b. Yoma 36b refers to full recitation of the Mishnah. See Zvi Zohar, "U-Mi Metaher ʾEtkhem—ʾAvikhem Ba-shamayim: Tefilat Seder ha-ʿAvodah shel Yom ha-Kippurim: Tokhen, Tifqud u-Mashmaʿut," *Association of Jewish Studies Review* 14 (1989): 1–28 [Hebrew section], 4–5.

51. Published in Ismar Elbogen, *Studien zur Geschichte des jüdischen Gottesdienstes* (Berlin: Mayer & Müller, 1907), 103–17; cf. the edition in Zvi Malachi, *Ha-"ʿAvodah" le-Yom ha-Kippurim—ʾOfiyah, Toledoteha ve-hitpatḥuta ba-Shirah ha-ʿIvrit* (Ph.D. diss., Hebrew University, 1974), 2:127–31.

crucial points.⁵² At some point it became customary for the congregation to prostrate themselves on hearing the report of the priest's confession, with its description of the divine name.

Shivʿat Yamim was apparently introduced by a poem called *Atah Barata* ("You Created"). This is the first Avodah poem known to us to introduce the theme of creation and the history of Israel into the structure of the liturgy. The period following these compositions, perhaps the fourth or fifth century C.E., which we call the preclassical period, saw the beginnings of the classical style, with its poetic treatments of liturgical themes, its network of allusive phrases, and its use of alphabetical acrostics. So too the form of the Avodah genre began to take shape. An early example of this pattern can be seen in the composition *Atah Konanta ʿOlam Me-Rosh* ("You established the world from the beginning"), the earliest extant true Avodah piyyut. This composition is still used in the Sephardic liturgy. Its combination of poetic style and directness stands in contrast to the later Avodah poems.

Other sources contributed directly to the development of the genre. Ben Sira, sage and poet of the second century B.C.E., devotes a pivotal chapter of his book, known as the Wisdom of Ben Sira, or Ecclesiasticus, to a description of the conduct of sacrifices by Simeon the high priest. His account is the only detailed Hebrew description of the Temple ritual surviving from the Second-Temple period written by an eyewitness.⁵³ Although it is a matter of debate whether Ben Sira is describing the Yom Kippur sacrifice or the perpetual daily offering (Tamid), the Book of Ben Sira influenced the Avodah genre deeply. The structure of the book, which prefaces its description of the sacrifice with a lengthy panegyric to Israel's heroes, prefigures that of the Avodah genre.⁵⁴ Indeed, a poem incorporated into the Book of Ben Sira describing the radiance on the face of the high priest as he emerged from the sanctuary found its way in an elaborate version into the Avodah corpus.

The Avodah piyyut is an epic form. The poems customarily begin

---

52. See J. N. Epstein, *Mavoʾ le-Nusaḥ ha-Mishnah* (Jerusalem: Magnes; Tel Aviv: Devir, 1964), 971–72.

53. For texts concerning the Temple from the Second-Temple period, see C. T. R. Hayward, *The Jewish Temple: A Non-Biblical Sourcebook* (London: Routledge, 1996).

54. See Cecil Roth, "Ecclesiasticus in the Synagogue Service," *Journal of Biblical Literature* 71 (1952): 171–78; cf. Mirsky, *Yose ben Yose*, 29–30; A. Zeidman, "Matbeaʿ Seder ha-ʿAvodah Le-Yom ha-Kippurim," *Sinai* 13 (1944): 173–82, 255–62; and Moshe Zvi Segal, *Sefer Ben Sira ha-Shalem* (Jerusalem: Mosad Bialik, 1976), 42–43 and 243–45.

with an account of creation, then describe each major generation, culminating in the selection of Aaron as priest. After this mythical-historical preamble the service in the Temple is described according to the order in the Mishnah. In these piyyutim, practically every major detail of the Mishnah is treated poetically, from the sequestering of the high priest in the Temple complex seven days before Yom Kippur[55] to the story of how the other priests used to rush up the ramp to deliver the daily sacrifice on that early morning, leading to violence between them,[56] to the ten separate times the high priest washes his hands and feet.[57]

This structure is best exemplified in two early masterpieces, *Az be-ʾEn Kol*, a massive anonymous piyyut published recently for the first time by Joseph Yahalom, and Yose ben Yose's *Azkir Gevurot Elohah* ("Let me recount the wonders of God"), first published critically in Daniel Goldschmidt's edition of the prayer manual of Saadia Gaon, then published in a full edition with extensive commentary several years ago by Aaron Mirsky.[58] These compositions form the heart of this volume. *Az be-ʾEn Kol* is the largest extant Avodah piyyut and apparently derives from the fourth or fifth century. This anonymous piyyut is remarkable as one of the earliest and most extensive examples of the Avodah genre in its full development. Each theme that it includes, from its praise of God's creation of the heavenly array to its extensive excursus on the priestly vestments, is elaborated at length. The artistry of the poet is also displayed in its careful choice of allusive words, alliteration, and unusual references. The poem is also significant as a source of myths and exegetical ideas known to us from few other sources. The poem *Aromem la-ʾEl* ("I will exalt God") follows the text and tradition of *Az be-ʾEn Kol* closely. Because the extant fragments of that poem include descriptions of the sacrifice lost to us in the manuscripts of *Az be-ʾEn Kol*, we have included excerpts from this composition as well.

Azkir Gevurot is the masterwork of Yose ben Yose, the first liturgical poet known to us by name. This poem, probably written in the fifth century, is particularly striking for its elegant style, which combines the allusions characteristic of classic piyyut with the stately depiction of the

---

55. Cf. m. Yoma 1:1.
56. Cf. m. Yoma 2:2.
57. Cf. m. Yoma 3:3.
58. I. Davidson, S. Assaf, and B. I. Joel, *Siddur Rav Saʿadiah Gaʾon* (Jerusalem: Reuben Mass, 1985), 264–75; Mirsky, *Yose ben Yose*, 127–72.

sacrificial drama. Yose ben Yose also wrote other Avodah compositions, including *Atah Konanta ʿOlam be-Rov Ḥesed* and is credited by tradition with *Az be-Daʿat Ḥaqar* and the lamentation *En Lanu Kohen Gadol*, "We have no high priest." We have included *Atah Konanta ʿOlam be-Rov Ḥesed* and *En Lanu Kohen Gadol* in this volume. It is likely that *Azkir Gevurot* was written after *Az be-ʾEn Kol* and influenced by it. However, *Azkir Gevurot* proved to be more influential than *Az be-ʾEn Kol* to later generations.

Yose ben Yose and the author of *Az be-ʾEn Kol* lived before the classical period of piyyut, the sixth to eighth centuries. We have no Avodah piyyutim by the celebrated seventh-century poet Eleazar ben Qallir, and probably only one fragmentary Avodah by Yannai. Moreover, the classical age saw the development of new genres of piyyut, such as the Qerovah, a piyyut for the Amidah, as well as the Qedushta and the Yoṣer, genres used for recitation as introductory pieces to versions of the Qedushah. Therefore, it would seem that the preclassical period, the fourth to fifth centuries, was the golden age of the Avodah.

Hebrew poets continued to produce Avodah compositions, even if the genre did not achieve the same prominence after the Islamic conquest of Palestine. Saadia Gaon, in some ways the founder of medieval Hebrew letters, composed Avodot in a new style that departed from the intricate wordplay of Eleazar ben Qallir and his school.[59] Some of the most prominent poets of medieval Spain, such as Solomon ibn Gabirol, Judah Halevy, and Moses ibn Ezra, composed Avodah piyyutim. In the southern Italian, Byzantine, and Franco-German (Ashkenazic) Jewish communities, this genre continued as well. One of these piyyutim, *Amiṣ Koah*, by the tenth-century Italian poet Meshullam ben Kalonymos, entered the standard Ashkenazic liturgy.[60]

The early anonymous composition *Atah Konanta ʿOlam Me-Rosh* (included in this volume) is used by the standard Sephardic liturgy and other Eastern liturgies. In the eighteenth century it was incorporated into the Hasidic liturgy, apparently because of that movement's adoption of the Sephardic rite, and only afterward was it used in other Ashkenazic liturgies.[61] The old French liturgy incorporates a poem by Yose ben Yose,

---

59. Davidson, Assaf, and Joel, *Siddur Rav Saʿadiah*, 409–12; Malachi, *Ha-"Avodah,"* 1:72–85.
60. See Daniel Goldschmidt, ed., *Maḥazor le-Yamim Noraʾim* (Jerusalem: Mosad Bialik, 1970), 2:435–46.
61. Ibid., 2:xviii–xix.

Eten Tehillah, and the Roman rite a poem by Yoḥanan ha-Kohen, the seventh-century Palestinian poet.[62]

In modern times, the Avodah has been a controversial genre. The last major poet to compose an Avodah poem was the nineteenth-century Italian scholar Samuel David Luzzatto. Because the Reform movement rejected the idea of the restoration of sacrifices, liturgical versions of the Avodah service called sacrifice into question.[63] The Avodah has been the subject of scholarly attention since the beginning of modern liturgical studies, and the literary history of the Avodah has been traced by such scholars as Ismar Elbogen, S. D. Luzzato, A. Zeidman, Cecil Roth, and Ezra Fleischer.[64] The most comprehensive study of the genre to date is Zvi Malachi's 1974 dissertation.[65] In recent years historians of religion and Judaism in late antiquity have recognized its importance for understanding the social and cultural history of Judaism in Byzantine Palestine.[66]

LITERARY TECHNIQUES

Avodah piyyutim follow most of the conventions of piyyut as a whole. The poems are based on an alphabetic acrostic. Occasionally the acrostic goes in reverse order of the alphabet, and often each letter of the alphabet is repeated several times. The lines follow patterns of rhythm and parallelism common to early piyyut and, like others, make liberal use of metonymy and other forms of allusion. However, there are several distinctive formal features to the Avodah piyyutim.

The most prominent feature of the Avodah genre is its overall lit-

---

62. For a fuller account of the liturgical history of the Avodah, see ibid., 2:xxiii.

63. See *The Union Prayer-Book for Jewish Worship* (New York: Central Conference of American Rabbis, 1906), 2:228–39; cf. especially *Dr. Einhorn's Olat Tamid: Book of Prayers for Jewish Congregations* (n.p., 1921), 178–208.

64. For summaries of the history of the Avodah, see Elbogen, *Jewish Liturgy*, 174, 217, 238–39, and 249–50; Goldschmidt, *Maḥzor*, 18–25; and Ezra Fleischer, *Shirat ha-Qodesh Ha-ʿIvrit Be-Yeme ha-Benayim* (Jerusalem: Keter, 1975), 173–77. An important early discussion is found in Elbogen, *Studien*; cf. also Zeidman, "Matbeaʿ Seder ha-ʿAvodah."

65. Malachi, *Ha-"ʿAvodah."* See also idem, *Be-Noʿam Siaḥ: Peraqim mi-Toldot Sifrutenu* (Lod: Haberman Institute for Literary Research, 1983), 46–113.

66. See, for example, Lawrence A. Hoffman, *Beyond the Text: A Holistic Approach to Liturgy* (Bloomington: Indiana University Press, 1987), 108–13; Zohar, "U-Mi Metaher ʾEtkhem"; Yahalom, *Az be-ʾEn Kol*; idem, *Piyyut u-Meṣiʾut*, 107–36; Michael D. Swartz, "Sage, Priest, and Poet: Typologies of Leadership in the Ancient Synagogue," in *Jews, Christians, and Polytheists in the Ancient Synagogue: Cultural Interaction During the Greco-Roman Period*, ed. Steven Fine (London: Routledge, 1999), 101–17; and idem, "Ritual About Myth About Ritual: Toward an Understanding of the *Avodah* in the Rabbinic Period," *Journal of Jewish Thought and Philosophy* 6 (1997): 135–55.

erary structure, particularly the progression from a mythical-historical preamble to the narration of the Yom Kippur sacrifice. The compositions usually begin with words of praise for God. These verses are often expressed in the first person, a feature that is usually facilitated by the acrostic, which begins with the letter aleph, which also begins verbs in the first-person imperfect or cohortative. Thus the poet begins with his declaration to praise God and commences by describing God in his heavenly array. From here the transition to description of God's creation is smooth. At this point the poet may linger on aspects of world and national history that suit the theme of the work, as we show below. A pivotal point is the narration of the selection of the tribe of Levi and the clan of Aaron. This allows the poet to focus on the process by which the high priest is instructed by the sages, officiates in the sacrifices, emerges from the inner sanctuary, and announces triumphantly Israel's redemption. The poems usually conclude with a declaration such as "happy is the eye that has seen these sights." Thus the listener is regaled with a panorama of Israel's history, led vicariously through the Yom Kippur sacrifice, and invited to recall the joy that greeted Israel's atonement upon its successful completion.

Other distinctive features of the Avodah have to do with its liturgical function. In the original Temple ritual commemorated by the Avodah, as by the Mishnah, the Tetragrammaton was pronounced by the high priest during his confession of sins. Description of this pronunciation plays a prominent part in the ritual—indeed, it seems to have been one of the first distinctive features of the liturgical Avodah.[67] Although Jewish law prevented the prayer leader from reciting the divine name, it became the custom for the synagogue congregation themselves to prostrate themselves as well at the report of the high priest's pronunciation of that name. In the Mishnah, and hence in subsequent Avodot, the priest's confession appears three times, along with the people's response, "Blessed be the name of His Majesty's glory for ever and ever." This liturgical declaration is presumably the people's response to the pronunciation of the divine name.[68] However, the third confession is the only one in which the Mishnah text says explicitly that the people heard

---

67. On this feature of the Avodah, see especially Zohar, "U-Mi Metaher ʾEtkhem."
68. On such formulae, see Saul Lieberman, "Some Notes on Adjurations in Israel," in *Texts and Studies* (New York: Ktav, 1974), 21–28, and Joseph Heinemann, "Qedushah u-Malkhut be-Qeriʾat Shemaʿ de-ʿAmidah," in *Shai le-Heman: Mehqarim li-Khevod A. M. Haberman* (Jerusalem: Reuben

the divine name and prostrated themselves. In fact, Jacob N. Epstein has suggested that this third passage was not original to the Mishnah but was added from the liturgy.[69] By contrast, the name and subsequent prostration are a key refrain in the Avodah.

Other techniques common to poetry of late antiquity are used in the Avodah to particular effect. As we have seen, the verbal expression of the "Jeweled Style" relies on the use of words and images in series. Detailed description by means of the patterned repetition of short sentences structured in parallel syntax is thus characteristic of the literature of late antiquity. As the medieval teacher of rhetoric Geoffrey of Vinsauf explained, patterned repetition makes it possible to pay closer attention to the choice of words and changes in meaning.[70] Biblical poetry had earlier relied on parallel structure to convey poetic meaning and style. Piyyut often extended the biblical tradition of parallelism by emphasizing relationships between hemistichs within lines of verse. Thus the opening of Yose ben Yose's *Azkir Gevurot* uses syntactic and semantic parallelism between the hemistichs as well as between whole lines. Here the lines are arranged from left to right so as to illustrate this technique:

Let me recount the wonders	of the magnificent God,
Who is unique, there is no other,	self-sufficient and none second to Him.
There is none beyond Him in the universe,	none prior to Him in heaven;
None preceded Him,	and none can supplant Him.
When the Lord conceived,	when God invented,
He consulted but none could prevent Him,	He spoke and none constrained Him.

The first line serves as the introduction to the whole poem and so does not use this form. But each of the following lines repeats a basic syntactical pattern. In most cases the parallelism serves synonymously (unique/self-sufficient, conceived/invented), but in the middle stanza

---

Mass, 1977), 107–17, repr. in Joseph Heinemann, *'Iyyune Tefilah*, ed. Avigdor Shinan (Jerusalem: Magnes, 1981), 12–21.

69. Epstein, *Mavo' le-Nusaḥ ha-Mishnah*, 2:971–72.

70. On this form in piyyut, see further Yahalom, *Piyyut u-Meṣi'ut*, 152–53.

the parallelism is antithetical (beyond/prior, preceded/supplant). The effect is to emphasize God's absolute sovereignty and eternal presence, before and after creation.

The poets are also capable of using simpler forms of repetition and listing for literary effect. In the *Atah Konanta ʿOlam Me-Rosh*, one of the earliest and most straightforward of the Avodah piyyutim, the anonymous composer details the steps in the Yom Kippur sacrifice in very direct language. The following passage consists of a series of nouns that culminate in verbs only in the fifth stich:

> Diadem, robe, and linen breeches,
> breastpiece, ephod, royal headdress, and sash;
>
> sacrifice of bulls and burnt offerings of sheep
> and the slaughter of goats and the cutting-up of rams;
>
> the perfumed aroma and the burning of coals
> correct enumeration and the dashing of blood;
>
> supplication at the incense and true prayer;
> and his holiness, which atones for our sins;
>
> the measurement of fine linen and the arrangement of jewels—
> he is girded in all of these like a ministering angel.
>
> You ordained all these for the glory of Aaron;
> You made him for Israel an instrument of atonement.[71]

On the face of it, this would seem to be a dry listing of objects and actions. However, there is significance in the list itself. For the audience, it serves as a reminder of the elements of the sacrifice and gives as well a swift overview of the Yom Kippur ceremony. But the list also serves the prosody of the composition; the nouns are arranged by twos according to the four-foot rhythm of the stichs. The last three hemistichs break this pattern. In the second hemistich of the fifth stich—

> he is girded in all of these like a ministering angel

—the poet loads both the holy vestments and ritual obligations onto the

---

71. MS add.: "and You placed the forgiveness of sins in his hand."

person of the high priest, who is likened to an angel. The next stich functions as a transition from the previous passage to the next unit.[72] This stich, in which the poet turns to the second person—

> You ordained all these for the glory of Aaron

—thus functions as a kind of zeugma, a construction used to tie together the objects that preceded it. It reminds the listener of God, who is the source of the sacrificial law and the object of the worship service as well. Thus the poet accomplishes one of the central goals of the Avodah piyyutim—the praise of the high priest and his intimacy with God.

SOURCES

The Avodah offers a good illustration of the range of sources that were available to the payetanim in ornamenting their discourse. At the same time, this genre raises questions for further research. In many cases we can see where the poets drew from the corpus of rabbinic literature, which was evolving in their time, and can detect influences and sources that were generally not used or known in the rabbinic academies.

The single most important source for the Avodah is the Mishnah. The entire genre can be described as a poetic elaboration of Mishnah Yoma. Yet its relationship to the Mishnaic source is not unambiguous. As we shall see, the piyyutim have a strong tendency to ascribe heroic qualities to the high priest. This places it somewhat in opposition to the Mishnah.

A major theme in Mishnah Yoma is the ongoing tension between the Zadokite high priest and the (presumably Pharisaic) sages, who, in the rabbis' telling, are essentially in charge of the sacrifice. In Lev 16, Aaron is the sole human character in the sacrificial drama. By contrast, the Mishnah is remarkable for its depiction of the high priest's passivity. In the opening of the tractate, the active verbs belong mainly to the anonymous priestly sages: They sequester the high priest, prepare a new wife for him in case he is suddenly bereft of a household to atone for, keep him awake while they lecture him, walk him from one chamber to another in the Temple complex, and even pass bulls and sheep before

---

72. This line, which begins with the letter *tav*, begins a new reverse acrostic.

him so that he will be familiar with them.⁷³ It is assumed that the high priest is likely to be an ignoramus or heretic, that he may not have the knowledge to expound on scripture on his own, or that he may follow Sadducean procedure in the sacrifice.

This picture is revised in the early Avodah piyyutim, which present the priest as an active and willing participant. *Atah Konanta ʿOlam Me-Rosh* is more direct in its language than the later piyyutim, and follows the Mishnah closely. Yet the author has certainly lent his editorial and ideological voice to the Mishnaic account. A striking feature of this poem is its emphasis on the volition, piety, and diligence of the priest; nowhere do we find the Mishnah's struggle between the sages and Zadokites. The priest is not lectured by the sages; rather, as the piyyut puts it:

> For seven days he studied, in our Temple,
> the laws of the procedure and the service of the day

To be sure, he is surrounded by the sages and warned of the solemn nature of what he is about to do; but he seems to take the lesson in good faith; he is soon performing specific acts joyously, and reverently:

> He performed the commandment in awe and fear
> and examined himself for interpositions (during) ablution.⁷⁴

> He rejoiced in the commandment to uphold His law
> and went down and immersed as he was instructed.⁷⁵

The controversies mentioned in the Mishnah find barely an echo. In the Mishnaic account, the Sadducean priest is warned by the Pharisaic sages to perform the ceremony properly—that is, according to Pharisaic law. Then, according to the Mishnah, "He turned aside and wept, and they turned aside and wept."⁷⁶ *Atah Konanta* omits this dramatic

---

73. We would like to acknowledge Kevin Osterloh for emphasizing this contrast in the use of verbs in a seminar paper for Michael Swartz at the Ohio State University.
74. That is, objects that prevent effective purification by their interposition between the water and the body.
75. Lines 7–8 of the second section.
76. M. Yoma 1:5.

moment entirely. This is one of several examples of how the Avodah uses its Mishnaic sources critically.

The relationship of piyyut to Midrash, rabbinic biblical interpretation, is so intimate that scholars in previous generations often argued that piyyut was simply a means to convey the content of rabbinic homilies at a time when they were forbidden.[77] While subsequent research has discredited this theory, the student of piyyut must be attuned to the complexities of rabbinic Midrash in order to understand piyyut thoroughly. The influence of Midrash on piyyut can be seen in innumerable turns of phrase, poetic figures, and themes expressed in the piyyutim. But there are also instances where a midrashic idea inspires an entire section or motif.

The idea, expressed in the fourth-century Midrash Genesis Rabbah 1:1, that God used Torah as a blueprint for the world forms the basis for a significant passage in *Az be-ʾEn Kol*. This section, which unfortunately is fragmentary in the extant manuscript, begins by describing the Torah as the instrument of creation. That is, God created the world

> With that which is longer than the earth,
> with that which is wider than the sea,
> with Your primordial possession,
> with that which is the beginning of all action.
>
> (lines 29–30)

In the first line the poet alludes to the esoteric idea, based on Job 11:9, that the Torah was larger than the world itself.[78] A few lines down, he details how the Torah served as the working plan for creation:

> Looking into it, You carved out
> the pillars of the heavens
> before there was primordial chaos
> on which the rafters could rest.[79]

---

77. On this argument and its sources, see Elbogen, *Jewish Liturgy*, 222–24; cf. especially the editors' notes there.

78. Cf. Tanḥuma Bereshit 1. On the idea of the size of the Torah, see S. H. Kook, "Godel ha-Torah ve-Yaḥasah le-Godel ha-ʿOlam," *Iyyunim u-Meḥqarim* (Jerusalem, 1967): 108–19, and Moshe Idel, "Tefisat ha-Torah be-Sifrut ha-Hekhalot ve-Gilguleha ba-Qabbalah," *Meḥqere Yerushalayim be-Maḥshevet Yisrael* (1981–82): 23–84.

79. Heb. *Tohu va-Vohu*, here referring apparently to the primordial waters, on which the rafters of heaven rest.

This myth is based on the exegetical equation of the word "beginning" (*reshit*) of Prov 8:22 with the same word in Gen 1:1. However, this association is found only in rabbinic sources[80] and obviously served as the inspiration for this passage in *Az be-'En Kol*.

Azkir Gevurot reflects a story, going back at least to the Second-Temple period[81] and preserved in Genesis Rabbah,[82] that the patriarch Abraham deduced monotheism by observing the ways of nature:

> When he saw the course
> of that which glides and shines,[83]
> eager as a hero when it emerges,
> and weak when it sets,
>
> the windows of the sky,
> in the east and the west
> through which the moon
> leaps every day,
>
> the arrows of lightning
> the rush of the stars
> dashing to and fro—
> and not one fails to appear—
>
> the unenlightened became wise
> and inferred by himself
> saying, "There is a Lord of these—
> Him I will follow."
>
> (lines 81–84)

Once again, the entire episode is dependent on an exegetical tradition. *Az be-'En Kol* describes God's guidance of Abraham in this way:

> You leapt toward him
> like a lover his companion

---

80. Cf., however, Philo, *On the Virtues* 62 and *On Drunkenness* 30–31.
81. See Apocalypse of Abraham ch. 7 (James H. Charlesworth, ed., *Pseudepigrapha of the Old Testament* [Garden City, N.Y.: Doubleday, 1983], 1:692).
82. Gen Rabbah 38:28 (ed. Theodor and Albeck, pp. 361–64). Note that the version in the piyyut is closer to the Apocalypse's version than to Genesis Rabbah's.
83. The sun.

and by the power of Your light[84]
he took his steps.

(lines 460-61)

At this point the piyyut quotes Isa 41:2, "Who has roused a victor from the East … ?" The idea that God's light guided Abraham is also found in Genesis Rabbah,[85] which interprets the same verse with regard to Abraham: "He who lives eternally would illuminate any place where he walked."[86] Here, as in innumerable instances, the meaning of the piyyut is dependent on a midrashic idea.

A more surprising feature of the Avodah piyyutim is the degree to which they preserve details and motifs found not in rabbinic literature but in Apocrypha and other Second-Temple texts. *Az be-ʾEn Kol* is a particularly striking example of this tendency. As Louis Ginzberg and Gary A. Anderson have shown, opinions in antiquity differed about whether Adam and Eve were celibate before their expulsion.[87] Rabbinic Midrash presupposes that they did engage in sexual relations before their disobedience of God—indeed, according to one story in Genesis Rabbah, they had just had sexual relations, and Adam had fallen asleep, when Eve spoke to the serpent.[88] But some texts from the Second-Temple period and the early centuries of the Common Era, as well as the Church Fathers, asserted that Adam and Eve had no sexual relations in the Garden. Jubilees, for example, sees to it that Adam and Eve have sexual relations before their entry into the garden but not after they have arrived, thus avoiding pollution of the sacred realm of Eden.[89] The *Syriac Apocalypse* of Baruch (*2 Baruch*), a Jewish text from the early second century, states that only after Adam's transgression did conception of children come into the world (56:6). *Az be-ʾEn Kol* reflects

---

84. Reading *nghk* for *nhgk*; see Yahalom, *Az be-ʾEn Kol*, 116.
85. Gen Rabbah 42:15 (ed. Theodor and Albeck, p. 418).
86. Playing on the sound of the word *meʿir*, "arouse," and the word *meʾir*, "illuminate." See Nahum M. Bronznick, review of *Az be-ʾEn Kol*, by Yahalom, *Lešonénu* 62 (1999): 152.
87. Louis Ginzberg, *The Legends of the Jews* (Philadelphia: Jewish Publication Society, 1909-38), 5:134 n. 4; Gary A. Anderson, "Celibacy or Consummation in the Garden? Reflections on Early Jewish and Christian Interpretations of the Garden of Eden," *Harvard Theological Review* 82 (1989): 121-48.
88. Gen Rabbah 19:3, on which, see Anderson, "Celibacy," 124.
89. Jubilees 3.2-5a, 6; see Anderson, "Celibacy," 128.

an opinion similar to that of the apocryphal literature. Describing the moment when God first brought forth Eve from Adam, the poet states:

> He set her opposite him
> and balanced his value with hers
> but still her desire for her husband
> had not been set.
>
> (lines 260–61)

Thus does he clearly reflect the opinion that sexual desire was one of the things brought on by the Fall of the first couple, and diverge from the rabbinic opinion that fertility and sexuality existed in Eden.

Elsewhere, the author seems to respond to sectarian sources polemically. In Jubilees (50:8), sexual intercourse is specifically prohibited on the Sabbath. The rabbis, on the other hand, considered marital relations to be praiseworthy on the Sabbath.[90] So too *Az be-ʾEn Kol* states:

> Tasting of the household table[91]
> were not prohibited on it
> for the inheritance of those who are blessed by Him
> is the reward of the fruit of His hosts.
>
> The fortress of the belly
> is not closed up on it,
> for He who opens the womb
> does not delay its time.
>
> (lines 218–21)

Thus, according to the author, God intended marital relations ("tasting of the table") and birth itself to occur on the Sabbath. There is evidence that Jubilees was known in late antiquity, sometimes under the name Little Genesis. The pointed nature of this statement may be an indication that the prohibition of sex on the Sabbath may still have been an issue in fourth-to-fifth-century Palestine.

There is also evidence that the Avodah literature influenced midrashic texts themselves. Pirqe de-Rabbi Eliezer is a narrative midrashic

---

90. See Anderson, "Celibacy," 131.
91. That is, the body.

composition, probably written in eighth- or ninth-century Palestine by a single author. Judging from its form and content, its context seems to be the synagogue. Pirqe de-Rabbi Eliezer, which by no means is a normative, conventional collection of rabbinic opinions, does have substantial affinities with *Az be-'En Kol* in structure, linguistic tendencies, and themes.[92] Since by its date it could not have preceded *Az be-'En Kol*, it is likely that the poem or others influenced by it formed one source from which the midrashic composition's author drew.[93] This is a further demonstration that the Avodah piyyutim cannot be ignored in writing the cultural history of Judaism in late antiquity and the early Middle Ages.

THEMES

Because of its unique function, the Avodah service can be seen as a series of systematic statements on the meaning of the ancient sacrificial cult and its place in the universe. Each of the components of the compositions—the historical preamble, the description of the Yom Kippur sacrifice, and its treatment of the Mishnah—attest to a priestly ideology in which the Temple is at the heart of Jewish religion.

A major theme in the poems is that creation itself took place for the sake of the cult. This notion complements the rabbinic idea, formulated most famously in Midrash Genesis Rabbah 1:1, that the world was created by the preexistent Torah and humankind was in turn created for the Torah's sake. This theme is manifest in subtle ways throughout the historical prelude, from the establishment of the heavenly prototype of the Temple to the election of the sons of Amram. For example, in *Azkir Gevurot*, the creation of vegetation and animals is depicted as the creation of food, a cultic notion:

> There grew out of the earth
> horned animals for slaughter
> edible beasts,
> both cattle and those that crawl.

---

92. See Yahalom, *Az be-'En Kol*, 46–53.

93. For a summary of arguments for the standard dating of the text, see Günter Stemberger, *Introduction to the Talmud and Midrash*, trans. and ed. Markus Bockmuehl (Edinburgh: T. & T. Clark, 1996), 329.

> He pastured the Behemoth
> with the produce of a thousand mountains,
> for on the day when it is slaughtered,
> He[94] will put His sword to it.
>
> (lines 31–32)

That is, God will slaughter the Behemoth to be used as food for the righteous in the world to come. This section therefore signals a teleological view of creation, one not self-evident in the Genesis narrative; each created thing has a future purpose in history and eschatology. This will serve the listener later on, when the history climaxes in the institution of God's Tabernacle. The poem continues:

> The Creator exulted
> and rejoiced in His deeds,
> when He saw
> that his work was good:
>
> grasses for rest
> and food of choice;
> the table was set,
> but there was no one to relish it.
>
> He said to Himself,
> "Who will approach
> for the butchered animals
> and blended wine?"
>
> (lines 33–35)

The purpose of the creation of humanity is the enjoyment of the food that God has created. The table is set, but there is no one to partake of it.

In another Avodah piyyut by Yose ben Yose, this teleological focus is even more pronounced. In his poem *Atah Konanta ʿOlam be-Rov Ḥesed*[95] creation of food is explicitly connected with God's intention in the details of creation:

---

94. That is, God himself.
95. On early discussion and publication of this piyyut, see Samuel David Luzzatto, *Mavo*

You made, as a sign for those who know You,[96]
those who are clad with scales,[97]
and a fleeing serpent[98]
for the meal in eternity.

Did you not make out of the earth
in great abundance
cattle and crawling creatures
and the beasts of the earth?[99]

You set signs to be known
of edibility and purity
and for the company of the righteous
you made the Behemoth fit to eat.[100]

And when the world was built,
in wisdom,
and when the table was set,
and its bounty,

You resolved[101]
to invite a guest
and to feed him
your choice food.

(lines 18–22)

Here too, all creation is arranged for human consumption. Creation is also associated in this composition with eschatology. Employing a common legend that the serpent and Behemoth will serve as meals for the righteous in the world to come, the poet portrays their creation as

---

le-Maḥazor Bene Roma, ed. Daniel Goldschmidt (Tel Aviv: Devir, 1966), 24 and n. 29. The piyyut itself is published in Goldschmidt, *Maḥazor*, 2:465–78, and in Mirsky, *Yose ben Yose*, 178–203. Mirsky's edition is used here. On this poem, see Elbogen, *Studien*, 79–81, and Malachi, *Ha-"Avodah,"* 2:20–22.

96. That is, for Israel.
97. Fish that are ritually pure.
98. See Isa 27:1. Here the poet is referring to the Leviathan; see below.
99. The rhetorical question is placed here for the sake of the acrostic; the first line in the stanza (line 19) begins *Ha-loʾ*.
100. Heb. *hikhsharta*; that is, "You made the Behemoth kosher."
101. Heb. *va-tishqod*.

having taken place for that purpose.[102] More than this, humankind is created for the purpose of praising God. In *Aromem la-ʾEl*, a piyyut influenced by *Az be-ʾEn Kol* and *Azkir Gevurot*, we read:

> This One[103] surveyed,
> and looked out at the world
> as a city without inhabitants,
> as an army without a commander.
>
> He considered this,
> and said, "What have I accomplished?
> I created and achieved,
> but who will recount My praises?"[104]

The idea that the creation of humankind has a cultic purpose is developed further, perhaps under the influence of our piyyutim, in Palestinian midrashim of late antiquity. In chapter 6 of Pirqe de-Rabbi Eliezer, the great size and glorious appearance lead the creatures of the world erroneously to worship Adam. In response Adam proposes: "Let us both go and clothe [God] in glory and might and enthrone the One who created us. For if there is no people to praise the King, will the King praise Himself?" This mythic idea, that God in fact needs creation to be God, is stated most boldly in an earlier Palestinian midrashic source. The midrash is based on the word order of Gen 1:1, which, following the

---

102. On the idea of the monsters as meal for the righteous, see *1 Enoch* 60:24, *2 Baruch* 29:4, and *4 Ezra* 6:49 (on which, see Michael E. Stone, *A Commentary on the Fourth Book of Ezra* [Minneapolis: Augsburg Fortress, 1990], 186–87); and Targum Pseudo-Jonathan to Gen 1:21, Num Rabbah 21:18, and Tanḥuma Shemini 7. Cf. especially Lev Rabbah 1:2, where it is explicitly stated that the intention to prepare a meal for the righteous in the world to come is built into creation. In contrast to those legends, note the following midrash on Isa 27:1 in b. Baba Batra 74b: "Everything that the Holy One, blessed be He, created, he created male and female; even the Leviathans He created male and female [Isa 27:1]; and if they had mated [*nizqaqin zeh la-zeh*], they would have destroyed the whole world. What did he do? The Holy One, blessed be He, castrated the male and killed the female and salted her for the righteous in the time to come [ibid.] and also the Behemoth." Note here that the use of the monsters as food for the righteous is a consequence of God's struggle with them and not the immediate objective of their creation. Our piyyut would thus be another comparatively early Jewish source for this idea; see Ginzberg, *Legends*, 5:43. On this idea, see further Ginzberg, *Legends*, 5:43–49, and Jefim Schirmann, "The Battle Between Behemoth and Leviathan According to an Ancient Hebrew Piyyut," *Proceedings of the Israel Academy of Sciences and Humanities* 4 (1969–70): 327–69.

103. God.

104. *Aromem la-ʾEl*, lines 125–28, in Yahalom, *Az be-ʾEn Kol*, 165.

usual order of subject and verb in biblical Hebrew, says literally, "In the beginning created God heaven and earth": "'In the beginning God created …' Fools say, God created the beginning. But it is not so. Why? God said: 'The owner of a ship is not called so unless he has a ship.' Thus I cannot be called God unless I have created a world for Myself. Thus, 'In the beginning created,' and then, 'God.'"[105]

That is, God could only become God through the fact of creation. Here then we can see the full development of an idea essential to the Avodah piyyutim, that the world and humankind were created for the sake of God's praise and that this function was essential to God's divinity.

One of the most significant features of the Avodah piyyutim is their systematic and elaborate glorification of the priest. This characteristic is consistent with their cultic nature in general but has wider implications. In stark contrast to the Mishnah, the Avodah endeavors to portray the high priest as a virtuous and heroic man, graced with piety, wisdom, and physical strength. We have already seen that whereas the Mishnah portrays the high priest as passive, ignorant, or heretical, the Avodah presents him as a pious man eager to perform the commandments and humble in his consciousness of the gravity of his office.

More than this, the high priest is portrayed in the Avodah as an extraordinary physical specimen. Building on rabbinic interpretations of Lev 21:10 that say the priest should be "greater than his brothers" in physical as well as moral virtues,[106] the poems emphasize the strength and stamina it takes to perform the sacrifice. Thus *Az be-ʾEn Kol* marvels how

> [h]is stature
> rose to the height of a cedar
> when he was fit with embroidered garments
> to ornament his body.
>
> (lines 551–52)

So too Yose ben Yose describes the moment when the high priest enters the holy of holies through the curtains:

> He displayed his great strength
> and pushed aside the curtain

---

105. See Ephraim Urbach, "Seride Tanḥuma-Yelamedenu," *Qoveṣ ʿal Yad*, n.s., 6 (1966): 12.
106. T. Kippurim 1:6; y. Yoma 1:3.

and entered without stepping
between the two rods.[107]

Elsewhere in that poem the priest is described in almost mythic terms:

Wrapped in a blue robe,
as bright as the firmament,
His rounded arms
filled the sleeves.

Az be-'En Kol and the piyyutim of Yose ben Yose contain extensive excursuses on the special vestments of the high priest.[108] These passages are remarkable for their elaborate imagery and symbolism. The following couplets from Yose's *Azkir Gevurot* exemplify the approach these sections take:

His strong body
filled his tunic,
doubled and woven
as far as the sleeves.

The sin of the house of Jacob
was atoned by this—
those who sold the righteous one[109]
over a sleeved tunic.

(lines 159-60)

These excursuses, based on Exodus chapters 28 and 39, lavish detail on the exact design of the clothes, the breastpiece and the ephod and the rings and cords that connect them. At the same time, they work out an intricate system of interpretation of the sacred garments by which each detail plays a specific role in atonement.

Az be-'En Kol takes the role of the vestments further. According to this poem, it is the duty of the garments not just to represent Israel but to arouse God's compassion for his people on the Day of Judgment so

---

107. Yose ben Yose, *Azkir Gevurot*, lines 229-30.
108. *Az Be-'En Kol*, lines 547-664; *Azkir Gevurot*, lines 151-84.
109. Joseph.

that He will dispel the malevolent forces. Thus the author says of the bells:

> He set golden bells
> and wove them into his hem
> to recall (God's) love
> of (the one of whom it is said): "How beautiful are your steps."
>   (Song 7:2)

(lines 559–60)

In *Az be-ʾEn Kol*, the active properties of the vestments extend to their role in dispelling the hostile forces preventing purification. Returning to the bells on the robe, the poem makes it clear that their function is not limited to atonement but that they also announce, noisily, the presence of the priest. As he steps into the sanctuary,

> When his soles moved
> they gave voice
> like him who called in the wilderness
> to make a path straight.[110]
>
> The servants of the Shekhinah
> were fearful of him
> for the robe is named
> after the One who wears justice.[111]

(lines 567–68)

That is, the hostile angels in the sanctuary—who are essentially bodyguards fending off intruders in the sacred precinct—are frightened by the sound of the bells, which carries with it divine authorization. Here, the high priest, like the travelers to the divine throne in early Jewish mysticism and Moses according to rabbinic legends, does battle with the angels.[112] In that same section, the priestly headdress is said to repel an

---

110. Cf. Isa 40:3 and Yahalom, *Az be-ʾEn Kol*, 32, where this passage is related to Aaron's intervention in Num 17.
111. Isa 59:17.
112. On this motif and its antecedents, see further Yahalom, *Az be-ʾEn Kol*, 17–18.

angelic personage called *zaʿaf*, meaning rage, perhaps signifying a fierce angel named Zaʿafiel:

> Rage, when he saw it,
> could not open his mouth
> for on the day of vengeance
> he will be swallowed up.
>
> (lines 647–48)

So too:

> And the supernal demigods
> made room for him
> lest their eyes be filled with (the sight of him)
> and grow dim.
>
> (lines 655–56)

Elsewhere in the piyyutim, the high priest himself is likened to an angel. Following a tradition that begins with Mal 2:7, the poems relate the priest's appearance and function to that of the angels on high serving God.[113] After its description of the high priest's garments and ritual actions quoted above, *Atah Konanta ʿOlam Me-Rosh* declares, "he is girded in all of these like a ministering angel." Likewise *Az be-ʾEn Kol* says of the high priest:

> You raised his stature
> from all the people of [   ]
> [for there is none so] great;
> he serves like an angel.
>
> (lines 540–41)

The theological significance of this correspondence of priest with angel is worth exploring. A long tradition in Jewish liturgy seeks to show that human and angelic rituals are equivalent before God. This tradition extends from the Dead Sea community at Qumran, whose members

---

113. Cf. also the Scroll of Blessings (Serekh ha-Berakhot) at Qumran: 25:5 (Megilat ha-Serakhim p. 284–85); Rule of Benedictions (1Q28b) 4/25–26.

composed hymns for the Sabbath in which they depicted angels offering sacrifices in the seven heavens, to the statutory Qedushah of the rabbinic liturgy, which describes the human community offering its praise while the angels offer theirs.[114] The Avodah, following an ancient tradition of identification of angel and priest, goes further by making the high priest superior to the angel in his ability to ward off angelic guardians of the divine presence. Sometime during this period or later, authors of the Hekhalot texts described journeys undertaken by rabbis through the heavenly palaces, in which they were to ward off malevolent angels guarding the divine throne, the Merkavah.[115] But whereas the Hekhalot texts described journeys undertaken for the sake of the vision of the Divine or perhaps the acquisition of divine secrets, the Avodah describes the high priest's journey into the divine presence to obtain forgiveness and well-being for all of Israel.

We have shown that in its structure and themes the Avodah genre strives to glorify the priesthood, to place the priest at the center of Judaism, and indeed to accord him a central place in the cosmic scheme of things. This pattern corresponds to what we have learned about the prominence of the priesthood in the social and cultural life of the synagogue. We have seen evidence that the social structure of the ancient Palestinian synagogue recognized the priestly caste as an important sector of its leadership. If this was so, the Avodah, coming as it did in a climactic moment at Yom Kippur, the most dramatic occasion in the liturgical calendar, was the priesthood's moment of glory. At the same

---

114. On the Qumran Sabbath Songs, see Carol Newsom, *Songs of the Sabbath Sacrifice: A Critical Edition* (Atlanta: Scholars Press, 1985); Bilhah Nitzan, *Qumran Prayer and Religious Poetry* (Leiden: Brill, 1994); and Esther Eshel, Hanan Eshel, Carol Newsom, Bilhah Nitzan, Eileen Schuller, and Ada Yardeni, *Qumran Cave 4.vi: Poetical and Liturgical Texts, Part i*, Discoveries in the Judaean Desert 11 (Oxford: Clarendon Press, 1998). On this idea in the liturgical Qedushah, see, for example, Moshe Weinfeld, "ʿIqvot shel Qedushat ha-Yoṣer u-Fesuqe de-Zimra bi-Megilot Midbar Yehudah u-ve-Sefer Ben Sirah," *Tarbiz* 45 (1976): 15–26. Cf. also Pirqe de-Rabbi Eliezer ch. 41 on the idea that the entire generation that received revelation at Sinai became like the angels; on this source, see Yahalom, *Az be-ʾEn Kol*, 139.

115. On the equivalence of angelic prayer with human prayer, see Swartz, *Mystical Prayer*. On the relationship of the Hekhalot literature to the Temple and priesthood, see Johann Maier, *Vom Kultus zum Gnosis: Bundeslade, Gottesthrone und Märkābāh* (Salzburg: Otto Müller, 1964); Martha Himmelfarb, *Ascent to Heaven in Jewish and Christian Apocalypses* (New York: Oxford University Press, 1993); Ithamar Gruenwald, "Meqoman shel Mesorot Kohaniot be-Yeṣiratah shel ha-Misṭiqah shel ha-Merkavah ve-shel Shiʿur Qomah," *Meḥqere Yerushalayim be-Maḥshevet Yisraʾel* 6 (1987): 65–120; Rachel Elior, "From Earthly Temple to Heavenly Shrines: Prayer and Sacred Song in the Hekhalot Literature and Its Relation to Temple Traditions," *Jewish Studies Quarterly* 4 (1997): 217–67.

INTRODUCTION 39

time, this liturgy strives to create a sense of identification with the high priest. Listeners to the Avodah would then follow the priest as he prepared for the sacrifice, dressed and undressed behind a sheet, slaughtered the bulls and goats for himself, his household, and Israel, entered the holy of holies, and would repeat the confessions with him. The Avodah, then, manages to exalt the high priest to the post of supreme emissary of Israel while at the same time allowing each congregant to participate in a kind of vicarious sacrifice.

THIS VOLUME

The purpose of this volume is to make the major early Avodah piyyutim available to readers of English. At the same time, we hope through our text, notes, and commentary to shed light on some long-standing questions of interpretation and meaning regarding this genre. Each of the translators has done research in a separate sphere in which the Avodah plays a key part. The results of this research are also reflected in this anthology.

We have not strived to produce a purely poetic translation. That is, where scholarly accuracy conflicts with grace of expression or where a turn of phrase may have changed the meaning of a line while making it more beautiful, we have usually opted for the more precise and less poetic. Nevertheless, we have endeavored to pay close attention to the poetic nature of the text—to the rhythms, assonance, and layers of meaning in the symbolic language of the poem. Thus the reader will notice alliteration, formal expressions or shifts in diction, and echoes of biblical phrases that reflect such tendencies in the Hebrew.

Early piyyut is most often written in a kind of basic rhythm, usually of four feet. It is not strict enough to be called meter, but it does create a sense of regularity. This rhythm also no doubt made piyyut conducive to singing. Listen, for example, to the sound of these lines from the beginning of *Azkir Gevurot* in the Hebrew, noting that in Hebrew the stress is usually placed on the last syllable of a word, and compare it to our translation:

    omer ve-ʿoseh
    yoʿeṣ u-meqayem
    amiṣ la-set
    ve-gibbor lis-bol

He speaks and fulfills,
decrees and enacts,
He is strong enough to support it,
Heroic enough to bear it.

This stanza divides neatly into two pairs of hemistichs that are perfectly parallel. The first pair consists of two pairs of two-syllable verbs (*omer*/*ʿoseh*) linked with conjunctions (*ve-*/*u-*). The second pair consists of adjectives (*ʾamiṣ*/*gibbor*) linked with infinitives (*la-set*/*lis-bol*), likewise of two syllables each. In our translation, we can duplicate the number of verbs, adjectives, and infinitives, but not the number of syllables. Furthermore, without the adverb "enough," the second half of the stanza makes no sense. Therefore, we have paid attention to stress rather than numbers of syllables. Often the need to fill in the syntax or make an allusion comprehensible prevailed over our wish to preserve a generally consistent rhythm. We have also not hesitated to reverse subject-verb order.

To the reader familiar with poetry translation, these comments should give the impression not that we have taken many liberties but rather the opposite—that we have been especially concerned to convey as much of the original as possible rather than let our poetic imaginations take flight. That impression would not be far from the truth. But we do so because of the nature of this literature. Early piyyut manages to combine a spareness of expression—as seen in the terse succession of verbs and adjectives in the stanza just quoted—with an elaborateness of ornamentation. It does so by its dense allusive quality, whereby no major noun or verb is allowed to stand for itself but is instead represented by a biblical figure or synonym (*kinnui*).

We have therefore worked to devise a special format appropriate for this complex allusive genre of poetry. In this edition the Hebrew and English are printed on facing pages. Most of the Hebrew texts have been reprinted from the standard editions. However, in certain cases, such as *Az be-ʾEn Kol* and *Azkir Gevurot*, we are making new manuscripts available to the public for the first time. At the same time, we hope through the translation to provide a means for nonspecialists to understand the biblical and rabbinic allusions, without compromising the poetic integrity of the composition. The glosses are printed in a column to the side of the page. Just as the ancient listener would hear the poem chanted in the synagogue and recall the biblical references and legends based on them, the modern reader will read the body of the poem and be able to consult the references without being distracted by footnotes. Further explanations and scholarly details, however, are provided in endnotes. Since the poems follow a prescribed order following biblical narrative (especially Genesis and Leviticus 16) and Mishnah Yoma, it may be helpful for the reader to have the appropriate texts at hand.

In a few cases we have left Hebrew terms untranslated, especially for specific sacrifices and sacrificial elements such as *Tamid*, the daily sacrifice, and *Minḥah* the grain offering. We define those in a brief glossary in the back, as well as a few uncommon English terms and translations of specific objects and places in the Temple system.

We have selected the following compositions for inclusion in this volume. This selection, we believe, conveys something of the history and variety of the Avodah as a genre in its early stages:

1. *Atah Barata*, "You Created," the first extant poetic expression of the Avodah and a preamble to *Shivʿat Yamim*;
2. *Shivʿat Yamim*, "Seven Days," the earliest Avodah liturgy, which restates the sacrificial procedure in language closely following the Mishnah;
3. *Atah Konanta ʿOlam Me-Rosh*, "You Established the World from the Beginning," the first fully poetic example of the Avodah;
4. *Az be-ʾEn Kol*, "When All Was Not," a massive anonymous composition distinguished by its extensive poetic treatment of cosmological and historical themes;
5. Selections from *Aromem la-ʾEl*, "Let Me Exalt God," an anonymous composition in the tradition of *Az be-ʾEn Kol*, which supplies details about the ritual not extant in *Az be-ʾEn Kol*;
6. *Azkir Gevurot Elohah*, "Let Me Recount the Wonders of God," by Yose ben Yose, the first Avodah piyyut by a named author and a composition of particular elegance;
7. *Atah Konanta ʿOlam be-Rov Ḥesed* "You Established the World in Great Mercy," another composition by Yose ben Yose;
8. *Emet Mah Nehedar*, "Truly, How Beautiful," a description of the radiance of the priest on his emergence from the sanctuary, based on a passage in the Book of Ben Sira;

9. *En Lanu Kohen Gadol*, "We Have No High Priest," a poignant lament by Yose ben Yose detailing the consequences of the destruction of the Temple.

1. Atah Barata
"You Created"

Atah Barata is perhaps the earliest poetic treatment of the themes of the Avodah. It is an introduction to the Avodah service and therefore ends not with a comprehensive description of the sacrifice but with the statement that God "informed [Aaron's sons] so that they might serve before [Him]." This leads naturally into the description of the sacrifice, which presumably takes place in a separate composition. In two manuscripts *Atah Barata* is used as the introduction to *Shiʿvat Yamim*, indicating a close relationship.[1] However, it is difficult to know if they were composed together. The main evidence for its antiquity is its literary style: like the earliest stage of piyyut, it employs lines composed of four feet, and it uses unrhymed acrostic. Unlike later piyyut, which is usually dense with allusions, this poem uses them more sparingly.[2] Despite its brevity, however, *Atah Barata* is not without interest. For example, the poem tells that the angels protested to God when he commanded Abraham to sacrifice his son Isaac, contrasting God's promise to Abraham with his command to kill his son. Although in Midrash Genesis Rabbah the angels are said to have wept when Abraham attempted to slaughter Isaac, their specific protest does not appear in that text. This is then an early attestation to the motif of the angels' protest to God.[3] Another interesting feature is the author's concentration on the genealogy of Aaron in his tracing of Israel's history, even to the exclusion of Moses.

This translation is based on Zvi Malachi's edition (*Ha-"ʿAvodah*," 2:125–26).

---

1. The known manuscripts of *Atah Barata* are TS H.5^A.6, TS H.10.122, and NS 156.172. Our thanks to Professor Ezra Fleischer for this information. According to Malachi, *Ha-"ʿAvodah*," 2:125, the composition serves as the introduction to *Shiʿvat* in MSS TS NS 156² and TS H5A¹⁹.
2. Malachi, *Ha-"ʿAvodah*," 1:13–15.
3. See Ginzberg, *Legends*, 1:281 and 5:251 n. 242.

You created
the entire world;
with great intelligence You established it
in love and mercy.

In wisdom and intelligence
You made the heavens
and spread out the earth
with understanding and knowledge.

Also from it
You formed Adam
and You caused his descendants to thrive
like the sands of the sea.

The generation of Nephilim
rejected Your word;
they also said to You,
"Go away from us."

You showed them
the magnitude of Your anger
and by **that which they vilified You**   water
You dealt with them.[4]

Then there arose among them
a small remnant:
this is Noah
whom You called "righteous."

From his descendants You produced
a pure and upright man:
Abraham, who loved You
with all his heart.

---

4. That is, the generation said, "We have our own water and we don't need God." Therefore, God punished them with water. See Mirsky, *Yose ben Yose*, 139, note to line 73 of *Azkir Gevurot*, citing Sifre Deut ʿEqev 43:16.

ATAH BARATA

אַתָּה בָּרָאתָ
אֶת כָּל הָעוֹלָם כֻּלּוֹ
בְּרוֹב שֵׂכֶל כּוֹנַנְתּוֹ
בְּחֶסֶד וּבְרַחֲמִים

בְּחָכְמָה וְהַשְׂכֵּל
שָׁמַיִם עָשִׂיתָה
וְרִקַּעְתָּ אֶרֶץ
בִּתְבוּנָה וּבְדַעַת

גַּם מִמֶּנָּה
אָדָם יָצַרְתָּה
וְצֶאֱצָאָיו הִרְבֵּיתָה
כְּחוֹל הַיָּם

דּוֹר הַנְּפִילִים
מָאֲסוּ דְּבָרֶיךָ
וְגַם אָמְרוּ לָךְ
סוּר מִמֶּנּוּ

הֶרְאֵיתָה אוֹתָם
אֶת רוֹב כַּעֲסֶיךָ
וּבַמָּה שֶׁחֵירְפוּךָ
בָּהֶם דַּנְתָּם

וְעָמַד מֵהֶם
שָׂרִיד כִּמְעַט
זֶה נֹחַ
שֶׁקְּרָאתָ צַדִּיק

זַךְ וְיָשָׁר
מִצֶּאֱצָאָיו הוֹצֵאתָה
זֶה אַבְרָהָם שֶׁאֲהֵבְךָ
בְּכָל לְבָבוֹ

מים

You announced Your devotion
to all who come into the world
and at one hundred years You gave him
the fruit of the womb.

Before **he** grew up   Isaac
You tested **him**   Abraham
when You said to him, "Offer him
before Me as a burnt offering."

Your angels became agitated
when they saw him bound;
when he arose to slaughter him,
they all cried out:

"'So shall your descendants be'[5]
is how You blessed his father,
and if this one is slaughtered
how can it be a blessing?"

So You decided
to spare him from the fire
and from the knife
You saved his offspring.

From him You produced
a beloved from the womb:
this is Jacob
whom You called firstborn.

You found comfort
in his children
so You created
what You created for their sake.[6]

---

5. Gen 15:5. The angels argue that God promised Abraham that his descendants would be as numerous as the stars in the sky, and that God would break his promise if Isaac were to be sacrificed.

חִיבַּתְךָ הוֹדַעְתָּ
לְכָל בָּאֵי חֶלֶד
וּלְמֵאָה שָׁנָה נָתַתָּה לוֹ
פְּרִי בָטֶן

טֶרֶם יִגְדַּל **יצחק**
אוֹתוֹ נִסִּיתָה
בְּאָמְרָךְ לוֹ הַעֲלֵיהוּ
לְפָנַי לְעוֹלָה

יְדוֹדוּן מַלְאָכֶיךָ **אברהם**
בִּרְאוֹתָם אוֹתוֹ נֶעֱקָד
וּבְקוּמוֹ לְשָׁחֲטוֹ
כֻּלָּם צָעֲקוּ

כֹּה יִהְיֶה זַרְעֲךָ
לְאָבִיו בֵּרַכְתָּ
וְאִם זֶה נִשְׁחָט
אֵיכָן הִיא בְרָכָה

לָכֵן רָצִיתָה
לְמַלְּטוֹ מִן הָאֵשׁ
וּמִן הַמַּאֲכֶלֶת
לִנִינוֹ הִצַּלְתָּה

מִמֶּנּוּ הוֹצֵאתָ
יָדִיד מִבֶּטֶן
זֶה יַעֲקֹב
שֶׁקְּרָאתוֹ בְּכוֹר

נַחַת רוּחַ
מִבָּנָיו מָצָאתָה
לָכֵן מַה שֶּׁבָּרָאתָ
כְּנֶגְדָּם בְּרָאתָה

---

6. The idea seems to be that the world was created for the sake of Israel.

You distinguished a treasure
from among his children:
this is Levi,
the third from the womb.

You looked favorably
on those who came forth from his loins:
this is Aaron,
the first holy man.

You specified to him with what[7]
he should enter the shrine
and informed him of what he should do
before You on the Day of Pardoning.

You clothed him in righteousness
in garments white as snow
and added **four**   garments
more than his brothers'.

You sanctified him
as You sanctified Your seraphim
for he appeases (You for)
the sins of Your people.

You made him a chief
for the descendants of the **father of a multitude**   Abraham
and an officer
for **the third seed**.[8]   Levi

The names of Your tribes
You placed on his two shoulders
so that when he entered before You
they could be remembered for good.

---

7. Heb. *be-ʾezeh;* cf. Lev 16:3, which specifies the conditions under which the high priest is to enter the holy of holies.

סְגוּלָה הִבְדַּלְתָּה
מִבֵּין בָּנָיו
זֶה לֵוִי
שְׁלִישִׁי לַבֶּטֶן

עֵינֶיךָ שַׂמְתָּה
בְּיוֹצְאֵי יְרֵכוֹ
זֶה אַהֲרֹן
רֹאשׁ קְדוֹשֶׁיךָ

פֵּרַשְׁתָּ לּוֹ בְּאֵיזֶה
יָבוֹא אֶל הַקֹּדֶשׁ
וְהוֹדַעְתּוֹ לְפָנֶיךָ
מַה יַּעֲשֶׂה בְּיוֹם הַסְּלִיחָה

צֶדֶק הִלְבַּשְׁתּוֹ
בְּגָדָיו כַּשֶּׁלֶג
וְלִיסוֹף **אַרְבָּעָה**   **בגדים**
יֶתֶר מֵאֶחָיו

קִדַּשְׁתּוֹ
כִּקְדוּשַׁת שְׂרָפֶיךָ
כִּי הוּא מְרַצֶּה
עֲווֹנוֹת עַמֶּךָ

רֹאשׁ עֲשִׂיתוֹ
לְצֶאֱצָאֵי **אַב הֲמוֹן**   **אברהם**
וְקָצִין
לְשַׁלֵּשׁ **זַרְעוֹ**   **לוי**

שְׁמוֹת שְׁבָטֶיךָ
עַל שְׁתֵּי כְתֵפָיו שַׂמְתָּה
שֶׁבִּכְנִיסָתוֹ לְפָנֶיךָ
יִזָּכְרוּ לְטוֹבָה

---

8. Levi is the third son. Heb. *le-shalesh*; alternatively, one might emend to *le-shamesh* (to serve).

As a substitute for atonement
you informed his sons
so that they might serve before you
following his example.

תְּמוּרַת כַּפָּרָה
לְבָנָיו הוֹדַעְתָּ
שֶׁיַּעֲשׂוּ לְפָנֶיךָ
כַּיּוֹצֵא בּוֹ

2. Shivʿat Yamim
"Seven Days"

This text is the earliest extant version of the Avodah service. It does not take the form of poetry but is rather a liturgical reworking of Mishnah Yoma. It gives us a reasonable picture of what kind of recitation of the Mishnah the Talmud might be describing.[1] The text is one of those Avodah services mentioned in the ninth-century rabbinic prayer manual of Rav Amram Gaon.[2]

Although *Shivʿat Yamim* follows the Mishnah closely, it omits much and introduces some changes. Most significantly, it omits minority opinions of individual sages and much legal detail. It also adds details found in the Tosefta and the Palestinian Talmud, as well as a section adapted from Mishnah Tamid. The text also features a full text of the confessions of the high priest. Some details and transitional phrases, however, seem to be original to this text.[3]

Shivʿat Yamim was first published by Ismar Elbogen in 1907.[4] This translation is based on an improved version of Zvi Malachi's edition.[5] Text included in *Shivʿat Yamim* that does not derive from the Mishnah is set in boldface type.

---

1. B. Yoma 36b, 56b; see the Introduction, above.
2. *Seder Rav Amram Gaon*, ed. Daniel Goldschmidt (Jerusalem: Mossad Harav Kook, 1971), § 127, p. 168.
3. See Malachi, *Ha-"Avodah,"* 1:12–14, and Menahem H. Schmeltzer, "How Was the High Priest Kept Awake on the Night of Yom ha-Kippurim?" in *Saul Lieberman (1898-1983), Talmudic Scholar*, ed. Meir Lubetski (Lewiston, N.Y.: Edwin Mellen, 2002), 59–70.
4. Elbogen, *Studien*.
5. Malachi, *Ha-"Avodah,"* 2:127–31. We have also consulted the translations of Mishnah Yoma by Herbert Danby, *The Mishnah Translated from the Hebrew with Introduction and Brief Explanatory Notes* (London: Oxford University Press, 1933; repr., 1974), and Jacob Neusner, *The Mishnah: A New Translation* (New Haven: Yale University Press, 1988), in our translation.

[1:1] Seven days before Yom Kippur they would remove the high priest from his house to the Councilors' Chamber, and prepare another priest in his place in case something happened to disqualify him. **The elders of the court handed him over to the elders of the priesthood,** and they read to him from the order of the day.[6]

[1:3] All those seven days **he would slaughter and** toss the blood, offer the incense, and repair the lamps and sacrifice the head and hind leg. Then they said to him: "Sir High Priest: Read, yourself," lest he forgot or did not learn.[7] On the eve of Yom Kippur, at dawn, they stood him at the eastern gate and passed bulls, rams, and sheep before him so that he could become familiar and accustomed to the sacrifice, **and so that he would know which to sacrifice first and which to sacrifice last**. All those seven days they would not forbid him food and drink.

The elders of the court then handed him to the elders of the priesthood **and led him** to the upper chamber of the house of Avtinas. Then they adjured him and departed and went their own way. **And they said to him:** "Sir High Priest: We are emissaries of the court, and you are our emissary and the emissary of the court, **and you are the messenger of the community.**[8] We adjure you by Him who caused His name to dwell in this house that you change nothing of all we have told you, **so that you do not sacrifice the first [animal] last and the last first, and that you do not burn the incense outside and bring it inside, and not do as the Sadducees, but do the first first and the last last, as we have adjured you to do and demonstrated it before you." He would** turn aside and weep, and they turned aside and wept.

If he was a sage, he would lecture. If not, they would lecture before him. If he was accustomed to reading, he would read. If not, they read before him from Job, Ezra, and Chronicles. **And if he was an ignoramus,**[9] **they would engage him with discourse about kings and discourse about the early pious men.**

---

6. The ritual procedure for Yom Kippur.
7. Mishnah: "lest you forgot or did not learn."

[א, א] שבעת ימים קודם ליום הכפורים מפרישין כהן גדול מביתו ללשכת פלהדרין ומתקינין לו כהן אחר תחתיו שמא יארע בו פסול. **מסרוהו זקני בית דין לזקני כהונה** וקורין לפניו בסדר היום ומלמדים אתו סדר יום הכפורים.

[א, ג] כל שבעת הימים **הוא שוחט** והוא זורק את הדם ומקטיר את הקטרת ומטיב את הנרות ומקריב את הראש ואת הרגל. ואומרים לו אישי כהן גדול קרא אתה בפיך שמא שכח ושמא לא למד. ערב יום הכפורים בשחרית מעמידין אותו בשער המזרח ומעבירין לפניו פרים ואלים וכבשים כדי שיהא מכיר ורגיל בעבודה **וכדי שיהא מכיר איזה מקריב ראשון ואיזה מקריב אחרון.** כל שבעת הימים לא היו מונעין ממנו מאכל ומשתה.

מסרוהו זקני בית דין לזקני כהונה **והוליכוהו** לעליית בית אבטינס והשביעוהו ונפטרו והלכו להם. **ואומרין לו אישי כהן גדול,** אנו שלוחי בית דין, ואתה שלוחנו ושלוח בית דין **ושלוח צבור אתה.** משביעין אנו עליך במי ששיכן את שמו בבית הזה, שלא תשנה דבר מכל שאמרנו לך **ושלא תחליף ותקריב ראשון אחרון ואחרון ראשון ולא תקטיר מבחוץ ותכניס לפנים ולא תעשה כמעשה הצידוקים אלא ראשון ראשון ואחרון אחרון כמה שהשבענוך ועבדנו לפניך.** היה פורש ובוכה והן פורשין ובוכין.

אם היה חכם דורש ואם לאו תלמידי חכמים דורשין לפניו. אם רגיל לקרות קורא ואם לאו קוראים לפניו באיוב ובעזרא ובדברי הימים. **ואם עם הארץ הוא, משיחין לפניו שיחת מלכים שיחת חסידים הראשונים.**

---

8. Heb. *sheliaḥ ṣibbur*, a term also used for the prayer leader in the synagogue; see the Introduction.

9. Heb. *ʿAm ha-ʾAreṣ*.

On the eve of Yom Kippur, toward nightfall, they would not let him eat too much, **so that he would not become drowsy or fall asleep and become impure and disqualified, and so his eyes would not see sleep and drowsiness.**[10] If he wanted to doze, young **Levites**[11] would make a noise with the middle finger. **And this is what they would say to him: "A song of ascents, by Solomon: Unless the Lord builds the house, its builders labor in vain on it."** (Ps 127:1): Then they would say to him: "Sir High Priest: Stand up and walk around the pavement, **so that you do not incur invalidation, for the purity of Israel is dependent on you." And all the Jerusalemites** would engage him **all night, group by group,** until the time came for the sacrifice. **When the time came for the sacrifice, he went to the place of immersion.**

They spread out a linen sheet between him and the people. He undressed, went down, immersed, went up, and dried himself. They brought him golden garments, and he put them on and washed his hands and feet. They brought him the **lamb** for the daily sacrifice (Tamid), **and dragged it and led it to the slaughtering place, and they gave it water to drink from a golden cup. Although it had been inspected the previous evening, they inspected it by the light of torches.**[12] **They brought him the knife,** he made an incision, and someone else finished the slaughtering. He collected the blood and tossed it, went to burn the incense[13] and repair the lamps, **as it is written, "On it Aaron shall burn the aromatic incense; he shall burn it every morning when he tends the lamps."** (Exod 30:7)—and to sacrifice the head, the limbs, the cakes, and the wine, [went] **to the ramp, and ascended the ramp. The prefect extended his hand and led him up with him to the altar,** took the limbs in order and arranged them on the pile of wood. He began to offer the wine libation, and the Levites would sing. The priests would blow trumpets—they would blow a *teruʿah*,[14] *teqiʿah*,[15] and *teruʿah*. Then the people would bow down after each break in the trumpeting and would bow down after each *teqiʿah*. **This was the order of the Tamid.**[16]

ערב יום הכפור' עם חשכה לא היו מניחין אותו לאכול הרבה **כדי שלא ינום ולא יישן ולא יטמא ולא יפסל ולא תראינה עיניו שינה ותנומה.** בקש להתנמנם פרחי לויה מכין לפניו באצבע צרדה. **וכן היו אומרין שיר המעלות לשלמה:** אם יייי לא יבנה בית שוא עמלו בוניו בו. ואומרין לו אישי כהן גדול עמוד והפוך אחת על הרצפה **כדי שלא תבוא לידי פסול מפני טהרת ישראל תלויה בך.** וכל אנשי ירושלם היו מעסיקין אותו **כל הלילה חבורה בחבורה** עד שמגיע זמן שחיטה. **כיון שהגיע זמן שחיטה בא לו לבית הטבילה.**

פרסו לו סדין של בוץ בינו לבין העם. פשט ירד וטבל עלה ונסתפג. הביאו לו בגדי זהב ולבש, וקידש ידיו ורגליו. הביאו לו **את הכבש** התמיד ומשכו והוליכו לבית המטבחיים והשקהו מים בכוס של זהב. **ואף על פי שמבוקר מבערב מבקרין אותו לאור האבוקות. הביאו לו את הסכין** קרצו ומירק אחר שחיטה על ידו. קבל את הדם וזרקו, נכנס להקטיר את הקטורת ולהטיב את הנרות **ככתוב: והקטיר עליו אהרן קטרת סמים בבקר בבקר בהטיבו את הנרות יקטירנה,** ולהקריב את הראש ואת האברין ואת החבתים ואת היין **לכבש ועלה לכבש. הושיט לו הסגן את ידו והעלהו עמו על גבי המזבח נטל את האברין כסדרן וסידרן על גבי מערכה. התחיל לנסך את היין והלוים מדברים בשיר. והכהנים תוקעים בחצוצרות הריעו תקעו והריעו. והשתחוו העם על כל פרק ופרק תקיעה ועל כל תקיעה השתחויה. זה סדר התמיד.**

---

10. If he fell asleep, there would be a danger of a seminal emission, which would render him impure.
11. Mishnah: priests.
12. Cf. m. Tamid 3:3–4.
13. Mishnah has here "of the morning."
14. Probably a tremolo of a series of staccato notes.
15. A long sound rising at the end.
16. Cf. m. Tamid 7:3.

After he finished (sacrificing) the lamb for the Tamid, they brought him to the chamber of Parvah, which was in the holy place. They spread out **for him** a linen sheet between him and the people. He washed his hands and feet and undressed, went down and immersed, went up and dried himself. They brought him linen garments, and he put them on and washed his hands and his feet.

They brought him a bull and a ram and two goats for the sin offering and a ram for the burnt offering from public property and the Temple treasury, as it is written, "With this shall Aaron enter [the Shrine: with a bull of the herd for a sin offering and a ram for a burnt offering]" (Lev 16:3), **and it is written: "And from the Israelite community [he shall take two he-goats for a sin offering and a ram for a burnt offering]. (Lev 16:5)"**[17] **He led the bull and stood it between the porch and the altar, then led the goats, and stood them in the north. Then** he approached his bull, which was standing between the porch and the altar, its head to the south and its face to the west. The priest was standing in the east with his face to the west. Then he laid his two hands on it and confessed.

> Thus he would say: "O Lord, I have sinned, I have done wrong, I have transgressed before You, I and my household. O, by the Lord,[18] forgive the sins and iniquities and transgressions that I have committed against You, I and my household, as it is written in the Torah of Moses, Your servant: 'For on this day [atonement shall be made for you to cleanse you of all your sins; before the Lord—'" (Lev 16:30)]

> And **when** the priests and the people standing in the court **and serving in the sanctuary heard the** explicit name coming forth from the mouth of the high priest **in holiness,** they would kneel, prostrate themselves, and fall to their faces and say: "Blessed is the name of His Majesty's glory for ever and ever."

---

17. Cf. Sifra Aḥare Mot 2 (ed. Weiss, fol. 80d).

לאחר שסיים את הכבש התמיד הביאוהו לבית הפרוה ובקדש היתה. פרסו **לו** סדין של בוץ בינו לבין העם. קדש ידיו ורגליו ופשט ירד וטבל עלה ונסתפג. הביאו לו בגדי לבן ולבש וקידש ידיו ורגליו.

הביאו לו פר ואיל ושני שעירים לחטאת ואיל לעולה מנכסי צבור ותרומת הלשכה, ככ' בזאת יבא אהרן וג': וככתוב: ומאת עדת בני יש' וגו'. משך את הפר והעמידו בין האולם למזבח ומשך את השעירים והעמידן בצפון. ואחר כך בא לו אצל פרו ופרו היה עומד בין האולם ולמזבח, ראשו לדרום ופניו למערב, והכהן עומד במזרח ופניו במערב. וסומך שתי ידיו עליו ומתודה.

וכך היה אומר: אנא השם חטאתי עויתי פשעתי לפניך אני וביתי. אנא בשם כפר נא על החטאים ועל העונות ועל הפשעים שחטאתי שעויתי שפשעתי לפניך אני וביתי, ככ' בתורת מש' עבדך כי ביום הזה יכפר עליכם לטהר אתכם מכל חטאתיכם לפני יהוה.

והכהנים והעם העומדים בעזרה והמשרתים בהיכל בזמן ששמעו את השם המפורש שהוא יוצא מפי כהן גדול **בקדושה** היו כורעים ומשתחוים ונופלים על פניהם ואומרים ברוך שם כבוד מלכותו לעולם ועד.

---

18. Heb. *ba-Shem*.

He would also aim to finish the name while facing those saying the blessing and say to them, "You shall be pure."

He approached the east of the court north of the altar, the prefect at his right and the head of the priestly division at his left. There were two goats there, and the urn was there. He shook the urn and took up two lots. On one was written "for the Lord" and on one was written "for Azazel." If the one for the Lord came up in his right hand, the prefect said, "Sir High Priest, raise your right hand," and if it came up in his left, the head of the priestly division said, "Sir High Priest, raise your left hand." Then he placed them on the two goats And he would say, "This is the ḥatta't for the Lord," **as it is written, "And Aaron shall take the two he-goats and let them stand before the Lord at the entrance of the Tent of Meeting; and he shall place lots upon the goats, [one marked for the Lord and the other marked for Azazel.] Aaron shall bring forward the goat designated by lot for the Lord, which he is to offer as a sin offering (Lev 16:7 9). And he left the goat designated for Azazel standing, as it is written, "while the goat which is designated for Azazel shall be left standing alive before the Lord, to make expiation with it and to send it off to the wilderness for Azazel" (Lev 16:10), to an inaccessible region, a desolate wilderness, it is written, "Thus the goat shall carry all their iniquities [to an inaccessible region]" (Lev 16:22).**

He tied a thread of crimson wool to the head of the scapegoat and stood it opposite the place where it was to be sent, and the one to be slaughtered toward the place of slaughter.

Afterward, he approached his second bull, **laid** his hands on it, and confessed.

> Thus he would say: "O Lord, I have sinned, I have done wrong, I have transgressed before You, I and my household and the children of Aaron, Your holy people. O Lord,[19] forgive the sins and iniquities and transgressions that I have committed against You, I and my household and the children

---

19. Heb. *ha-Shem*.

אף הוא מתכון לגמור את השם כנגד המברכים ואומר להם תטהרו.

בא לו למזרח העזרה בצפון המזבח הסגן מימינו וראש בית אב משמאלו. ושם שני שעירים וקלפי היתה שם. טרף בקלפי והעלה שני גורלות, אחד כתוב עליו של שם, ואחד כתוב עליו לעזאזל. אם שם עלה בימינו הסגן אומר לו אישי כהן גדול הגבה ימינך ואם בשמאלו עלה ראש בית אב אומר לו אישי כהן גדול הגבה שמאלך. ונתנן על שני השעירים ואומר לה׳ חטאת, **ככ׳ ולקח את שני השעירים והעמיד אותם לפני יייי פתח אהל מועד, ונתן אהרן על שני השעירים גורלות וג׳, והקריב אהרן את השעיר אשר עלה עליו הגורל לייי ועשהו חטאת. ושל עזאזל יעמידנו, ככ׳ והשעיר אשר עלה וג׳, לשלח אתו המדברה, לארץ גזירה למדבר שומם, ככ׳ ונשא השעיר עליו את כל עונ׳ וג׳.**

קשר לשון של זהורית בראש שעיר המשתלח העמידו כנגד בית שלוחו ולנשחט כנגד בית שחיטתו.

ואחר כן בא לו אצל פרו שניה, **סומך** שתי ידיו עליו ומתודה,

וכך היה אומר אנא השם חטאתי עויתי פשעתי לפניך אני וביתי ובני אהרן עם קדושיך. אנא בשם כפר נא על החטאים ועל העונות ועל הפשעים שחטאתי שעויתי שפשעתי לפניך אני וביתי ובני

of Aaron, Your holy people, as it is written in the Torah of Moses, Your servant: 'For on this day [atonement shall be made for you to cleanse you of all your sins; before the Lord—'" (Lev 16:30)

And **when** the priests and the people standing in the court **and serving in the sanctuary heard the** explicit name coming forth from the mouth of the high priest **in holiness,** they would kneel, prostrate themselves, and fall to their faces and say: "Blessed is the name of His Majesty's glory for ever and ever."]

He slaughtered it and collected its blood in a basin, and gave it to the one who would stir it, on the fourth terrace in the sanctuary, so that it would not curdle. He took the fire-pan and went up to the top of the altar and cleared [some of the coals inside], and went down and put it on the fourth terrace of the court.

They brought out the ladle and the fire-pan; he took a handful and put it into the ladle. **As it is written, "He shall take a panful"** (Lev 16:12)each according to the size (of his hand).[20] [He placed the fire-pan in his right hand and the ladle in his left, **and** walked in the sanctuary until he came between the two curtains that divide the holy place from the holy of holies. There was a cubit between them. **When he went in between the curtains**—the outer one was fastened from the south and the inner one from the north—he walked between them until he got to the north. When he got to the north, he turned, facing the south. **He faced** the curtain until he arrived at the ark. When he arrived at the altar, he placed the fire-pan between the two rods of the ark. He piled up the incense **and placed it** on the coals, and the house was filled with smoke. He came out the way he had gone in, and said a short prayer in the outer chamber. He would not extend his prayer, so as not to frighten Israel.

---

20. Lit., "the large according to his large size, and the small according to his small size."

אהרן, ככ׳ בתורת מש׳ עבדך כי ביום הזה יכפר עליכם לטהר אתכם מכל חטאתיכם לפני יהוה

והכהנים והעם העומדים בעזרה **והמשרתים בהיכל בזמן ששמעו את** השם המפורש שהוא יוצא מפי כהן גדול **בקדושה** היו כורעים ומשתחוים ונופלים על פניהם ואומרים ברוך שם כבוד מלכותו לעולם ועד.

שחטו וקבל במזרק את דמו ונותנו למי שהוא ממרס בו על הרובד הרביעי שבהיכל, כדי שלא יקרוש. נטל את המחתה ועלה לראש המזבח, וחתה מן המעוכלות הפנימיות וירד והניחה על הרובד הרביעי שבעזרה.

הוציאו לו את הכף ואת המחתה וחפן מלא חפניו ונתן לתוך הכף, ככ׳ **ולקח מלא המחתה,** הגדול לפי גודלו והקטן לפי קוטנו. נטל את המחתה בימינו ואת הכף בשמאלו ומהלך בהיכל עד שמגיע לבין שתי הפרכות המבדילות בין הקדש ובין קדש הקדשים וביניהם אמה. **כיון שהגיע לבין שתי הפרכות** החיצונה פרופה מן הדרום והפנימית מן הצפון מהלך ביניהן עד שמגיע לצפון. הגיע לצפון הפך פניו לדרום. **הפך פניו** עם הפרוכת עד שמגיע לארון. הגיע לארון נתן את המחתה בין שני בדי ארון. צבר את הקטורת **ונתן** על גבי גחלים נתמלא הבית עשן. יצא לו ובא לו דרך בית כניסתו ומתפלל תפלה קצרה בבית החיצון. ולא היה מאריך בתפלתו כדי שלא להבעית את ישראל.

This is what he would pray: May it be Your will, that this year be a year [of abundance],[21] and let not the prayers of travelers[22] enter before You.[23]

Afterward, he went out and took the blood from the one who was stirring it. He went in [to the place where he went in] and stood at the place where he stood, and sprinkled some of it, once up and seven times down. He did not aim to sprinkle either up or down, but as if he were whipping. And this is how he would count: "one, one and two, one and three, one and four, one and five, one and six, one and seven." He went out and set it down on the golden stand in the sanctuary.

They brought him the goat, he slaughtered it and collected its blood in a basin, **as it is written, "He shall slaughter the people's goat of sin offering, bring its blood [behind the curtain, and do with its blood as he had done with the blood of the bull]"** (Lev 16:15). He went in [to the place where he went in] and stood at the place where he stood, and sprinkled some of it, once up and seven times down. He did not aim to sprinkle either up or down, but as if he were whipping. And this is how he would count: "one, one and two, one and three, one and four, one and five, one and six, one and seven." He went out and set it down on the second stand in the sanctuary.

He set down the blood of the goat and took up the blood of the bull and sprinkled some of it on the curtain opposite the ark, once up and seven times down. He did not aim to sprinkle either up or down, but as if he were whipping.

He took the blood of the goat and set down the blood of the bull and sprinkled some of it on the curtain opposite the ark from outside, once up and seven times down. He did aim to sprinkle up or down, but as if he were whipping. And this is how he would count: "one, one and two," etc. He poured the blood of the bull into the blood of the goat and he transferred (the contents of) the full (vessel) into the empty one.

---

21. The manuscript has only the letter *shin* or *sin*, which, judging from the parallels, could stand either for *sheḥunah* (heat) or for *sova* (abundance). Cf. y. Yoma 5:3 (42c).

וכך היה מתפלל: יהי רצון מלפניך שתהא השנה הזאת שנת שובע וכו' ולא תכנס לפניך תפלת עוברי דרכים

אחר כך יצא ונטל את הדם ממי שהוא ממריס בו. נכנס למקום שנכנס ועמד במקום שעמד והזה ממנו אחת למעלה ושבע למטה. ולא היה מתכוין להזות לא למעלה ולא למטה אלא כמצליף. וכך היה מונה אחת ואחת ושתים, א' וג', א' וד', א' וה', א' וו', אחת ושבע. יצא והניחו על כן זהב שבהיכל.

הביאו לו את השעיר, שחטו וקבל במזרק את דמו, **כב' ושחט את שעיר החטאת אשר לעם והביא א' דמו אל וג'.** ונכנס למקום שנכנס ועמד במקום שעמד, והזה ממנו אחת למעלה ושבע למטה. ולא היה מתכוין להזות לא למעלה ולא למטה אלא כמצליף. וכך היה מונה אחת, א' וא' וכ' יצא והניחו על כן השני שהיה בהיכל.

הניח דם השעיר ונטל דם הפר והזה ממנו על הפרוכת שכנגד הארון מבחוץ אחת למעלה ושבע למטה, ולא היה מתכוין להזות לא למעלה ולא למטה אלא כמצליף.

נטל דם השעיר והניח דם הפר והזה ממנו על הפרוכת כנגד הארון מבחוץ אחת למעלה וש' למטה ולא היה מתכוין להזות לא למעלה ולא למטה אלא כמצליף. וכך היה כו'. עירה דם הפר לתוך דם השעיר ונתן את המלא בריקן.

---

22. Who pray that it not rain.
23. Cf. y. Yoma 5:3 (42c); t. Kippurim 2:1; b. Yoma 53b.

He then went to the altar that was before the Lord **and purged it**—this is the golden altar, **as it is written: He shall go out to the altar** (Lev 16:18). He began to purge the altar from sin[24] (and continue). And from where would he begin? From the northeastern horn (of the altar), the northwestern, the southwestern, to the southeastern. The places where he would begin purging the outer altar were where he would finish on the inner altar.

He sprinkled on the top of the altar seven times. Then he poured [the rest of the blood] on the western base of the outside altar, and poured [the rest of the blood] from the outside altar on the southern base.

Afterward, he approached the scapegoat **and said a confession over it for the guilt of the community.** He laid his hands on it **and confessed.**

> Thus he would say: "O Lord, **they have sinned, they have done wrong, they have transgressed** before You, Your people, the house of Israel. O by the Lord,[25] forgive the sins and iniquities and transgressions that I have committed against You, I, my household, and the sons of Aaron, as it is written in the Torah of Moses, Your servant: 'For on this day atonement shall be made for you to cleanse you of all your sins; you shall be pure before the Lord.'" (Lev 16:30)

> And **when** the priests and the people standing in the court **and serving in the sanctuary heard the** explicit name coming forth from the mouth of the high priest **in holiness,** they would kneel, prostrate themselves, and fall to their faces and say: "Blessed is the name of His Majesty's glory for ever and ever."

Thus it is written: Aaron shall lay both his hands upon the head of the live goat and confess over it all the iniquities and transgressions [of the Israelites] (Lev 16:21).

---

24. Heb. *meḥatṭe*, "purged [the altar] from sin," as opposed to *mekhapper*, "purged," above in the same paragraph.

ויצא אל המזבח אשר לפני ה' **וכפר עליו** זה מזבח הזהב, כך **ויצא אל המזבח וג'**. התחיל מחטא ויורד. מאיכן הוא מתחיל, מקרן מזרחית צפונית מערבית צפונית מערבית דרומית דרומית מזרחית. מקום שהוא מתחיל בחטאת על מזבח החיצון שם הוא גומר על מזבח הפנימי.

הזה על טהרו של המזבח שבע פעמים ושירי הדם היה שופך על יסוד מערבי של מזבח החיצון, ושל מזבח החיצון היה שופך על יסוד דרומי.

ואחר כך בא לו אצל שעיר המשתלח **והתודה עליו אשמת קהילה**. סומך שתי ידיו עליו **נתודה**.

וכך היה אומר אנא השם **חטאו עוו פשעו** לפניך עמך בית ישראל. אנא השם כפר נא על **החטאים ועל העוונות ועל הפשעים שחטאו שעוו שפשעו** לפניך עמך בית ישראל ככתוב בתורת משה עבדך כי ביום הזה יכפר עליכם לטהר אתכם מכל חטאתיכם לפני יהוה

והכהנים והעם העומדים בעזרה **בזמן** ששמעו את השם המפורש שהוא יוצא מפי כהן גדול **בקדושה** היו כורעים ומשתחוים ונופלים על פניהם ואומרים ברוך שם כבוד מלכותו לעולם ועד.

וכך כת' וסמך אהרן את שתי ידיו על ראש השעיר החי והתודה עליו את כל עונת [...]

---

25. Heb. *ha-Shem*.

3. Atah Konanta ʿOlam Me-Rosh
"You Established the World from the Beginning"

This anonymous composition is the earliest true Avodah piyyut extant. It contains all the elements that became characteristic of the genre: the historical preamble, selection of Aaron, praise of the priesthood, and the reworking of Mishnah Yoma into a poetic narrative. It is popular in the Sephardic and Middle Eastern liturgies, but not Ashkenaz and France. In the eighteenth century the Hasidic liturgy, which was based in part on the Sephardic liturgy, took it up. The piyyut is printed in Daniel Goldschmidt's edition of the Maḥzor and in the liturgical handbook of Saadia Gaon.[1] This translation is based on Goldschmidt's edition.

The poem is in the form of an acrostic, forward and then backward. In keeping with the style of preclassical piyyut, each line consists of four feet. The language, however, is fairly straightforward; it lacks the constant circumlocutions and substitutions that begin with the early classical piyyutim we shall see in the following texts. Yet the poem does not lack artfulness, and there is certainly editorial and ideological treatment of the Mishnaic account. One example of this is the poem's emphasis on the volition, piety, and diligence of the priest, in contrast to the Mishnah's portrayal of him as a passive recipient of the sages' instructions.[2]

---

[1]. Goldschmidt, *Maḥazor*, 2:19–23 [Hebrew numbering]; Davidson, Assaf, and Joel, *Siddur Rav Saʿadiah*, 275–80. A prose translation appears in *Ḥazon Yeḥezkel: A Prayerbook for Yom Kippur According to the Oriental Sephardic Rite*, ed. and trans. Earl Klein (Los Angeles: Kahal Joseph Sephardic Congregation, 1994), 435–51.

[2]. See the Introduction, above.

You established
the world from the beginning;
You founded the earth
and formed creatures.

When You surveyed the world
of chaos and confusion
You banished gloom
and put light in place.

You formed from the earth
a lump of soil in Your image
and commanded him
concerning the tree of life.

He forsook Your word
and he was forsaken from Eden
but You did not destroy him
for the sake of the work of Your hands.[3]

You increased his fruit
and blessed his seed
and let them flourish in Your goodness
and let them live in quiet.

But they broke the yoke
and said to God, "Go away,"[4]
then You took away Your hand
and they withered[5] instantly like grass.

You remembered Your covenant
with **the one who was blameless in his generation**   Noah
and as a reward You made him
a remnant forever.

You made a permanent covenant
of the rainbow for his sake
and in Your love for his fragrant offering
You blessed his children.

---

3. Heb. *yegiaʿ kappekha*; cf. Job 10:3, where Job asks God, "Does it benefit You … to despise the work of Your hands?"

אַתָּה כּוֹנַנְתָּ
עוֹלָם מֵרֹאשׁ
יָסַדְתָּ תֵבֵל
וּבְרִיּוֹת יָצַרְתָּ

בְּשׁוּרְךָ עוֹלָם
תֹּהוּ וָבֹהוּ
גֵּרַשְׁתָּ אֹפֶל
וְהִצַּבְתָּ נֹגַהּ

גֹּלֶם תַּבְנִיתְךָ
מִן הָאֲדָמָה יָצַרְתָּ
וְעַל עֵץ הַדַּעַת
אוֹתוֹ הִפְקַדְתָּ

דְּבָרְךָ זָנַח
וְנִזְנַח מֵעֵדֶן
וְלֹא כִלִּיתוֹ
לְמַעַן יְגִיעַ כַּפֶּיהָ

הִגְדַּלְתָּ פִּרְיוֹ
וּבֵרַכְתָּ זַרְעוֹ
וְהִפְרִיתָם בְּטוּבְךָ
וְהוֹשַׁבְתָּם שָׁקֵט

וַיִּפְרְקוּ עֹל
וַיֹּאמְרוּ לָאֵל סוּר
וַהֲסִירוֹת יָד
כְּרֶגַע אָמְלָלוּ כֶּחָצִיר

זָכַרְתָּ בְּרִית
לְתָמִים בְּדוֹרוֹ
וּבִשְׁכָרוֹ שַׂמְתָּ
לְעוֹלָם שְׁאֵרִית

חֹק בְּרִית קֶשֶׁת
לְמַעֲנוֹ כָּרַתָּ
וּבְאַהֲבַת נִיחוֹחוֹ
בָּנָיו בֵּרַכְתָּ

נוֹחַ

---

4. The generation of the flood rejected God, thus "breaking the yoke" of God's commandments.
5. Following Klein's translation in *Ḥazon Yeḥezkel*.

They erred in their wealth
and built a tower
and said, "Let us split the firmament
and fight against Him."

The **father of a multitude**   Abraham
shined forth like a star,
suddenly, from Ur of the Chaldees,
to illuminate in darkness.

You deferred Your anger
when You surveyed his deeds
and when he was old
You looked into his heart.

You brought forth from him
a fair garland,[6]   Isaac
a pure lamb
from a choice sheep.

From his root
you brought forth **a perfect man**[7]   Jacob
sealed with Your covenant
when he was taken from the womb.[8]

You gave him
twelve tribes,
beloved by the Most High,
they were called from the womb.

You placed a fair garland
of favor upon Levi,
and of all his brothers
You placed **a crown** on him.   the priesthood

---

6. See Prov 1:9.

7. The Hebrew word *tam*, applied to Jacob in Gen 25:27, can mean "simple" or "perfect." On the implication of his "perfection," see the following note.

	טָעוּ בְעָשְׁרָם
	וּבָנוּ מִגְדָּל
	וַיֹּאמְרוּ נַבְקִיעַ הָרָקִיעַ
	לְהִלָּחֶם בּוֹ
אברהם	**יָחִיד אַב הָמוֹן**
	פִּתְאוֹם כְּכוֹכָב
	זָרַח מֵאוּר כַּשְׂדִּים
	לְהָאִיר בַּחֹשֶׁךְ
	כַּעֲסֹךְ הַפְרָתְּ
	בְּשׁוּרָךְ פָּעֲלוֹ
	וּלְעֵת שַׁבָּתוֹ
	לְבָבוֹ חָקַרְתָּ
יצחק	**לִוְיַת חֵן**
	מִמֶּנּוּ הוֹצֵאתָ
	טָלֶה טָהוֹר
	מְכֻבָּשׁ נִבְחָר
	מִגִּזְעוֹ
יעקב	**אִישׁ תָּם** הוֹצֵאתָ
	חִתַּם בִּבְרִיתְךָ
	מֵרֶחֶם לָקַח
	נָתַתָּ לּוֹ
	שְׁנֵים עָשָׂר שְׁבָטִים
	אֲהוּבֵי עֶלְיוֹן
	מִבֶּטֶן נִקְרָאוּ
	שַׂמְתָּ עַל לֵוִי
	לִוְיַת חֵן וָחֶסֶד
	וּמִכָּל אֶחָיו
הכהונה	**כֶּתֶר** לוֹ עִטַּרְתָּ

---

8. Alluding to a legend that Jacob was born circumcised and therefore complete ("perfect"). See Avot de-Rabbi Natan A ch. 2 (ed. Schechter, p. 12); cf. the other sources cited in Ginzberg, *Legends*, 5:273 n. 26.

Amram was chosen
from the seed of Levi;
Aaron, holy to the Lord,
You sanctified from his stock.[9]

You adorned him
in woven garments,
and by his sacrifices
he annulled Your anger.

Diadem, robe,
and linen breeches,
breastpiece, ephod,
royal headdress, and sash;

sacrifice of bulls
and burnt offerings of sheep
and the slaughter of goats
and the cutting-up of rams;

the perfumed aroma
and the burning of coals
correct enumeration[10]
and the dashing of blood;

supplication at the incense
and true prayer;[11]
and his holiness,
which atones for our sins;

the measurement of fine linen
and the arrangement of jewels—
he is girded in all of these
like a ministering angel.

You ordained all these
for the glory of Aaron;
You made him for Israel
an instrument of atonement.

---

9. Cf. Klein's translation in *Ḥazon Yeḥezkel*.
10. Of the times the blood is sprinkled.

עַמְרָם נִבְחַר
מִזֶּרַע לֵוִי
אַהֲרֹן קְדוֹשׁ יְיָ
מִשָּׁרְשָׁיו קִדַּשְׁתָּ

פֵּאַרְתּוֹ
בְּבִגְדֵי שְׂרָד
וּבְקָרְבְּנוֹתָיו
הֵפֵר מַעֲשֵׂה

צִיץ וּמְעִיל
כֻּתֹּנֶת וּמִכְנְסֵי בַד
חֹשֶׁן וְאֵפוֹד
מִצְנֶפֶת וְאַבְנֵט

קָרְבְּנוֹת פָּרִים
וְעוֹלוֹת כְּבָשִׂים
וּשְׁחִיטַת עַתּוּדִים
וְנִתּוּחַ אֵלִים

רֵיחַ מִרְקַחַת
וּבְעוּר גֶּחָלִים
וּסְפִירַת יֹשֶׁר
וּזְרִיקַת דָּם

שַׁוְעַת קְטֹרֶת
וּתְפִלַּת אֱמֶת
וּקְדָשָׁתוֹ
מְכַפֶּרֶת עֲוֹנוֹתֵינוּ

תִּכֶּן בּוּץ
וַעֲרִיכַת אֶבֶן
מָחְגָּר בְּכֻלָּם
כְּמַלְאָךְ מְשָׁרֵת

תִּכַּנְתָּ כָּל אֵלֶּה
לִכְבוֹד אַהֲרֹן
כְּלִי כַפָּרָה
לְיִשְׂרָאֵל שַׂמְתּוֹ

11. See m. Yoma 5:1.

In Aaron's place
stood one of his clan
to serve before You
on the day of forgiveness.

For seven days
he studied in our Temple,
the laws of the procedure
and the service of the day.

For the elders of his people
and the sages of his brothers
perpetually surrounded him
until the day arrived.

"See before whom
you are entering,
to a place of fire,
a burning flame.

Our community's congregation
relies on you
and by your hands
will be our forgiveness."

They commanded him and taught
him until the tenth day
so that he would be accustomed
to the order of the Avodah.

They spread out for him a sheet
when he slaughtered the sheep
to make a separation
between him and the people.

He performed the commandment
in awe and fear
and examined himself
for interpositions (during) ablution.[12]

---

12. That is, for objects that prevent effective purification by their interposition between the water and the body.

תַּחַת אַהֲרֹן
מִגִּזְעוֹ יַעֲמֹד
לְשָׁרֵת לְפָנֶיךָ
בְּיוֹם הַסְּלִיחָה

תּוֹרַת מַעֲשֵׂה
וַעֲבוֹדַת הַיּוֹם
שִׁבְעַת יָמִים
בִּזְבוּלֵנוּ יִלְמַד

שֶׁזִּקְנֵי עָם
וְחַכְמֵי אֶחָיו
תָּמִיד יְסוֹבְבוּהוּ
עַד בּוֹא הַיּוֹם

"רְאֵה לִפְנֵי מִי
אַתָּה נִכְנָס
לִמְקוֹם אֵשׁ
לֶהָבַת שַׁלְהֶבֶת

קְהַל עֲדָתֵנוּ
עָלֶיךָ יִסְמֹכוּ
וְעַל יָדְךָ
תְּהֵא סְלִיחָתֵנוּ"

צִוּוּהוּ וְלִמְּדוּהוּ
עַד יוֹם הֶעָשׂוֹר
כְּדֵי שֶׁיְּהֵא מָרְגָּל
בְּסִדְרֵי עֲבוֹדָה

פֵּרְשׂוּ לוֹ סָדִין
בְּעֵת שְׁחִיטַת כֶּבֶשׂ
לַעֲשׂוֹת מְחִיצָה
בֵּינוֹ לְבֵין הָעָם

עוֹשֶׂה מִצְוָה
בְּאֵימָה וּבְיִרְאָה
וּבוֹדֵק עַצְמוֹ
מֵחוּצְצֵי טְבִילָה

He rejoiced in the commandment
to uphold His law
and went down and immersed
as he was instructed.

They gave him
golden garments,
and he put them on and washed
his hands and his feet.

Immediately he received
the sheep for the Tamid
and performed it as required,
as for the whole year.

Inside he entered
to offer the incense
and to repair the lamps
and to sacrifice limbs.

As commanded every day
he made cakes[13]
and offered the wine libation
in all proper vessels.

He came at once
to the house of Parvah,
and they spread for him
a sheet as before.

Before he took off
his golden garments,
he washed clean
his hands and his feet.

He began to take off
his golden garments
and went down and immersed
as he had immersed.

---

13. Heb. *ḥavitin*, referring to the griddle cakes baked for the daily offering. See Lev 6:13 (on

שָׂשׂ עַל מִצְוָה
לְקַיֵּם דָּתוֹ
וְיָרַד וְטָבַל
כְּמוֹ שֶׁהֻזְהַר

נָתְנוּ לוֹ
בִּגְדֵי זָהָב
וְלָבַשׁ וְקִדַּשׁ
יָדָיו וְרַגְלָיו

מִיָּד יְקַבֵּל
אֶת כֶּבֶשׂ הַתָּמִיד
וַעֲשָׂאוֹ כְּהִלְכָתוֹ
כְּכָל הַשָּׁנָה כֻּלָּהּ

לִפְנִים יִכָּנֵס
לְהַקְטִיר אֶת הַקְּטֹרֶת
וּלְהֵטִיב אֶת הַנֵּרוֹת
וּלְהַקְרִיב הָאֵבָרִים

כְּמִצְוָתָן בְּכָל יוֹם
יַעֲשֶׂה חֲבִתִּין
וִינַסֵּךְ אֶת הַיַּיִן
בְּכָל כְּלִי יֹשֶׁר

יָבוֹא מִיָּד
לְבֵית הַפַּרְוָה
וְיִפְרְשׂוּ לוֹ
סָדִין כְּבָרִאשׁוֹנָה

טֶרֶם יִפְשֹׁט
בִּגְדֵי זָהָב
מְקַדֵּשׁ בִּנְקִיּוּת
יָדָיו וְרַגְלָיו

חָל וּפָשַׁט
בִּגְדֵי זָהָב
וְיָרַד וְטָבַל
כְּמוֹ שֶׁטָּבַל

---

which, see Levine, *Leviticus*, 38-39); Jastrow, *Dictionary*, s.v. ḥavitin.

He set aside the gold
and put on white,
for the service of the day is
to be performed in white garments.

He hurried and washed
his hands and his feet
and first approached
toward his bull.

He stood in awe
before the Most High
and said over it
words of confession.

Then he placed his hands on it and confessed. Thus he would say: ["O Lord, I have sinned, I have done wrong, I have transgressed before You, I and my household. O Lord, forgive the sins and iniquities and transgressions that I have committed against you, I and my household, as it is written in the Torah of Moses, Your servant: 'For on this day atonement shall be made for you to cleanse you of all your sins; before the Lord—' ". And when the priests and the people standing in the court and serving in the Sanctuary heard the explicit name coming forth from the mouth of the high priest in holiness and purity, they would kneel, prostrate themselves, and fall to their faces and say: "Blessed is the name of His Majesty's glory for ever and ever." He would also intend to finish the name while facing those saying the blessing and say to them, "You shall be pure."]

He spoke; then they brought him
two goats,
and over them he cast
two lots.

The right lot,
which was for the Lord,
he placed on the goat
and made it a sin offering.

זְהוּבִים מַעֲבִיר
וּלְבָנִים לוֹבֵשׁ
שֶׁעֲבוֹדַת הַיּוֹם
בְּבִגְדֵי לָבָן

וּמְמַהֵר וְקִדֵּשׁ
יָדָיו וְרַגְלָיו
וּבָא לוֹ תְּחִלָּה
אֵצֶל פָּרוֹ

הוּא עוֹמֵד בְּאֵימָה
לִפְנֵי עֶלְיוֹן
וְאוֹמֵר עָלָיו
דִּבְרֵי וִדּוּי

וְסָמַךְ שְׁתֵּי יָדָיו עָלָיו וְהִתְוַדָּה. וְכָךְ הָיָה אוֹמֵר. ‹אָנָּא הַשֵּׁם. חָטָאתִי, עָוִיתִי, פָּשַׁעְתִּי לְפָנֶיךָ אֲנִי וּבֵיתִי: אָנָּא בַשֵּׁם, כַּפֶּר נָא לַחֲטָאִים וְלַעֲוֹנוֹת וְלַפְּשָׁעִים. שֶׁחָטָאתִי וְשֶׁעָוִיתִי וְשֶׁפָּשַׁעְתִּי לְפָנֶיךָ אֲנִי וּבֵיתִי. כַּכָּתוּב בְּתוֹרַת מֹשֶׁה עַבְדֶּךָ מִפִּי כְבוֹדֶךָ. כִּי בַיּוֹם הַזֶּה יְכַפֵּר עֲלֵיכֶם לְטַהֵר אֶתְכֶם מִכֹּל חַטֹּאתֵיכֶם לִפְנֵי יְהֹוָה: וְהַכֹּהֲנִים וְהָעָם הָעוֹמְדִים בָּעֲזָרָה כְּשֶׁהָיוּ שׁוֹמְעִים אֶת הַשֵּׁם הַנִּכְבָּד וְהַנּוֹרָא מְפֹרָשׁ יוֹצֵא מִפִּי כֹהֵן גָּדוֹל בִּקְדֻשָּׁה וּבְטָהֳרָה הָיוּ כּוֹרְעִים וּמִשְׁתַּחֲוִים וְנוֹפְלִים עַל פְּנֵיהֶם וְאוֹמְרִים: בָּרוּךְ שֵׁם כְּבוֹד מַלְכוּתוֹ לְעוֹלָם וָעֶד: וְאַף הוּא הָיָה מִתְכַּוֵּן כְּנֶגֶד הַמְבָרְכִים לִגְמֹר אֶת הַשֵּׁם, וְאוֹמֵר לָהֶם תִּטְהָרוּ›

דִּבֵּר וְהֵבִיאוּ לוֹ
שְׁנֵי שְׂעִירִים
וְהִגְרִיל עֲלֵיהֶם
שְׁנֵי גוֹרָלוֹת

גּוֹרַל יָמִין
שֶׁהוּא שֶׁלַּשֵּׁם
יִתְּנֵהוּ עַל הַשָּׂעִיר
וְיַעֲשֵׂהוּ חַטָּאת

He tied a crimson thread
on the goat for Azazel
and stood it opposite
the place where it was to be sent.

Then the goat
that was for the Lord
he placed opposite
the house of slaughter.

Then he approached his bull
a second time
and said over it the confession
of his brothers.

Then he placed his hands on it and confessed. And thus he would say: [O Lord, I have sinned, I have done wrong, I have transgressed before You, I and my household and the children of Aaron, Your holy people. O Lord, forgive the sins and iniquities and transgressions that I have committed against You, I and my household and the children of Aaron, Your holy people, as it is written in the Torah of Moses, Your servant: 'For on this day atonement shall be made for you to cleanse you of all your sins; before the Lord—'" (Lev. 16:30). And when the priests and the people standing in the court and serving in the Sanctuary heard the explicit name coming forth from the mouth of the high priest in holiness and purity, they would kneel, prostrate themselves, and fall to their faces and say: "Blessed is the name of His Majesty's glory for ever and ever." He would also intend to finish the name while facing those saying the blessing and say to them, "You shall be pure."]

After the confession
he was very diligent
in performing his sin offering
and the sin offering of the people.

He examined the knife
and slaughtered his bull
and collected the blood
in the pure basin.

בִּשְׂעִיר עֲזָאזֵל
לְשׁוֹן זְהוֹרִית יִקְשֹׁר
וְיַעֲמִידֵהוּ כְּנֶגֶד
בֵּית שִׁלּוּחוֹ

אַף שָׂעִיר
שֶׁהוּא שְׁלִּשֵּׁם
יַעֲמִידֵהוּ כְּנֶגֶד
בֵּית שְׁחִיטָתוֹ

וּבָא לוֹ שְׁנִיָּה
אֵצֶל פָּרוֹ
וְאוֹמֵר עָלָיו
וִדּוּי אֶחָיו

וְסָמַךְ שְׁתֵּי יָדָיו עָלָיו וְהִתְוַדָּה. וְכָךְ הָיָה אוֹמֵר. ‹אָנָּא הַשֵּׁם. חָטָאתִי, עָוִיתִי, פָּשַׁעְתִּי לְפָנֶיךָ אֲנִי וּבֵיתִי וּבְנֵי אַהֲרֹן עַם קְדוֹשֶׁךָ: אָנָּא בַשֵּׁם, כַּפֶּר נָא לַחֲטָאִים וְלַעֲוֹנוֹת וְלַפְּשָׁעִים. שֶׁחָטָאתִי וְשֶׁעָוִיתִי וְשֶׁפָּשַׁעְתִּי לְפָנֶיךָ אֲנִי וּבֵיתִי וּבְנֵי אַהֲרֹן עַם קְדוֹשֶׁךָ. כַּכָּתוּב בְּתוֹרַת מֹשֶׁה עַבְדֶּךָ מִפִּי כְבוֹדֶךָ. כִּי בַיּוֹם הַזֶּה יְכַפֵּר עֲלֵיכֶם לְטַהֵר אֶתְכֶם מִכֹּל חַטֹּאתֵיכֶם לִפְנֵי יְהֹוָה (וי׳ טז, ל): וְהַכֹּהֲנִים וְהָעָם הָעוֹמְדִים בָּעֲזָרָה כְּשֶׁהָיוּ שׁוֹמְעִים אֶת הַשֵּׁם הַנִּכְבָּד וְהַנּוֹרָא מְפֹרָשׁ יוֹצֵא מִפִּי כֹהֵן גָּדוֹל בִּקְדֻשָּׁה וּבְטָהֳרָה הָיוּ כּוֹרְעִים וּמִשְׁתַּחֲוִים וְנוֹפְלִים עַל פְּנֵיהֶם וְאוֹמְרִים: בָּרוּךְ שֵׁם כְּבוֹד מַלְכוּתוֹ לְעוֹלָם וָעֶד: וְאַף הוּא הָיָה מִתְכַּוֵּן כְּנֶגֶד הַמְבָרְכִים לִגְמֹר אֶת הַשֵּׁם, וְאוֹמֵר לָהֶם תִּטְהָרוּ›

אַחַר וִדּוּי
שָׁקַד בְּחָזְקָה
לַעֲשׂוֹת חַטָּאתוֹ
וְחַטָּאת הָעָם

בָּדַק סַכִּין
וְשָׁחַט פָּרוֹ
וְקִבֵּל דָּמוֹ
בְּמִזְרָק טָהוֹר

He also gave it
to his colleague[14] at once
to stir its blood
so that it would not curdle.

He laid the blood of his bull
on the terrace
and took the golden (fire-pan)
and went up to the head of the altar.

He took it down
filled with fiery coals
and laid it down
on the terrace in the court.

Then he added a handful (of incense)
of an everyday measure,
in his right hand the fire-pan
and in his left the shovel.

He fortified himself
and went into the holy (shrine)
and laid down the fire-pan
between the poles of the ark.

He took a handful
and placed it on the coals,
and because of it the house
was filled with smoke.

He closed his eyes
and turned back around
and said a short prayer
in the sanctuary.

He went out and took
the blood of the bull
and sprinkled it on the curtain
opposite the ark.

---

14. The assisting priest.

גַּם לַחֲבֵרוֹ
מִיָּד יִתְּנֵהוּ
לְמָרֵס בְּדָמוֹ
שֶׁלֹּא יִקְרֹשׁ

דַּם פָּרוֹ
הִנִּיחַ עַל הָרוֹבֵד
וְנָטַל זְהוּבָה
וְעָלָה לְרֹאשׁ הַמִּזְבֵּחַ

הוֹרִידָהּ מְלֵאָה
גַּחֲלֵי אֵשׁ
וְהִנִּיחָהּ
עַל הָרוֹבֵד שֶׁבָּעֲזָרָה

וּמוֹסִיף מְלֹא חָפְנָיו
עַל מִדַּת כָּל יוֹם
בִּימִינוֹ מַחְתָּה
וּבִשְׂמֹאלוֹ כַּף

זֵרֵז עַצְמוֹ
וְנִכְנַס לַקֹּדֶשׁ
וְהִנִּיחַ מַחְתָּה
בֵּין בַּדֵּי הָאָרוֹן

חָפַן וְנָתַן
עַל הַגֶּחָלִים
וּמִמֶּנָּה נִתְמַלֵּא
הַבַּיִת עָשָׁן

טִמְטֵם עֵינָיו
וְשָׁב לַאֲחוֹרָיו
וּמִתְפַּלֵּל בַּהֵיכָל
תְּפִלָּה קְצָרָה

יָצָא וְנָטַל
אֶת דַּם הַפָּר
וְהִזָּה עַל הַפָּרֹכֶת
כְּנֶגֶד הָאָרוֹן

Like a bereaved bear[15]
he brought the goat for the sin offering;
he slaughtered it and collected
its blood in a basin.

He went inside
to sprinkle some of its blood
in the order in which he sprinkled
the blood of the bull.

He hurried and took
the blood of the bull
and sprinkled opposite
the ark from outside.

He urgently laid
the blood of the bull down
and took the blood of the goat
and sprinkled some of it.

Gladly he poured out
the blood of the bull into the blood of the goat
and approached and stood
over the golden altar.

He put [the blood] in order
on the four horns (of the altar)
and on its top
he dashed it seven times.

He strode and went
outside the portico
and poured the remainder
on the western foundation.

He commanded, and they brought him
the goat to be sent out,
and he confessed over it
the guilt of the community.

---

15. Fiercely; see 2 Sam 17:8.

כְּדֹב שַׁכּוּל
שְׂעִיר חַטָּאת יָבִיא
שְׁחָטוֹ וְקִבֵּל
דָּמוֹ בְּמִזְרָק

לִפְנִים יְכַנֵּס
לְהַזּוֹת מִדָּמוֹ
כְּסֵדֶר שֶׁהִזָּה
דַּם הַפָּר

מִהַר וְנָטַל
דַּם הַפָּר
וְהִזָּה כְּנֶגֶד
הָאָרוֹן מִבַּחוּץ

נָחַץ וְהִנִּיחַ
דַּם הַפָּר
וְנָטַל דַּם הַשָּׂעִיר
וְהִזָּה מִמֶּנּוּ

שָׁשׁ וְעֵרָה
דַּם הַפָּר לְתוֹךְ דַּם הַשָּׂעִיר
וּבָא וְעָמַד
עַל מִזְבַּח הַזָּהָב

עַל אַרְבַּע קַרְנוֹתָיו
יִתֵּן כְּסִדְרָן
וְעַל טָהֳרוֹ יַזֶּה
שֶׁבַע פְּעָמִים

פָּסַע וְיָצָא
חוּץ לָאוּלָם
וְשָׁפַךְ אֶת הַשִּׁירַיִם
אֶל יְסוֹד מַעֲרָבִי

צִוָּה וְהֵבִיאוּ לוֹ
אֶת הַשָּׂעִיר הַמִּשְׁתַּלֵּחַ
לְהִתְוַדּוֹת עָלָיו
אַשְׁמַת קְהִלָּה

Then he placed his hands on it and confessed. Thus he would say: ["O Lord, they have sinned, they have done wrong, they have transgressed before You, Your people, the house of Israel. O Lord, forgive the sins and iniquities and transgressions that they have committed against you, Your people, the house of Israel, as it is written in the Torah of Moses, Your servant: 'For on this day atonement shall be made for you to cleanse you of all your sins; before the Lord—'" (Lev. 16:30). And when the priests and the people standing in the court and serving in the Sanctuary heard the explicit name coming forth from the mouth of the high priest in holiness and purity, they would kneel, prostrate themselves, and fall to their faces and say: "Blessed is the name of His Majesty's glory for ever and ever." He would also intend to finish the name while facing those saying the blessing and say to them, "You shall be pure."]

He called to one
of the priests
to lead it to an inaccessible land,
to a desolate wilderness.

He ran to the bull
and the goat that were to be burned
and tore them up and placed them
in a bowl to be sent up in smoke.[16]

He returned to read	
from **the Priestly Teaching**	Leviticus
from the portion **"after the death of Aaron"**[17]	Lev 16
and also from **"on the tenth day."**	Num 29:7

He directed his steps
to the place of immersion
and went down and immersed
and went up and dried himself.

---

16. See m. Yoma 6:7.

וְסָמַךְ שְׁתֵּי יָדָיו עָלָיו וְהִתְוַדָּה. וְכָךְ הָיָה אוֹמֵר. חָטְאוּ הַשֵּׁם. אָנָּא הַשֵּׁם. חָטָאוּ ‹עָו›ּוּ. ‹פָּ›שְׁעוּ
לְפָנֶיךָ עַמְּךָ בֵּית יִשְׂרָאֵל: כַּפֶּר נָא עַל הַחֲטָאִים וְעַל הֶעָוֹ' וְעַל הַפְּשָׁעִים.
שֶׁחָטְאוּ שֶׁעָווּ ‹וְשֶׁפָּ›שְׁעוּ לְפָנֶיךָ עַמְּךָ בֵּית יִשְׂרָאֵל. כַּכָּתוּב בְּתוֹרַת מֹשֶׁה עַבְדֶּךָ מִפִּי
כְבוֹדֶךָ. כִּי בַיּוֹם הַזֶּה יְכַפֵּר עֲלֵיכֶם לְטַהֵר אֶתְכֶם מִכֹּל חַטֹּאתֵיכֶם לִפְנֵי יְהֹוָה:
וְהַכֹּהֲנִים וְהָעָם הָעוֹמְדִים בָּעֲזָרָה כְּשֶׁהָיוּ שׁוֹמְעִים אֶת הַשֵּׁם הַנִּכְבָּד וְהַנּוֹרָא מְפֹרָשׁ
יוֹצֵא מִפִּי כֹהֵן גָּדוֹל בִּקְדֻשָּׁה וּבְטָהֳרָה הָיוּ כּוֹרְעִים וּמִשְׁתַּחֲוִים וְנוֹפְלִים עַל פְּנֵיהֶם
וְאוֹמְרִים: בָּרוּךְ שֵׁם כְּבוֹד מַלְכוּתוֹ לְעוֹלָם וָעֶד: וְאַף הוּא הָיָה מִתְכַּוֵּן כְּנֶגֶד
הַמְבָרְכִים לִגְמֹר אֶת הַשֵּׁם וְאוֹמֵר לָהֶם תִּטְהָרוּ. וְאַתָּה בְּטוּבְךָ מְעוֹרֵר רַחֲמֶיךָ וְסוֹלֵחַ
לַעֲדַת יְשֻׁרוּן›

קָרָא לְאֶחָד
מִן הַכֹּהֲנִים
לְהוֹלִיכוֹ אֶל אֶרֶץ גְּזֵרָה
לְמִדְבָּר שָׁמֵם

רָץ לוֹ אֵצֶל הַפָּר
וְהַשָּׂעִיר הַנִּשְׂרָפִים
וּקְרָעָן וּנְתָנָם
בְּמַגָּס לְהַקְטִירָם

שָׁב לִקְרוֹא

ספר ויקרא   בְּתוֹרַת כֹּהֲנִים
ויקרא טז   בְּפָרָשַׁת אַחֲרֵי מוֹת
במדבר כט, ז   וּבָאָךְ בֶּעָשׂוֹר

תִּכֶּן צְעָדָיו
לְבֵית הַטְּבִילָה
וְיָרַד וְטָבַל
וְעָלָה וְנִסְתַּפָּג

17. This and the following line list the designated Torah portions for Yom Kippur.

Then they brought him
golden garments,
and he dressed and washed
his hands and his feet.

Then he went out and sacrificed his ram
and the ram of the people
and the bull for the sin offering
and the bull for the burnt offering.

When he was finished
doing all of these,
he went again
to the place of immersion.

And he washed his hands and his feet
and undressed
and went down and immersed,
went up and dried himself.

And they brought him
white garments,
and he dressed
and washed his hands and his feet.

He entered
to take out the shovel
and the fire-pan,
which he had put in in the morning,

and he went again
to the place of immersion
and undressed and and immersed,
and went up and dried himself,

and they brought him
golden garments,
and he dressed and washed
his hands and his feet.

He entered to offer
the incense

הֵבִיאוּ לוֹ
בִּגְדֵי זָהָב
וְלָבַשׁ וְקִדֵּשׁ
יָדָיו וְרַגְלָיו

וְיָצָא וְעָשָׂה אֶת אֵילוֹ
וְאֶת אֵיל הָעָם
וְאֶת פַּר הַחַטָּאת
וְאֶת פַּר הָעֹלָה

אַחַר כַּלּוֹתוֹ
מֵעֲשׂוֹת כָּל אֵלֶּה
וְעוֹד בָּא לוֹ
לְבֵית הַטְּבִילָה

וְקִדֵּשׁ יָדָיו וְרַגְלָיו
וּפָשַׁט
וְיָרַד וְטָבַל
עָלָה וְנִסְתַּפֵּג

הֵבִיאוּ לוֹ
בִּגְדֵי לָבָן
וְלָבַשׁ וְקִדֵּשׁ
יָדָיו וְרַגְלָיו

נִכְנַס לְהוֹצִיא
אֶת הַכַּף
וְאֶת הַמַּחְתָּה
שֶׁהִכְנִיס בְּשַׁחֲרִית

וְעוֹד בָּא לוֹ
לְבֵית הַטְּבִילָה
וּפָשַׁט וְטָבַל
וְעָלָה וְנִסְתַּפֵּג

הֵבִיאוּ לוֹ
בִּגְדֵי זָהָב
וְלָבַשׁ וְקִדֵּשׁ
יָדָיו וְרַגְלָיו

נִכְנַס לְהַקְטִיר
אֶת הַקְּטֹרֶת

of the afternoon
and to repair the lamps.

Then he went again
to the place of immersion
and undressed and immersed,
and went up and dried himself.

They brought him
his own clothes,
and he put them on;
then they accompanied him to his house.

Then he celebrated the holiday
for **those who love him**   his family
when he went out safely
from the holy [shrine].

Happy is the people
who have it so;
happy is the people
whose God is the Lord.[18]

---

18. Ps 144:15.

וּלְהֵטִיב אֶת הַנֵּרוֹת
שֶׁל בֵּין הָעַרְבַּיִם

וְעוֹד בָּא לוֹ
לְבֵית הַטְּבִילָה
וּפָשַׁט וְטָבַל
וְעָלָה וְנִסְתַּפָּג

הֵבִיאוּ לוֹ
בִּגְדֵי עַצְמוֹ
וּלְבָשָׁן
וּמְלַוִּין אוֹתוֹ עַד בֵּיתוֹ

וְיוֹם טוֹב
הָיָה עוֹשֶׂה **לְאוֹהֲבָיו** **משפחתו**
בְּצֵאתוֹ בְשָׁלוֹם
מִן הַקֹּדֶשׁ

אַשְׁרֵי הָעָם
שֶׁכָּכָה לוֹ
אַשְׁרֵי הָעָם
שֶׁיְיָ אֱלֹהָיו

4. Az be-ʾEn Kol
"When All Was Not"

This massive composition is one of the most comprehensive of the extant ancient Avodah piyyutim. It is distinguished for its thorough treatment of every major theme in the Avodah, for its extensive use of poetic figures such as metonymy, alliteration, and parallelism, for its use of mythology in its retelling of the history of the world, and above all for its ingeniousness in formulating poetic figures and forms. As described in our Introduction, above, this composition abounds in legends and details known to us from Apocrypha and other nonrabbinic sources. Unlike most of the other Avodah piyyutim, *Az be-ʾEn Kol* deals with all of the major episodes in Israel's early history, and not just those most relevant to the Temple cult. For example, a remarkable amount of esoteric cosmological and angelological lore is embedded in the opening sections praising God and his work of creation. The composition also uses unusual poetic forms in its portrayal of individual episodes, such as its description of the agency of the Torah in creating the world and in its listing of auspicious events that may occur on the Sabbath.

Although mentioned in at least two liturgical sources,[1] this composition did not enter any of the standard liturgies of the last several centuries and so remained undiscovered until recently. Fragments were published by Zvi Malachi in 1974.[2] In 1998, Joseph Yahalom reconstructed the composition from Genizah fragments and published it in an annotated edition.[3] Still, not all of the poem has been found, and several portions remain fragmentary. Although the poem has been attributed erroneously to Yose ben Yose and Eleazar ben Qallir, its author is unknown. It may have preceded and influenced Yose ben Yose's *Azkir Gevurot*. It is also notable for its affinities with the eighth- or ninth-

---

1. See Mirsky, *Yose ben Yose*, 245; A. M. Haberman, "Sefer Qerovah," *Yediʿot ha-Makhon le-Madaʿe ha-Yahadut* 3 (1927): 104; Malachi, *Ha-"Avodah,"* 34.
2. Malachi, *Ha-"Avodah,"* 2:15–35.
3. Yahalom, *Az be-ʾEn Kol*.

century midrash Pirqe de-Rabbi Eliezer and may have influenced that composition.

This translation and edition are based on Yahalom's, with the addition of newly discovered fragments.[4] Text that has been restored from parallel manuscripts appears in braces { }. Restorations from context or from biblical citations are placed in brackets [ ]. Explanatory phrases are placed in parentheses ( ).

The extant fragments end at line 792. However, since there is much more of the ceremony to go, it is obvious that the poem went on extensively. Following the extant text of *Az be-ʾEn Kol*, we have appended portions of another piyyut, possibly *Aromem la-ʾEl*, which is apparently a reworking of *Az be-ʾEn Kol*. The text is based on a newly discovered fragment, MS Firkovitch, Heb. iiA 897, and Joseph Yahalom's edition in *Az be-ʾEn Kol*, 186–88, lines 439–60. We translate from the portion that completes some of what is missing at the end of *Az be-ʾEn Kol*.

>   When all was not,
>   You were all that was,
>   {and when You prepared all}
>   You filled all.
>
>   When You [   ] all,
>   You are ever renewing,
>   for in the beginning You were aged,
>   and in the end youthful.
>
> 5 No eye can behold
>   the place of Your desired dwelling
>   For You have dwelt
>   above **the mighty** since ancient times.   **water** or **angels**
>
>   Or perhaps some rooster[5]
>   might search out Your dwelling place;
>   You have snatched up a fire consuming fire
>   from the fiery waters.[6]

---

4. MS TS NS 324.86; Firkovitch, Heb. iiA 897. Both manuscripts were referred to us by Mr. B. Löffler of the Academy of the Hebrew Language, to whom we are indebted.

⟨אָז בְּאֵין כֹּל⟩
⟨אַ⟩תָּה כֹּל הָיִיתָ
⟨וּבַהֲכִינְךָ כֹּל⟩
⟨אַ⟩תָּה כֹּל נִמְלֵאתָ

⟨א.. ..⟩ךְ כֹּל
אַתָּה חָדָשׁ לְחַדְּשׁוֹ
כִּי יְשׁוּשֶׁיךָ בְּרֵאשִׁית
וּבְחוּרוֹתֶיךָ בְּאַחֲרִית

אֵין עַיִן לָשׁוּר   5
אוּי חֲנָיֶיתָךְ
המים או המלאכים   כִּי עַל **אַדִּירִים**
אָז מִקֶּדֶם חָנִיתָ

אוֹ אֵיזֶה שֶׂכְוִי
יַחְקוֹר מְקוֹם שְׁכֶנְךָ
וְאֵשׁ אוֹכְלָה אֵשׁ
בְּלַבַּת מַיִם הַחְתִּיתָ

---

5. Said to be the wisest bird, since it distinguishes between day and night.
6. That is, Your dwelling place is above the river of fire (cf. Dan 7:9–10).

Only **those who are seized
with fear** can serve You.   *the angels*
For in a contrite heart
and a humble spirit You can be found.

They have no father,
and no mother bore them;[7]
{they were conceived from fire,
and they were born of the snow.

You carved **Erelim**[8]   *a class of angels*
from flames of fire;
You engendered the Creatures[9]
out of the River of the Chariot.[10]

They are enveloped in fear,
encircled with awe,
belted with writing cases;[11]
their loins are girded with sighing.

They are the image of fire;
their bodies are like the streams of Rahab;[12]
Their eyes are like lightning;
their roar is like the rush of waves.

You caused their heads
to flash like sapphire;[13]
the radiance at their feet
flashes incandescently.[14]

"Amen" is their vocation.
"Blessed" is their labor.[15]
Their utterance is "Righteousness."
"Holiness" is their proclamation.

---

7. The text in braces that follows is from MS TS NS 324.86.
8. Cf. Isa 33:7.
9. The Ḥayyot of Ezek 1.
10. Cf. the river of fire, Dan 7:10; cf. also the Hekhalot text *3 Enoch* in Peter Schäfer, *Synopse zur Hekhalot-Literatur* (Tübingen: Mohr, 1981), §§ 50 and 916.
11. See Ezek 9:2.

AZ BE-'EN KOL

המלאכים	אֲחוּזֵי אֵימָה
	הֵם לְבַד יְשַׁמְּשׁוּךָ
	כִּי בְּלֵב דַּכָּא
	וּבִשְׁפַל רוּחַ תִּמָּצֵא
	אָב אֵין לָמוֹ
	אֵם לֹא יְלָדָתַם
	הוֹרָתָם אֵשׁ
	וְיוֹלַדְם שֶׁלֶג
קבוצת מלאכים	אֶרְאֶלִים חֲצַבְתָּה
	מִלַּהֲבוֹת אֵשׁ
	וְחוֹלַלְתָּה חַיּוֹת
	מִנְּהַר מִרְכְּבָ‹ת›
	אֲפוּדִים פַּחַד
	אֲזוּרִים יִרְאָה
	חֲגוּרִים קֶסֶת
	וּמָת‹נַ›יִם אֲנוּחִים
	אִישִׁים דְּמוּתָן
	גּוִיָּ‹תָם› כְּפַלְגֵי רַהַב
	עַפְעַפָּם כִּ‹בְ›רָק
	שַׁאֲגָם כֶּהָמוֹן
	אֶבֶן סַפִּיר
	הִקְדַּחְתָּה מֵרָאשׁוֹתָם
	זִיו מַרְגְּלוֹתָם
	נוֹצְצִים כְּקָלָל
	אָמֵן מְלַאכְתָּם
	בָּרוּךְ עֲבוֹדָתָם
	צֶדֶק הֲגִיָּ‹תָם›
	קָדוֹשׁ קְרִיאָתָם

12. Cf. Job 9:13, 26.
13. Cf. Isa 54:12.
14. Cf. Ezek 1:7, Dan 10:6.
15. The angels say the doxology "Blessed is the presence of the Lord from His place"; see Ezek 3:12.

They serve their Leader
and do not behold Him;
they cannot turn their heads,[16]
and they all acclaim Him.

Vast power and station,
the demigods of **Senir**   Mount Hermon
disperse to all remote places
and say, "Here we are."

Thousands upon thousands
and myriads of holy ones
are transformed into wind,
turned into fire.

They do not mourn,
and grieving does not seize them,
for they will not give birth
nor will they die.

There is no enmity among them,
nor are they convulsed by hatred;
they know nothing of antagonism,
for their camp is tranquil.

They do not scrape for food,
nor do they imbibe drink.
They are supplied with abundance
and radiant with goodwill.

Scarlet does not stain them,   blood
nor does **white**[17] affect them.   semen
Flux cannot pollute them;
they are not whitened with any blemish.[18]

---

16. Lit., "necks."
17. The idea that the angels do not suffer menstrual and seminal pollution is attested in several

אַלּוּפָם יְשָׁרֵתוּ
וּבוֹ לֹא יְשׁוּרוּ
וְעוֹרֶף אַל יַפְנוּ
וּבוֹ כֻּלָּם ‹עוֹנִ›ם

הר חרמון

אַמִּיצֵי כֹחַ וּמַעֲמָד
אֱלֵי שִׂ‹נִי›ר
מְשׁוֹטְטִים בְּכָל קְצָווֹת
וְאוֹמְ[רִים] לְךָ "הִנֶּנּוּ"

אַלְפֵי שִׂ‹נְ›אָן
וְרִבְבוֹת קְדוֹשִׁים
מוּתָמָרִים לָ‹רוּחַ›
וּמוּחְלָפִים לָאֵשׁ

אֲבָל אֵין לָמוֹ
אוֹנָן לֹא יַשִּׂיגֵן
כִּי לֹא יוֹלִידוּ
אַף לֹא יָמוּתוּ

אֵיבָה אֵין בֵּינֵימוֹ
בְּ‹שִׂנְ›אָה בַּל יִשְׂטוֹמוּ
וְרִיב בַּל יֵדְעוּ
כִּי שֶׁקֶט מַחֲנָם

אוֹכֶל בַּל יוּגְרְדוּ
שָׁאָב בַּל יָמוֹצוּ
כִּי אֲסוּמֵי טוֹב
וּמְפִיקִים רָצוֹן

דם
זרע

אוֹדֶם אַל יְגָעֲלֵם
לוֹבֶן אַל יְקָרֵם
זוֹב לֹא יְנַדֵּם
נֶגַע לֹא יְבַהֲקֵם

---

midrashim and esoteric sources. See Michael D. Swartz, *Scholastic Magic: Ritual and Revelation in Early Jewish Mysticism* (Princeton: Princeton University Press, 1996), 166–69.

18. Heb. *negaʿ*, referring to impurity of the skin.

15 Their tent is pure;[19]
    their place is holiness—
    their ritual bath is a river of fire,
    and they immerse in flames.[20]

    The mighty of the world are Your confidants,   the angels
    yet You did not consult them
    when You made up Your mind[21]
    to create the world.

    The fear of Your [   ]
    fell upon them,
    for no servant
    can tell his master what to do.

    God [   ],
    and no one delayed,
    for [there is no one] besides You
    and no other god [   ].

    No god coerced You.
    No companion advised You.
    No master [taught You].
    No sage [instructed You].[22]

25 As it is written: Who has plumbed [the mind of God?] (Isa 40:13);
    and it is said: Whom did he consult? (Isa 40:14).

    [GOD USED TORAH TO CREATE THE UNIVERSE]

    You relied on Your knowledge;
    You trusted Your discernment;
    in Your power You were revealed;
    and on Your strength You depended.

---

19. The angels are not affected by "tent-impurity," a type of corpse impurity derived from Num 19:14 and described in the Mishnah tractate *Ahelot*.
20. Cf. Seder Rabbah de-Bereshit (Schäfer, *Synopse*, § 181), in which the angels who go down to

אָֽוהֳלָם טַהֲרָה
מְקוֹמָם קְדוֹשָׁה
מְקוֹנָם נְהַר אֵשׁ
[וּ]טְבִילָתָם לַהַט

המלאכים

[אֵילֵי] אֶרֶץ סוֹדָךְ
וּבָם לֹא נִמְלַכְתָּה
בְּנָוְשָׂאָךְ לִבָּךְ
לִבְ‹ר›וֹת עוֹלָם

‹אֵימַת ..›מךְ
עֲלֵיהֶם נָפָלָה
שֶׁאֵין עֶבֶד
אוֹמֵר לְקוֹנוֹ מַה תַּעֲשֶׂה

[אֶל] ‹... ..›תה
וְאַחֵר לֹא אִיחַר
כִּי ‹...› אַחֵר
וְאֵל זָר ‹... בָךְ›

אֵל לֹא אֲנָסָךְ
רֵיעַ לֹא יְעָצָךְ
רָב לֹא ‹לִימְּדָךְ›
סוֹפֵר לֹא ‹הוֹדִיעָךְ›

25 ככ' מי תיכן (יש' מ, יג)
וו' את מי נוע‹ץ› (שם יד)

[ואהיה אצלו אמון]

בְּדַעְתְּךָ נִשְׁעַנְתָּה
בְּבִינָתְךָ בָּטַחְתָּה
בְּעוּזְךָ נִגְלֵ‹י›תָה
בְּ‹כֹחֲ›ךָ [נִסְמַכְתָּה]

---

earth purify themselves in the river of fire; see note 17 above. Cf. Zvi M. Rabbinowitz, *Maḥazor Piyyute Rabbi Yannai le-Torah u-Moʿadim* (Jerusalem: Mosad Bialik, 1985), 459.

21. Lit., "lifted up Your heart."
22. That is, a court administrator.

With that which is longer than the earth,[23]　　　　　　　Torah
with that which is wider than the sea,
with Your primordial possession,
with that which is the beginning of all action,

with the measuring line of judgment,
and with the scales of mercy,
with the right hand of life,
with riches and honor;[24]

It was hidden in Your heart
and brought forth from Your mouth.
By Your hand [   ]
as [by the hand of a] craftsman.

35　Looking into it, You carved out
the pillars of the heavens
before there was primordial chaos
on which the rafters could rest.[25]

By[26] [its] weaving
loops and twisted chains
until You were to [   ]
to build Your Tent.[27]

By [   ]
rings of the earth[28]
before Your winds
were to refine [   ].

You [clothed Yourself]
with light as a garment[29]
before You made
a sweet delight to the eyes.　　　　　　　　　　　　　　　light

---

23. Job 11:9, here referring to the Torah. This section refers to the idea, found in rabbinic literature, that God used the Torah as the blueprint for the world; see page 26 in the Introduction. On the idea of the size of the Torah, see Kook, "Godel ha-Torah."

24. Prov 3:16.

25. Heb. *tohu va-Vohu*, here referring apparently to the primordial waters, which support the rafters of heaven.

התורה

בַּאֲרוּכָה מֵאֶרֶץ
בִּרְחָבָה מִנִּי יָם
בְּקִנְיָן קֶדֶם
בְּרֵ‹אשִׁ›ית [לְכָל פּוֹעַל]

בְּקַוֵּו צְדָקָה
‹וּ›מִשְׁקוֹלֶת חֶסֶד
בִּימִין חַיִּים
בְּעֹ‹ו›שֶׁר וְכָבוֹד

בְּלִבְּךָ הוּצְפָּנָה
וּמִפִּיךָ הוּנְבָּעָה
בְּיָדְךָ ה‹..ב›תה
כְּ‹בְיַד... חָ›רָשׁ

‹בַּמָּה׳אֵיָּה חָצַבְתָּה   35
עַמּוּדֵי שְׁחָקִים
עַד לֹא תֹהוּ ‹וָבֹהוּ›
לִקָרוֹת עֲלִיּוֹת

בְּ‹.. ..›תה טְוֻוִי
לוּלָאוֹ‹ת› וְשַׁרְשָׁרוֹת
עַד לֹא ‹...›
‹..לְבִ›נוֹת אֹהָלָךְ

‹בְּ.. ..›תה
טַבָּעוֹת נְשִׁ‹יָּ›ה
עַד לֹא ר‹וּ›חָיִךְ
מְצָ‹רֵ›ף צָ‹..›ה

‹בְּ... ›
אוֹר כַּשַּׂלְמָה
עַד לֹא הִמְתַּקְתָּה
טוֹב לַעֵינַיִם

אור

26. The preposition *b-* beginning each stanza is translated in this section as "by" or "with," according to the structure described in the Introduction above; see page 26–27.

27. B. Shabbat 99a: The clasps in the loops looked like stars in the sky. The reference is to the loops that held the curtains of the Tabernacle to each other. This may be expressing the idea that the earthly Tabernacle that was to be built had a primordial supernal counterpart.

28. Heb. *neshiyyah*; in the Bible, "oblivion"; here, "the earth."

29. See Ps 104:2

[   ]
light above
before You hid
primordial chaos in the depths.

45   [   ]
snow and smoke[30]
until You kept them ready
for the day of war and battle.[31]

[   ]
[   ]
until dust was kneaded
so that clods of earth stuck fast together.   to make Adam

[   ] to the earth
until You made song heard
on the wing[32]
to the one who spreads it forth.

[   ]
[that which is gathered in] the hollow of Your hand[33]   water
until it fled
from Your rebuke.[34]

By its design You depressed
that which flows from a vessel[35]   water
until You broke down
the **humble** as required.[36]   waters

55   By its fullness You closed
the sluiced windows
until they were to open
on the day of **the furious rain**.   the Flood

---

30. According to y. Ḥagigah 2:1 and Gen Rabbah 10:3 (ed. Theodor and Albeck, p. 75), snow was used to create the world.
31. See Job 38:23.
32. See Isa 24:16.
33. The expression derives from Isa 40:12. On these stanzas, cf. especially Job 38:8–16.

AZ BE-ʾEN KOL

⟨ב..⟩ ..⟩ה
אוֹר מַ⟨עְ⟩לָה
עַד לֹא הִטְמַנְתָּה
תֹּהוּ וָבֹהוּ בִּתְהוֹמוֹת

⟨ב..⟩ ⟨...   45
⟨שֶׁלֶג⟩ וְקִיטוֹר
עַד לֹא תְּחַסְּכֵם
לְיוֹם קְרָב וּמִלְחָמֶת

⟨ב..⟩ ⟨...
⟨... ..⟩ת
עַד לֹא יוּצַק עָפָר
לְדַבֵּק רְגָבִים   ליצירת אדם

⟨ב..⟩ ⟨...
⟨..ת⟩ה לְאַרְקָא
עַד לֹא תַּשְׁמִיעַ בְּכָנָף
זֶמֶר לְרוֹקְעָהּ

⟨ב..⟩ ⟨...
⟨..⟩רִי שָׁעֳלֶךְ   המים
עַד לֹא יָנוּסוּ
מִגַּעֲרָתֶךָ

בְּחוֹטְבָהּ הִנְבַּכְתָּה
שָׁפַךְ בִּדְלִי   המים
עַד לֹא תֶחֱצֶה
חֲפוּיִים לְחוֹקָם   המים

בִּכְלוּלֶיהָ נַעֲלְתָּה   55
אֶשְׁנַבֵּי אֲרוּבּוֹת
עַד לֹא יוּפְתָּחוּ
בְּיוֹם גִּשְׁמַת זַעַם   המבול

---

34. Ps 104:7. Cf. Tanḥuma Ḥaye Sarah 3: God trampled down the water to make space for the earth and killed its designated angel (*sar*). When the rest of the waters saw this, they fled.

35. In Tanḥuma Ḥaye Sarah 3 interpreting Job 38:16 ("Have you penetrated to the depths of the sea?"), it is said that the waters cried when He killed the angel appointed over them.

36. Job 38:10.

With its compass You set a limit
on the great springs of the deep
until they were to open
to blot out [all] existence in anger.

With its nectar You sweetened
produce, choice fruit, and crops
until You were to plant a tree
for tasting death and life.

With [its   ] You made [   ]
white as fleece
until You were to draw Your bow
and lead an arrow to attack.[37]

With its whetstone You sharpened
a **sword** for the Twisting Serpent[38]   Leviathan's fin
until He locked up,
with his bar, the deep sea.[39]

65 With its pools You increased
fins and fowl
until You were to give commands
concerning a **fish** and a **raven**.[40]   the fish that swallowed Jonah;
                                              the ravens that fed Elijah

With its granary You nipped
leaven from the earth[41]   Adam
until You were to pour [him][42] like milk,
to curdle [him like] cheese.

By its delight
You created the world in six days,
until repose came to You,
and You rested from labor.

---

37. Cf. Ps 18:13–16, where God disperses the darkness and destroys enemies with arrows of lightning.

38. According to Isa 27:1.

39. See Pirqe de-Rabbi Eliezer ch. 9. The idea here is that the Twisting Serpent used Leviathan's fin as a bolt to fasten the sea.

בְּחוּגָהּ חַקְתָּהּ
עֵינוֹת תְּהוֹם רַבָּה
עַד לֹא יֻבְקָעוּ
לִמְחוֹת יְקוּמִים [בְּזַעַף]

בְּנוֹפְתָּהּ הַמְתַּק‹תָּ›הּ
יְבוּל מֶגֶד וּתְנוּב
עַד לֹא תִטַּע אֶשֶׁל
לִטְעוֹם מָוֶת וְחַיִּים

בחרי‹..› הֶ‹חֱ›וַורְתָהּ
צֶמֶר מ‹רו..› ב‹›עת
עַד לֹא תְתָאֵיר קֶשֶׁת
וְתַדְרִיךְ חֵץ לְפָגַ‹ע›

סנפירי לויתן [בְּשִׁנְנָהּ] ‹לְ›טַשְׁתָּהּ
 חֶרֶב עֲקַלְ‹תוֹן›
 עַד לֹא יַבְרִיחַ
 עַל בְּרִיחֵי מְצוּלָה

[בִּבְרִיכָתָהּ] הָעֲצַמְ‹תָּ›הּ 65
‹סַ›נַּפִּירִים וְדָאִים
עַד לֹא תִתֵּן סִיחַ
הדג שבלע את יונה; העורבים שהאכילו את אליהו **לְדָג וְעוֹרֵב**

אדם [בְּקוּמְצָהּ] קָרַצְתָּהּ
‹שֶׁ›**אוֹר** מֵאֲדָמָה
עַד לֹא תַתִּיךְ חָלָב
לְהַקְפִּיא גְבִינָה

[בְּשַׁעַשׁוּ]עֶיהָ
[שַׁשְׁתָּ] יְמֵי הַמַּעֲשֶׂה
עַד לֹא יַגִּיעַ נוֹפֵשׁ
וְתִשְׁבּוֹת עֲבוֹדָה

---

40. See 1 Kgs 17:2–6.
41. See Job 33:6.
42. Cf. Job 10:10. The idea here is that after God created man from the first "batch of dough," he was able to use that "leavening" to make every subsequent human being.

With **perfection**[43] [   ]   Torah
each action according to plan
and afterward, like a wise man,
You started to build.

> As it is written: The Lord founded the earth by wisdom; He established the heavens by understanding. (Prov. 3:19)

[THE FIRST DAY]

You clothed Yourself in might;
You girded Yourself in strength;
and You stood like an expert
to do Your work.

You exalted Yourself
and hung the foundations
without establishing
and erecting afterward.[44]

You placed the rooftop
over the upper story;
then You made firm
the outer edges of the skies.[45]

80   You spread out the heights of heaven
like a cloth tent
with pegs of storm
on the wheels of wind.

You solidified **the ravine**[46]   earth
in the springs of the deep,
and it was placed in the midst of water
and [   ] liquid.

---

43. See Ps 19:8.
44. That is, unlike human builders, You did not erect the building after the foundation.
45. Cf. Prov 8:28. Cf. Pirqe de-Rabbi Eliezer ch. 3. The idea here is that God, not following the

התורה

[בְּתְמִימָה] ⟨...⟩
כָּל פּוֹעַל בְּמַחְשָׁבֶת
וְאַחַר כָּךְ כְּחָכָם
הִתְחַלְתָּהּ לִבְנוֹת

⟨ככ'⟩ ייי בחכמה (מש' ג, יט)

[מעשה היום הראשון]

גְּבוּרָה לָבַ⟨שְׁתָּ⟩
⟨וְעֹז⟩ הִתְאַזָּרְתָּה
וְנִצַּבְתָּה כְּמָהִיר
לַעֲשׂוֹת מְלַאכְתֶּךָ

גָּאֹה גָּא⟨יתָ⟩
⟨וִיסוֹדוֹתֶיהָ תָּ⟩לִיתָה
בְּלִי לְיַסֵּד
וְאַחַר כָּךְ לָשֵׂאת

גַּגֵּי עָלֶיהָ
⟨לְמַעְלָה⟩ קֵירִיתָה
וְאָז אִימַּצְתָּה
⟨יַ⟩רְכְּתֵי שְׁחָקִים

גָּבְהֵי שָׁמַיִם   80
כְּאֹהֶל דּוֹק מָתַחְתָּה
בִּיתֵידוֹת שְׂעָרָה
עַל גַּלְגַּ⟨לֵּ⟩י רוּחַ⟩

הארץ

גֵּיא הִקְרַשְׁתָּה
בְּנִיבְכֵי תְּהוֹמוֹת
וְהוּשְׁ⟨מָ⟩ה בְּתוֹךְ מַיִם
וְ⟨נוֹזְלִים ...⟩

usual way of erecting a tent, placed the central support in place first and then spread out the expanse of the tent.

46. Heb. *gy'*.

You made its peaks level
with leveling tools,
and it was sunk
[   ]

You weighed its hills
in a balance, and constructed it,
[   ]
[   ]

You stored up **that which hovers**[47]   the wind
in its four directions
by measure and by weight
[   ]

90   You rolled back the primordial chaos
to the chambers of the depths,
and from darkness You illumined
[   ]

[   ]
[   ]
They recoiled for fear of You,   the primordial waters
and heeding You, they rolled back.

95   [THE THIRD DAY]

[   ]
strong [   ]
to gather [   ]
[   ]

You made thunder
[   ]
[   ]
[   ]

You made known [   ]
[   ]

---

47. Cf. Gen 1:2.

גְּבְנוּנֶּיהָ פִּלַּסְתָּה
בְּמְסוּרֵי פֶלֶס
וְהוּטְבָּע⟨וּ ...⟩
⟨... ...⟩

גְּבָעוֹתֶיהָ בְּמֹאזְנַיִם
עִיַּנְתָּה וְהִצְבַּתָּה
או⟨.. ...⟩
⟨... ...⟩

הרוח

גְּנָזְתָה מְרַחֶפֶת
בְּאַרְבַּע פִּנּוֹתֶיהָ
בְּמִדָּה בְּמִשְׁקָל
בְ⟨... ...⟩

גַּלַּלְתָּה תֹהוּ וָבֹהוּ   90
לְחַדְרֵי מְצֻלוֹת
וּמַחְשָׁךְ הֶאֱרַצְתָּ⟨ה⟩
⟨... ...⟩
⟨ג.. ...⟩
⟨... ...⟩

המים

הֵן מִפַּחְדְּךָ חָלוּ
וּמִקְּשָׁבָךְ הִתְגַּלְגָּלוּ

[מעשה היום השלישי]   95

⟨ה.. ...⟩
⟨... ⟩ עַזִּים
לֶאֱסוֹף ⟨...⟩
⟨... ...⟩

הִרְעַמְתָּה בְק⟨וֹל⟩
⟨... ...⟩
⟨... ...⟩
⟨... ..⟩ם

⟨ה..⟩ וְהוֹעַדְתָּה
⟨... ...⟩

[   ]
[   ] they poured
[   ]
[   ]
to inform to those who were to go down
[   ]

You commanded the water
that if **a stutterer** should come,   Moses
it should honor him
and stand at his right hand['s command].

105 And You made Your tempestuous storm
rule over it;
against the will of a demigod,[48]
You put it to rest.

You informed it
of the integrity of **the Servant**,   Joshua
when he lifted his heart to You (in prayer)
that it should turn backward.[49]

You told it
that if **a prophet**[50] should spread his mantle   Elijah
it should stay low, near the riverbed,[51]
for the one who ascended in a whirlwind.

You set down a rule for it,
not to be ignored,
to show the path through the Red Sea
to **him who was thrown into the sea.**[52]   Jonah

You marked its tongue
to be divided into seven[53]
to clean off the dust of the road
from **the one whose feet are lovely.** Israel at the Red Sea

---

48. An archangel, possibly Metatron, known from early Jewish magical and mystical literature. Cf. Gen Rabbah 5:4.
49. Cf. Ps 114:3.
50. See 2 Kgs 2:8, in which the Jordan divides for Elijah and Elisha.

⟨... ...⟩
יִשְׁטְפוּ ⟨...⟩

ה⟨⟩.. ...⟩

⟨... ...⟩
וְהוֹ⟨דִיעַ⟩ (ליהודים) [לַיּוֹרְדִים]
⟨..ר⟩או פ⟨ס..⟩

⟨הַמַּיִם⟩ לָמוֹ צִוִּיתָה
אִם יָבֹא אִלֵּם
יִתְּנוּ יָק⟨ר⟩
⟨וְיַעַמְדוּ⟩ לִימִינוֹ

משה

(וְ)הִמְשַׁלְתָּה עֲלֵיהֶם 105
סַעַר סוּפָתֶךָ
⟨בְּעַל כּוֹ⟩רַח אֵל
יִשְׁתּוֹקוּ לָנוּחַ

הוֹדַעְתָּ לָמוֹ
תֻּמַּת מְשָׁרֵת
בְּנָשְׂאוֹ [לֵב] אֵלֶיךָ
יֵהָפְכוּ לְאָחוֹר

יהושע

הִשְׁמַעְתָּה לָמוֹ
אַדֶּרֶת אִם יִגְלוֹם נָבִיא
יַעֲבוֹר בֶּחָרָבָה
לַעֲלוֹת ⟨בַּסְּעָרָה⟩

אליהו

הוֹרֵ⟨י⟩תָם חוֹק
וְלָעַד לֹא נֶעְדָּר
לְהַרְאוֹת אוֹרַח סוּף
לְמוֹשְׁלָךְ יַמִּים

יונה

הִתְוֵותָה עַל לְשׁוֹנוֹ
לְחַתְּכוֹ לְשִׁבְעָה
לְהַדִּיחַ אֲבַק אוֹרַח
מִיפַת ⟨פְּ⟩עָמִים

ישראל בים סוף

---

51. That is, should stay low so that they could pass.
52. That is, Jonah was given a guided tour through the ocean, during which he was shown the place in the Red Sea where the waters had divided.
53. See Isa 11:15.

115 The roaring waves
appealed to You when they fled,
for You set a limit for them,
not to be transgressed.

You illuminated **that which is covered**　　　　　　　earth
and refreshed it with fruit,
made it redolent with fragrance
in honor of God and human being.

It conceived and carried
but did not give birth
until it overflowed
and gave birth and raised a man.

On that day, by Your word You created three—
those born by Your decree.
It was called the third [day]
by **the third [man]**.　　　　　　　　　　　　　　　**Moses**

As it is written: Who measured the waters with the hollow of His hand, and gouged the skies with a span, and meted earth's dust with a measure, and weighed the mountains with a scale? (Isa 40:12).

[THE FOURTH DAY]

You resolved to form
two illuminating lights
to display Your creations,
for there is no flaw in Your handiwork.

You commanded and they stood
like faithful emissaries
to tell Your mercies
and to recount Your faithfulness.

And You opened, for their departure,
windows in the east
to make (the sun) shine heroically
so that laborers could to go to their work.

115 ⟨הֲמ⟨ו⟩ן גַּלִּים
בְּנוּסָם יְשַׁבֵּרוּ
כִּי חַקְתָּה בַעֲדָם
בְּלִי חוֹק יַעֲבֹרוּ

אדמה   הֶיאַרְתָּה ⟨כְּסוּיָה⟩
⟨וְהוּעַדְנָה בְּכָל מֶגֶד⟩
וְהִרְקַחְתָּה רֵיחַ בּוֹשֶׂם
לִכְבוֹד אֱלֹהִים וְאִישִׁים

הָרָה וְעִיבְּרָה
אֲבָל לֹא הִמְלִיטָה
עַד עֵת הוּחְשָׁרָה
וְיָלְדָה וְגִידְלָה אִישׁ

הַשְּׁלַשְׁתָּה יוֹם בְּקִיּוּ
בְּרוּאֵי בְּמ[וֹ]צָא
וְה[וּ]קְרָא שְׁלִישִׁי
מִפִּ⟨י שְׁלִישִׁי⟩

משה

כ״כ' מי מדד בשעלו מים ושמים בזרת תיכן וכל בשליש עפר הא⟨רץ⟩ ושקל בפלס הר⟨ים⟩ (יש' מ, יב)

[מעשה היום הרביעי]

וְאָמַרְתָּה לַצּוּר
שְׁנֵי מְאוֹרֵי אוֹר
לְהַרְאוֹת מַעֲשֶׂיךָ
שֶׁאֵין מוּם בְּפָעֳלָהּ

וְצִוִּיתָה וְעָמְדוּ
כְּצִירֵי אֱמוּנָה
לְהַגִּיד חֲסָדֶיךָ
וּלְסַפֵּר אֱמוּנָתֶיךָ

וּפָתַחְתָּה לְצֵאתָם
חַלּוֹנִים בְּמִזְרָח
לְהוֹפִיעַ בִּגְבוּרָה
לָצֵאת עֲמֵלִים לְפָעֳלָם

130	And in the west You blazed paths for them to enter to lower their prominence before the **Rider of the heavens**.[54]	God
	And You arranged **those numbered above**, corresponding to **the hosts below**,[55] and appointed them to the Kishon, to the beating of horses' hooves.[56]	stars Israel
	And they were given as omens of the day of war and battle,[57] for the time when You will no longer incline Your ear, heeding prayer.	
	And **a youth** would command them in the mighty battle to be still at Gibeon and to halt at Ayalon.	Joshua
	And if **a sick man** should cry out[58] and You added days to his life, the Healer would reverse them,[59] and they would not be obstinate.[60]	Hezekiah
140	And when You bind up the wounds of Your burdened [people],[61] they will place balm on its wings.[62]	
	And when You cover them with sackcloth to humiliate **those who serve them**,[63] You will renew their light forty-nine-fold.	idolaters

---

54. The divine presence (Shekhinah) resides in the west, so that when the sun sets in the west, it bows down to God. See Pirqe de-Rabbi Eliezer ch. 6 (fol. 14b).
55. Likened to the stars in Gen 15:5.
56. See the Song of Deborah (Judg 5:20–22), in which the stars are said to fight against Sisera.
57. Joel 2:10; the stars dimmed in anticipation of the Day of the Lord.
58. See Isa 38:1–8, in which God extends Hezekiah's life in response to his prayer.

AZ BE-ʾEN KOL

	וְחָתַרְתָּה בַּמַּעֲרָב 130
	אֲשָׁנַבִּים לְבוֹאָם
	לְשׂוֹחֵיחַ גָּבְהָם
הָאֵל	לִפְנֵי **רוֹכֵב בָּעֲרָבוֹת**
כּוֹכָבִים	וְעָרַכְתָּה **סְפוּרֵי מַעֲלָה**
יִשְׂרָאֵל	מְשׁוּלֵי **בְּצִבְאוֹת מַטָּה**
	וְהִזְמַנּוּ לְקִישׁוֹן
	לְהֶלֶם עִקְּבֵי סוּס
	וְנִ[י]תְּנוּ לְאוֹתוֹת
	לְיוֹם קְרָב וּמִלְחֶמֶת
	לְעֵת תָּסִיר אוֹזֶן
	מִשְּׁמוֹעַ תְּפִילָה
יְהוֹשֻׁעַ	וְנַעַר יִמְשָׁל בָּם
	בְּמִלְחֶמֶת עֵזּוּז
	וְיִדּוֹמוּ בְּגִבְעוֹן
	וְיַעַמְדוּ בְּאַיָּלוֹן
חִזְקִיָּהוּ	וְאִם יִבְכֶּה **חוֹלֶה**
	וְתוֹסִיף לוֹ יָמִים
	יַהֲפְכֵם רוֹפֵא
	וּבַל יַקְשׁוּ עוֹרֶף
	וּבְעֵת תַּחֲבוֹשׁ 140
	מַכַּת עֲמוּסֶיךָ
	הֵם יִתְּנוּ לָמוֹ
	צָרֵי בְּכַנְפֵיהֶם
עוֹבְדֵי אֱלִילִים	וּבְעֵת תְּכַסֵּם שַׂק
	לְהַחְפִּיר **עוֹבְדֵיהֶם**
	תְּחַדֵּשׁ אוֹרָם
	לְאַרְבָּעִים וְתִשְׁעָה

59. God would reverse the progression of the sun and the stars.
60. The passage plays on the root *rph*, which can mean "to soften" (here, perhaps, "to massage") and "stiff-necked."
61. These stanzas deal with the eschatological future.
62. See Mal 3:20.
63. The reference is to those who worship the stars.

And when Your elders calculate
the times of month and year,
the **Younger one** will be diminished   the moon
so that it can be sanctified.

And their dominion is over
the four corners of the earth.
So the One who rules over every day
ordained them on the fourth day.

As it is written: He made the moon to mark the seasons (Ps 104:19);
and it is written: He reckoned the number of stars; to each He gave its name (Ps 147:4).

[THE FIFTH DAY]

150   There is a great sea,
which You made vast and spacious
and which was commanded to bring forth swarms,
with creatures beyond number.

You established within it
the offspring of scaled fish
and those that grow fins
so that no one can fathom.

There arose from the waters of the sea
swooping and flying,[64] abundant,
for when they perish,
they bring tidings to their captor.[65]

You bestowed a blessing on them,
and they were fruitful and multiplied,
and from then until now
they look to You for their bounty.

You appointed over them
great chiefs:

---

64. An allusion to two kinds of birds, birds of prey and the others.

הירח

וּבִמְנוֹת זְקֵינֶיךָ
רִגְעֵי חוֹדֶשׁ וְשָׁנִים
יַמְעִיטוּ צְעִידָה
לְמַעַן תִּתְקַדֵּשׁ

וּמֶמְשַׁלְתָּם בְּאַרְבַּע
קְצוֹת הָאָרֶץ
לָכֵן מוֹשֵׁל בְּכָל יוֹם
בָּרְבִיעִי חֲקָקוֹ

ככ' עשה יריח למועדים (תה' קד, יט)

ונא' מונה מספר לכוכבים לכולם שמות יקרא (תה' קמז, ד)

[מעשה היום החמישי]

150 זֶה הַיָּם [הַ]גָּדוֹל
הִ[רְ]חַבְתָּה לְיָדַיִם
וְהָוְזְמַן לְהַשְׁרִיץ
רֶמֶשׂ בְּלִי מִסְפָּר

זֶרַע קַשְׂקַשִּׂים
וּמִגְדְּלֵי סְנַפִּיר
הֲכִינוֹתָה בְתוֹכוֹ
בְּלִי אִישׁ יַחְקוֹר

זֶהוּ מִמֵּי יָם
עֵיטִים וּמְעוֹפְפִים [לָרוֹב]
כִּי בְּעֵת יְלַקּוֹטוּן
בְּשֹׁ(וֹ)[י]רָה יִתְּנוּ לְמַלְכָּם

זִבַּדְתָּם בְּרָכָה
וּפָרוּ וְרָבוּ
וּמֵאָז וְעַד עַתָּה
לִלְקָטְךָ יְשַׁבֵּרוּן

זִמַּנְתָּה עֲלֵיהֶם
שָׂרִים גְּדוֹלִים

---

65. This reading is from the variant, by which the birds' function is to provide good omens to their owners by means of organ divination.

the elusive serpent[66]
and the twisting Leviathan.

160 No stranger can rouse him[67]
nor ascertain his dwelling place,
for like the hinge sockets of doors,
the depths are sealed.

O God,[68] when You wish
to draw him out with a fishhook,[69]
[You make him sink][70] by piercing
his tongue with a rope.

You prepared his muzzle
and pierced his cheek
to provide food
for the holy [people].

When You play with him
like a pet bird,
he will plead with You
not to leash him for young girls.[71]

The virtuous shall feast on him;
the pious shall divide him up;
those who eat him will [   ];
[   ] will say blessings.

170 What You propose, O Lord,
cannot be reversed,
for Your thoughts
are the deeds of Your hands.

The breaking waves
sing praise to You;
for Your part[72] You blessed
the fifth day of creation.

---

66. Cf. Isa 37:1.
67. Referring to the Leviathan.
68. Lit., "this," from Exod 15:2: "This is my God."
69. In the end of days, when God will capture Leviathan as a feast for the righteous.

AZ BE-ʾEN KOL

נָחָשׁ בָּרִ‹י›חַ
[וְ]ל‹י›וְיָתָן ‹מְעוֹ›קָל

160 זָר לֹא יְעִירֶנּוּ
וְלֹא יָבִין רִבְצוֹ
כִּי כְּפוּתוֹת לִדְלָתוֹת
תְּהוֹ‹ם סָ›גוּר

האל

זֶה עֵת תִּרְצֶה
לְמָשְׁכוֹ בְּחַכָּה
לְהַשְׁקִיעַ לְשׁוֹנוֹ
בְּחֶ‹בֶל רוֹ›צְצוֹ

זִמְּמוֹ הֵיכַנְתָּה
וְנָקְבָתָּה לְחָיוֹ
לְתִתּוֹ מַאֲכָל
לְ‹...› קוֹדֶשׁ

זְמָן תְּשַׂחֶק בּוֹ
כְּצִפּוֹר לְשַׁעֲשֵׁיעַ
יַפִּיל תְּחִינָה
‹בַּל לַעֲלֵ›מוֹת יָקְשַׁר

זַכִּים יְכָרוּהוּ
חֲסִידִים יֶחֱצוּהוּ
אוֹכְלָיו יְשׁו‹...›
‹...› יְ‹בָרֲכוּ

170 זְמָמָתָהּ אָדוֹן
אָחוֹר לֹא הוּשָׁבָה
כִּי מַחְשְׁבֹ‹וֹתֶי›ךָ
‹פְּעוּלַ›ת יָדֶיךָ

זֶמֶר נָתְנוּ לָךְ
מְשַׁבְּרֵי רְהָבִים
כְּיַחַסְךָ ‹בֵּירַכְתָּ›
‹יוֹם חֲמִישִׁ›י לְרֵאשִׁית

---

70. Restored from the fragmentary text in line 162.
71. Cf. Job 40:29.
72. The creatures created on that day praise You. Therefore, You blessed them in return.

As it is written: Above the thunder of the mighty waters,
   more majestic than the breakers of the sea (Ps 93:4);
and it is said: All of them look to you (Ps 104:27);
and it is said: Give it to them, they gather it up; open your hand,
   they are well satisfied (Ps 104:28).

[THE SIXTH DAY]

Congealed cream,
crawling creatures:
most of them **unfavored**   impure
and some of them **favored**.   pure

You made from it
the first of Your works.   behemoth
Its crib[73] is a thousand mountains,
and its watering place is the Jordan.

[   ]
to struggle together
for the blessing of the Creator,
for the entertainment of the faithful.

You made his strength as great
as bronze armor;[74]
His limbs are like iron;
his thighs are knit together.

185 Holy Creatures and angels
are in dread as he rears up,[75]
but only the One who made him
will put His sword to him.

He who lives forever
consulted His heart
to make in [His] image
to have dominion over all these.

---

73. Or feeding trough.
74. Lit., "tubes of bronze." See Job 40:18.

ככ' מקולות מים רבים אדירים משברי ים (תה' צג, ד)
ונא' כ⟨-⟩ולם אליך ישבר⟨ון⟩ (תה' קד, כז)
ונא' תתן להם וג' (שם שם, כח)

[מעשה היום השישי]

חֵמָה קְפוּיָה
רִמְשֵׂי חַיּוֹת
רוּבָּם ⟨לְחָרוֹן⟩   טמאים
⟨וּמֵהֶם⟩ לְרָצוֹן   טהורים

⟨חוֹלַלְתָּ מִמֶּנָּה⟩
רֵאשִׁית דַּרְכֶּךָ   בהמות
אֲבוּסָיו אֶלֶף הַר
וּמַשְׁקָיו יַרְדֵּן

⟨ח.. ..⟩ם
לְהִתְגָּר יַחַד
לְבִרְכַּת יוֹצֵר
לְשַׁעֲשׁוּעַ אֱמוּנִים

⟨חֵילוֹ הֶעֱרַץ⟩תָּה
כַּאֲפִיקֵי נְחוּשָׁה
אֲבָרָיו כַּבַּרְזֶל
פֶּחָדָיו שְׂרוּגִים

⟨חַיּוֹת וּמַלְ⟩אָכִים   185
מִשֵּׂאתוֹ יָגוּרוּ
אֲבָל לְבַד הָעוֹשׂוֹ
יַגֵּשׁ חַרְבּוֹ

⟨חַי עוֹ⟩לָמִים
בְּלִבּוֹ נוֹעַץ
לַעֲשׂוֹת בְּצֶלֶם
לִרְדוֹת בְּכָל אֵלֶּה

---

75. Cf. NJV's translation of Job 41:17.

The Merciful One saw
a lonely earth
sitting silently
like a widowed woman.

He willingly made
a human being in His image
and set him to govern all creation
and commanded him to protect it.

Fat and milk,
cream and honey,
he shall eat and enjoy
and say praise to his Creator.

195 No anger shall come to him,
or theft trouble him;
"I will protect his life
if he will observe my laws."

You carved him out in wisdom
in the image of divine beings[76]
and made him a little less
than the image of his Maker.

He was nipped from clay
but his soul is a lamp;
"if he becomes arrogant, I will snuff him out,
and he will sleep in his darkness."

He fathomed skillfully
and brought forth from the earth
and blew with his mouth
the breath of life.

You joined with him
a woman who loved to steal,
and You rejoiced on the day that he was made
and placed him on the sixth day.

---

76. See sources in Yahalom, *Az be-ʾEn Kol*, 85.

〈חַ〉נוּן רָאָה
אֲדָמָה בּוֹדֶדֶת
יוֹשֶׁבֶת וְשׁוֹמֵמֶת
כְּאִשָּׁה אַלְמָנָה

חָפֵץ וְעָשָׂה
אָדָם בְּצֶלֶם
וְהִשְׁלִיטוֹ בְּכָל מַעַשׂ
וְצִוָּה הוּא לִשְׁמוֹר

חֵלֶב וְחָלָב
חֶמְאָה וּדְבַשׁ
יֹאכַל וְיִתְעַנַּג
וְיֹאמַר הַלֵּל לְבוֹרְאוֹ

חָרוֹן בַּל יְבוֹאֵינוּ
שׁוֹד בַּל יְדָאִיגֶנּוּ
"אֵעָצִים חַיָּיו
אִם חֻקַּי יִשְׁמוֹר"

חֲקָקָתוֹ בְחָכְמָה
בְּצֶלֶם בְּנֵי אֱלֹהִים
וְחִיסַּרְתּוֹ מְעַט
מִדְּמוּת יוֹצְרוֹ

חוֹמֶר קְרִיצָתוֹ
נֵר נִשְׁמָתוֹ
אִם יִתְגָּאֶה אֲכַבֶּנּוּ
וְיָלִין בָּאֲפֵילוֹ

חָקַר 〈בְּ〉חָכְמָה
וְהוֹצִיא מֵאָרֶץ
וְנָפַח מִפִּיו
נִשְׁמַת חַיִּים

חוֹמֶדֶת לִגְנוֹב
עֲמוֹ חִיבַּרְתָּהּ
וְשִׁשַּׁתָּהּ בְּיוֹם נַעֲשָׂה
וְשַׂמְתּוֹ 〈יוֹם שִׁשִּׁי〉

195

205   As it is written: How many are the things You have made, O Lord,
   [You have made them all in wisdom] (Ps 104:24);
and it is said: You alone are the Lord. You made the heavens, the
   highest heavens, and all their host, the earth and everything
   upon it, the seas and everything in them (Neh 9:6).
May the glory of the Lord endure forever; may the Lord rejoice in
   His works (Ps 104:31).

[THE SABBATH]

The Good One gazed,
the Adorned One looked out,
Shaddai's rest,
and God's repose.

210   The good and the bad,
The oppressed and the free,   non-Jews and Jews
those who enter and those who accompany,[77]   converts and
all desire it.   "God-fearers"

A decree was issued
to those who enjoy it forever
so that those who rest on it can stride
the heights of the earth.

Daubers of plaster[78]   heathens
will not enjoy its quiet,
for its light
is denied to the wicked.

Ghostly impurity
will not prevail on it,[79]
for the wicked
have no opportunity to succeed.[80]

---

77. This seems to be a reference to converts to Judaism and other sympathizers known as "God-fearers," who participated in Jewish beliefs and attended the synagogue.

78. Cf. Ezek 13:11. Perhaps Christians who add Sunday to the Sabbath. Cf. the prayer *ve-lo netatto le-goye ha-ʾaraṣot* in the Sabbath Amidah, in which it is said that God did not give the Sabbath to the other nations of the world.

205　ככ' מה רבו מעשיך י"י (תה' קד, כד)

ונא' אתה הוא י"י לבדך אתה עשיתה את השמים שמי השמים וג' (נח' ט, ו)
יהי כבוד י"י לעולם וג' (תה' קד, לא)

[מעשה השבת]

טוֹב הֵצִיץ
הַדּוּר הִשְׁקִיף
מְנוּחַת שַׁדַּי
וּנְפִישַׁת אֱלֹהִים

210　טוֹבִים וְרֵעִים
חָפְשִׁים וּרְצוּצִים　　נוכרים ויהודים
בָּאִים וְנִלְוִים　　גוים ויראי אלוהים
בָּהּ חָשָׁקוּ

טַעַם נָתַן
לְתַעֲנוּגֵי עַד
לִדְרוֹךְ שׁוֹבְתָיו
עַל בָּמֳתֵי אָרֶץ

טָחֵי תָפֵל　　עובדי אלילים
בּוֹ לֹא יִשְׁקֹטוּ
כִּי מְאוֹרוֹ
נִמְנְעוּ רְשָׁעִים

טֻמְאַת אוֹב
בּוֹ לֹא תִרְדֶּה
כִּי אֵין לָרֶשַׁע
פִּתְחוֹן פֶּה בְּצֶדֶק

---

79. This section uses *bo* to refer to the Sabbath, listing the auspicious events that cannot be prevented on that day.

80. That is, evil spirits have no dominion over the Sabbath observer.

Tasting the household table[81]
was not prohibited on it,
for the inheritance of those who are blessed by Him
is **the reward of the fruit of His hosts.**[82]   **children of Israel**

220 The fortress of the belly
is not closed up on it,
for He who opens the womb
does not delay its time.

Dew and rain
do not cease up on it,
for they provide for the banquet
like wine and nectar.

Flowing manna, with its taste,
did not rain down on it,
for a second portion was prepared
and was preserved in its honor.[83]

The pure of heart
do not sigh on it,
for it has been given forever
for the joy of those who honor it.

the **Pure One** crowned (it)   **God**
with "remember" and "observe";[84]
so like a ring,
he sealed his works with it.

230 He who is good to all [perfected on the sixth]
and made rest on the seventh.
Then He blessed it and sanctified it,
for he rested on it.

As it is written: It shall be a sign for all time between Me and the people of Israel (Exod 31:17);

---

81. Perhaps marital intercourse.
82. See Ps 129:3. Marital intercourse was not prohibited on the Sabbath, because children are the reward of those blessed by God.

ילדי ישראל

טָרֵף שֻׁלְחַן בַּיִת
בּוֹ לֹא נֶאֱסַר
כִּי נַחֲלַת מְבוֹרָכָיו
שְׂכַר פְּרִי צְבָאָיו

220 טִירַת בֶּטֶן
בּוֹ לֹא הֻסְגְּרָה
כִּי פוֹתֵיחַ רֶחֶם
לֹא יְאַחֵר קֵץ

טַל וּמָטָר
בּוֹ לֹא הֻעֲצְרוּ
כִּי כְיַיִן וּכְעָסִיס
לְמִשְׁתֶּה נְוֹתָנוּ

טַעַם שִׁכְבַת טַל
בּוֹ לֹא הֻמְטְרָה
כִּי הוּכַן בְּמִשְׁנֶה
וְלִכְבוֹדוֹ נִשְׁמַר

טְהוֹרֵי לְבָ‹בוֹת›
בּוֹ לֹא ‹נָא›נָחוּ
כִּי לָעַד נִיתַּן
לְ[שִׂ]מְחַת מְכַבְּדָיו

האל

טָהוֹר עִיטֵּר
בְּ'זָכוֹר' וְ'שָׁמוֹר'
לָכֵן כְּטַבַּעַת
חָתַם בּוֹ מַעֲשָׂיו

230 טוֹב לַכֹּל ‹...›
וְהִשְׁקִיט בְּיוֹם שְׁבִיעִי
וּבֵרְכוֹ וְקִדְּשׁוֹ
כִּי בוֹ שָׁבַת

ככ' ביני ובין בני ‹...› (שמות לא, יז)

---

83. The Sabbath. Here the reference is to the legend that in the Sinai wilderness an extra portion of manna descended every Friday and was miraculously preserved for the Sabbath.

84. In the two versions of the Ten Commandments Israel is commanded to "remember" the Sabbath (Exod 20:8) and "observe" it (Deut 5:12).

and it is said: Happy is the man who does this, the man who holds fast to it: who keeps the Sabbath and does not profane it (Isa 56:2).

[ADAM AND EVE]

God abided
to tell his deeds
to make his benevolence known
when he nipped the clay.[85]

Fine stature,
chambers [of] organs,
twisting channels,
were prepared when he was created.[86]

The supernal servants
were afraid of him,
for they were all created with speech,
and he with the hand of God.

240 **Fiery creatures**   angels
   [   ]
   regarded him
   and said: "What is man?"[87]

The Creator crafted[88] it
   [   ]
and he perfected his body
in the recesses of the earth.[89]

The molding of his body
   [   ]
and his spirit and breath
from the God of faith.

---

85. In chapter 2 of Genesis God interrupts the story of creation to go back and tell of the creation of humankind.
86. Cf. Ezek 28:13.
87. Ps 8:5.

וּנָא׳ אשרי אנוש יעשה זאת ובן אדם יחזיק בה שומר וג׳ (יש׳ נו, ב)

[אדם וחוה]

יָשַׁב אֵל
⟨לְסַפֵּר מַעֲשָׂ⟩יו
לְהוֹדִיעַ חֲסָדָיו
בְּעֵת קָרַץ חוֹמֶר

יָופִי קוֹמָה
⟨חַדְרֵי נְקוּבָ⟩יו
וּפִיתּוּחַ[י] תָּוָפָיו
בְּהִבָּרְאוֹ כּוֹנְנוּ

יָרְאוּ מִמֶּנּוּ
⟨מְשָׁרְתֵי עֶלְיוֹ⟩ן
כִּי כֹל בְּאוֹמֶר נִבְרָא
וְהוּא בְּכַף אֵל

יְצוּרֵי לַהֶבֶת   מלאכים   240
⟨... ..ת⟩
הִתְבּוֹנְנוּ בוֹ
וְשָׂחוּ "מָה אֱנוֹשׁ"

יוֹצֵר רִיקֵם
⟨... ..בּ⟩וּ
וְהִקְרִים גִּיוָיו
בְּתַחְתִּית אֲדָמָה

יְצִיקַת גּוּפוֹ
⟨... ...⟩
וְרוּחוֹ וְנִשְׁמָתוֹ
מֵאֵל אֱמוּנָה

---

88. Lit., "knit." See Ps 139:15.

89. The stanza deals with two stages of God's formation of the human being: the first, the stage of "weaving" or "molding," is the basic; the second, the "finishing" or "glazing," is the completion of the work.

They were all astonished
when God blew into his nostrils,
for [they were] of fire and flammable,
and he of the breath of life.

Reptiles and birds
were alerted and came,
and he who was named by his Creator
gave each its pedigree.

250 God, as he arranged them,
had joined one to the other,
but for his[90] bodily pleasure,
no one was found.[91]

God, wondrous and exalted,
said, "It is not good.
I am one,
so how can he be one?"

"I created him to honor Me—
how can I test him?[92]
Let **fire** come forth from him   **woman**
and through her he will be refined."

God put him to sleep
and cast a pleasant slumber over him
and took a rib away,
but she led him astray.[93]

He awoke from his sleep
and said, "This one at last
is formed from my bone
and given to me for intimacy."

260 He set her opposite him
and balanced his value with hers,

---

90. That is, Adam's.
91. That is, God had provided a mate for every creature except the man.

יַחַ(יָ)ד תָּמָהוּ
בִּינְפוֹחַ אֵל בְּאַפָּיו
כִּי מֵאֵשׁ וּשְׂרוּפִים
וְהוּא בְּנִשְׁמַת חַיִּים

יֵעוֹרוּ וְיָבוֹאוּ
רְחוּשִׁים וְעוֹפִים
וּלְכֻלָּם יְחַסֵּם
נִיקְרָא בְשֵׁם ⟨מִ⟩פִּי בּוֹרְאָם

יָהּ כְּסִידְּרָם 250
וְהוּחְבַּר זֶה לָזֶה
וּלְנַחַת שְׁאֵירוֹ
עוֹד לֹא נִמְצָה

יָהּ נוֹרָא עֲלִילָה
נָם "לֹא טוֹב
אֲנִי אֶחָד
וְזֶה אֵיךְ יִהְיֶה אֶחָד"

"יְצַרְתִּיו לְכַבְּדֵנִי
וְאֵיךְ אֲבְחָנֶנּוּ
תֵּצֵא מִמֶּנּוּ אֵשׁ
וּבָהּ יְצָרֵף"

אישה

יֵשְׁנוֹ אֵל וְהִנְעִים
תְּנוּמַת רִדְמוֹ
וְשָׁלַף מֶנּוּ צֵלָע
וּבָהּ נִצְלַע

[יָקַץ מִתְּנוּמָה
וְשָׂח "זֹאת הַפַּעַם
אֲצוּלָה מֵעֶצֶם
נְתוּנָה לִי שְׁאֵר"]

יְשַׁבָּהּ כְּנֶגְדּוֹ 260
וּשְׁקָלָהּ כְּעֶרְכּוֹ

---

92. That is, how can God distinguish Adam from Himself? Cf. Gen Rabbah 8:10, in which the creatures mistake Adam for God and bow down to him until God casts sleep upon him.

93. Heb. ṣr̄, the same root as "rib."

but still her desire for her husband
had not been set.

As it is written: Men are mere breath (Ps 62:10).

[THE GARDEN OF EDEN]

Ruby and turquoise,
sapphire and amethyst,
beryl and lapis lazuli,
jacinth and emerald:

265 With those gems
You adorned his dwelling,
and You paved his chambers
with shining foundation stones.

A dome of fire
was his canopy,
and You guided his steps
over coals of fire.[94]

You crowned the bride;
You wreathed the bridegroom;
and like a cantor[95] You blessed them
and said, "Be fruitful and multiply."

You called their name
Adam when they were created,
for the generations of Adam
would sprout from them.

All the heavenly hosts
shook like celebrants
when they saw the Creator
making His creatures happy.

275 All the fruits of Eden
and the bounty of the garden—

---

94. Cf. Ezek 28:14.

וַעֲדַיִן לֹא שָׁת
תְּשׁוּקָתָהּ אֶצְלוֹ

ככ׳ אך הבל בני (תה׳ סב, י)

[גן העדן והפיתוי]

כַּדְכֹּד וְנוֹפֶךְ
סַפִּיר וְיָהֲלֹם
תַּרְשִׁישׁ וְשֹׁהַם
לֶשֶׁם וּבָרֶקֶת

כָּל אֶבֶן יְקָרָה 265
סַכְתָה דִּירָתוֹ
וְרִצְּפָתָה חֲדָרָיו
בְּבֹהַק אַבְנֵי בַחַן

כִּפַּת אֵשׁ
חֻפָּתוֹ הָיְתָה
וְעַל גַּחֲלֵי אֵשׁ
הִילַּכְתָה צְעָדָיו

כִּילַּלְתָה כַּלָּה
עִיטְּרַתָה חָתָן
וְכַסּוֹפֵר בֵּרַכְתָה
וְנַמְתָה "פְּרוּ וּרְבוּ"

[כֻּנִּיתָ שְׁמָם
אָדָם בְּהִבָּרְאָם]
[כִּי מֵהֶם יִפְרוּ
תּוֹלְדוֹת אָדָם]

כָּל צְבָא מָרוֹם
כִּבְנֵי מִשְׁתֶּה שִׁיקְשְׁקוּ
בְּשׁוּרָם לְיוֹצֵר
מְשַׂמֵּחַ יְצוּרָיו

כָּל פֵּירוֹת [עֵדֶן] 275
וּתְנוּבַת הַגָּן

---

95. Lit., "scribe." Cf. Pirqe de-Rabbi Eliezer ch. 12, which describes the *ḥazzan*'s blessing of the bride at a wedding.

You permitted them
except for the tree of knowledge.

"If you do not taste of
the bough of good and evil,
you will succeed in doing good
and be saved from evil."

You created the **instrument**　　　　　　　　　　the snake
for the **destroyer** to make havoc　　　　　　　　Satan
and he came with smooth speech
to arouse the **arouser**.⁹⁶　　　　　　　　　　　　Eve

He flattered the innocent
and misled the upright
and ascribed flaws
to the Perfect One's work.

"You shall be like gods
if you listen to me;
for if it were not so,
why would He begrudge you?"

285　As it is written: Let slanderers have no place in the land; let the evil of the lawless man drive him into corrals (Ps 140:12).
As it is written: A lawless man misleads his friend, making him take the wrong way (Prov 16:29).

He was stripped of steps
by smooth speech;
and the one who misled the upright
fell in his depravity.

As it is written: He who misleads the upright into an evil course [will fall into his own pit] (Prov 28:10).

[THE FIRST SIN AND ITS PUNISHMENT]

290　She who is snares and nets⁹⁷
listened to the evil one,

---

96. Eve disturbed Adam, lit., "ringing his bell" all night.

הִתְרַתָּה לָהֶם
חוּץ מֵעֵץ הַדַּעַת

"כַּנַּת טוֹב וָרָע
אִם לֹא תִטְעֲמוּ
הֵן בַּטּוֹב תִּצְלָחוּ
וּמֵרָע תִּוָּצֵלוּ"

הנחש; שטן	כְּלִי [הַ]מַּשְׁחִית
	בָּרָאתָהּ לְחַבֵּל
	וּבָא וְהֶחֱלִיק פֶּה
חווה	לְפַעַם הַמִּפְעֶמֶת

כִּחֵשׁ בִּתְמִימִים
וְהִשְׂגִּיא יְשָׁרִים
וְנָתַן דֹּפִי
בִּפְעוּלַת תָּמִים

"כְּאִם תִּהְיוּ
אִם לִי תַאֲזִינוּ
כִּי לוּלֵי שֶׁכֵּן
לָמָּה [מִכֶּם] כְּלָאוּ"

285 ככ' איש לשון בל יכון בארץ איש חמס רע יצודנו למדחפות (תה' קמ, יב)
ככ' איש חמס יפתה רעהו להוליכו בדרך לא טוב (מש' טז, כט)

[כִּלִּיתָה פְעָמָיו
בִּשְׂפַת חֲלָקוֹת]
[וְנָפַל בִּשְׁחוּתוֹ
מַשְׁגֶּה יְשָׁרִים]

[ככ' משגה ישרים (מש' כח, י)]

[החטא הראשון ועונשו]

290 לַמֵּרֵעַ הֶאֱזִינָה
מְצוּדַת חֲרָמִים

---

97. See Eccl 7:26.

and the **innocent one** was caught 　　　　　　Adam
in the trap of the devious.

A heart of flesh[98] turned away from them, 　**an obedient heart**
and they understood evil;
they girded themselves with leaves from the tree
when they stole the fruit of that tree.

You took a walk in the cool of the day,
and they heard Your voice,
and they hid in their shame,
for they recognized their defiance.

To the end of their generations
at the beginning You tested them;
so that You might judge them favorably,
You asked, "Where are you?"[99]

You said to them,
"Perhaps you erred in eating,"
so that You might answer, "You made a mistake—
you have acted ignorantly."[100]

300　The boor did not understand
the soft answer.
He was undone by his folly
and raged against You.

To **her who drips endlessly**[101] 　　　　　woman
You said, "What have you done?"
and she answered You,
"The **cunning one** deceived me." 　　　　　snake

To the base plotter
You accused and cursed,
and his lying mouth
You filled with dust.

---

98. See Ezek 36:26.
99. That is, in asking this question, God hoped they would repent.

AZ BE-ʾEN KOL

          וְנוֹקַשׁ תָּמִים   **אדם**
בְּמַלְכּוֹדֶת עִיקְשִׁים

לֵב בָּשָׂר סָר מֵהֶם   **לב כנוע**
וְהֵבִינוּ בְרָעָה
וַעֲלֵי עֵץ חָגְרוּ
כְּגוֹנְבֵים פְּרִי עֵץ

לְרוּחַ הַיּוֹם הִילַּכְתָּה
וְשָׁמְעוּ קוֹלֶךָ
וְנֶחְבְּאוּ בְּבָשְׁתָּם
כִּי יָדְעוּ מִרְיָם

לְסוֹף דּוֹרוֹתָם
מֵרֹאשׁ חֲקַרְתָּם
וּלְמַעַן תְּחָנֵּם
בְּ"אַיֶּיכָּה" שְׁאַלְתָּם

לָמוֹ אָמַרְתָּה:
"שֶׁמָּא בְּאוֹכֶל תְּעִיתֶם"
לְהָשִׁיב "שֶׁגַּגְתֶּם
בִּבְלִי דַעַת עֲשִׂיתֶם"

לְמַעֲנֵה רַךְ   300
בַּעַר לֹא הֵבִין
וּבְאִיוַּלְתּוֹ סוֹלֵף
וְעָלֶיהָ נִזְעַף

לְדֶלֶף טוֹרֵד   **אישה**
אָמַרְתָּה "מֶה עָשִׂית"
וְהֵשִׁיבָה לָךְ
"עָרוּם הִשִּׁיאַנִי"   **הנחש**

לְיוֹעֵץ בְּלִיַּעַל
הִרְשַׁעְתָּהּ וְקִילַּלְתָּהּ
וּמִלֵּאתָהּ עָפָר
פִּי דּוֹבֵר שֶׁקֶר

---

100. God gave Adam and Eve an opportunity to say that they sinned inadvertently and so be spared punishment.
101. See Prov 19:13.

The devisor of evil[102]
You threatened with "enmity"[103]
and he was punished with[104] striking at the head
and striking at the heel.[105]

That which begets a dullard   the earth; man
You enveloped in grief
as it was condemned to give forth thorns
and to grow thistles.

310 With convulsions in childbearing
and labor pains
and with the helpmeet's urge to lust
You punished her.

Who can plumb the mind[106]
of the one who searches the inward parts?
For three sinned
and four were punished.

You prepared a remedy
for the affliction of all of them
except for the slithering
of **the one who speaks impiety.**[107]   the snake

Thus in all Your ways
there is faithfulness and justice.
And You are merciful,
not destroying Your deeds.

As it is written in Your holy scriptures: The Lord is beneficent in all His ways (Ps 145:17).

---

102. Lit., "him who wove the love of evil."
103. Between the woman and the snake; See Gen 3:15.
104. Lit., "[his punishment] was tied to."

לְאוֹגֵר אַהֲבַת [רֶשַׁע]
הִתְרֵיתָהּ בְּ"אֵיבָה"
וְהֻקְשַׁר בְּשׁוּף רֹאשׁ
וּ[בְ]שׁוּפַת עָקֵב

לְיוֹלֶדֶת כְּסִיל   האדמה; האדם
תּוּגָה הֶעֱטֵיתָהּ
[וְהָרָשַׁת] לִיתֵּן קוֹץ
וּלְגַדֵּל דַּרְדַּר

לְשִׁבְרֵי הֵרָיוֹן   310
וְהֶפְכֵי צִירִים
וּתְשׁוּקַת עֵזֶר
לְרָעֵב(ת)[נָ]ת עֲנֻשָּׁתָהּ

לְבוֹחֵן כְּלָיוֹת
מִי יְתַכֵּן דַּעַת
כִּי שְׁלֹשָׁה חָטְאוּ
וְאַרְבָּעָה לָקוּ

לְמַכַּת כֻּלָּם
צֳרִי (לָעַד) הֵיכַנְתָּהּ
חוּץ מִלְחִיכַת
דּוֹבֵר נְבָלָה   הנחש

לָכֵן בְּכָל דְּרָכֶיךָ
אֱמוּנָה וּמִשְׁפָּט
וְחָסִיד בְּכָל מַעֲשֶׂיךָ
בְּלִי לְחַבֵּל פּוֹעַל

ככ' בד' ק' צדיק י"י בכל (תה' קמה, יז)

---

105. That is, as the snake strikes at a person's heel, so human beings will strike at his head. See Gen 3:15.
106. Isa 40:13.
107. According to legend, the snake will not be restored to its former self in the world to come.

[SIBLING RIVALRY]

They did not sleep
one night in honor,
for **the one who is like a beast**   Adam
did not understand honor.[108]

They were expelled from Eden
to devour food[109] in sweat,[110]
for pleasure
is not fitting for a fool.

{From the path of life,
the fools were expelled;
with a fiery ever-turning sword,[111]
the tree of life was protected.}

Those aware of good and evil   Adam and Eve
became acquainted with the bed,
and their belly gave forth
children, one good and one evil.

325   The occupation of each
was different from the other's;
neither resented
the other's vocation.

The one who causes the honest to stray   the snake
cast jealousy between them
and sowed discord
between the children of **those who stayed.**   Adam and Eve

The elder hatched a cunning plan
with his offering
and presented fruit,
recalling his parents' sin.

The younger hurried
to arrange an offering;

---

108. Cf. Ps 49:21.
109. Lit., "taste."

[שנאת אחים]

מָלוֹן אֶחָד
בְּכָבוֹד לֹא לָנוּ
כִּי לֹא בָן
מָשׁוּל בַּהֵמָה בִּיקָּר   אדם

מֵעֵדֶן גּוֹרְשׁוּ
לִלְעוֹט טַעַם בְּזֵיעָה
כִּי לֹא נָאֶה
לִכְסִיל תַּעֲנוּג

⟨מִדֶּרֶךְ חַיִּים
אֱוִילִים נִגְרְשׁוּ
וּבְלַהֲטַת מִתְהַפֶּכֶת
עֵץ חַיִּים נִשְׁמַר⟩

מִשְׁכַּב יָדְעוּ
מַכִּירֵי טוֹב וָרָע   אדם וחווה
וְהִמְלִיטָה בְּטָנָם
יַלְדֵי טוֹב וָרָע

מְלֶאכֶת שְׁנֵיהֶם   325
זֶה מִזֶּה הִפְרִדַתָּה
בְּלִי יִשְׁטוֹמוּ
זֶה אֶת זֶה בְּעָבְדָם

מְשַׁגֵּה יְשָׁרִים   הנחש
שָׁת בֵּינֵימוֹ קִנְאָה
וְשִׁלַּח מְדָנִים
בְּנֵינֵי שִׁיגְיוֹ   אדם וחווה

מַחֲשֶׁבֶת הֶעָרִים
גָּדוֹל בְּמַשְׂאָתוֹ
וְהִגִּישׁ פֵּירוֹת
וְהִזְכִּיר עֲווֹן הוֹרָיו

מִיהַר קָטוֹן
וְעָרַךְ מִנְחָה

---

110. Cf. Gen 3:19.
111. This stanza is restored from MS ENA 2147.22-23. See Gen 3:24.

You took comfort in the aroma[112]
and looked with favor on the sacrifice.

You did not want
the malefactor's offering,
for the wicked's sacrifice
is considered an abomination.

335 His countenance
changed to downfallen,
for he did not turn
to the Merciful to plead mercy.

"Why are you enraged?"
You said to him,
"Bar **the lurking at the door**;[113]   sin
return and I will return you."

O King, to You are revealed
the [inner] details of the vital parts,
counting steps
and repaying deeds in kind.

As it is written by Your prophet: Most devious is the heart (Jer 17:9);
and it is said: I, the Lord, probe the heart (Jer 17:10).

[MURDER COMES INTO THE WORLD]

Livid revenge
and a vicious grudge[114]
were borne in the inner chambers
of the born criminal.

345 With words of enmity
and hateful speech
he assaulted him in the field,
to find a way to harm him.[115]

---

112. Playing here on the words *minḥah* (offering) and *niḥoaḥ* (aroma).
113. Cf. Gen 4:7.

וְנָחֲתָה עַל נִיחוֹחַ
וְשָׁעֲתָה עַל קָרְבָּן

מִיַּד עַוָּל
מִנְחָה לֹא רָצִיתָה
כִּי זֶבַח רְשָׁעִים
לְתוֹעֵבָה נִיתָּן

מַרְאֵה פָּנָיו 335
בִּנְפוֹל נִשְׁתַּנּוּ
כִּי לֹא פָנָה
חַנּוּן לְחָנְנוּ

"מַה לְּךָ נִזְעַמְתָּה"
אָמַרְתָּה לוֹ
"סָגוּר אוֹרֵב בַּפֶּתַח
שׁוּב וַאֲשִׁיבָה"

החטא

[מֶלֶךְ] לְךָ גְלוּיִים
מֶחְקְרֵי כְלָיוֹת
לִסְפּוֹר צְעָדִים
[וּלְשַׁלֵּם גְּמוּלִים]

ככ' ע' י' נ' עקוב הלב (יר' יז, ט)
ונ' אני יי״י חוקר (יר' יז, י)

[רצח בעולם]

נְקִימַת אַף
וּנְטִירַת חָרוֹן
הוֹצִפָנוּ בְחַדְרֵי
פּוֹשֵׁעַ מִבָּטֶן

נוֹאֲמֵי אֵיבָה 345
וְדִבְרֵי שִׂנְאָה
הִתְעַלֵּל בַּשָּׂדֶה
[לְהִתְאַנּוֹת לוֹ]

114. Cf. Lev 19:18.
115. See Gen 4:8.

He turned a blind eye
before **the One that no eye can see**[116]   God
and did not set
the God of hidden things before him.

The child of thieves[117]   Cain
taught murder,[118]
wounded the righteous,
and stoned the immaculate.

He who is exalted on high
stood up to plead the cause;
He demanded the victim
from the murderer.[119]

The arrogant one retorted,
answering his Maker,
"Am I an employee—
hired to watch over my brother?"

355   He hid his face
when God rebuked him—
"Could he who is not watching
ambush someone more innocent?"[120]

"You shall surely be
a destructive curse
along with **that which opened its mouth**[121]   earth
to share **that which you stole.**"[122]   Abel's blood

A ceaseless wanderer,
his insolence was humbled.
And he replied to the Exalted One,
"My guilt is too much to bear."

---

116. See Job 24:15.
117. Because Adam and Eve stole the fruit, Cain was the "son of thieves."
118. That is, taught the rest of the world to murder.
119. God demanded to know where Abel, the victim, was.
120. The lines play on the word *shomer* in Gen 4:9, which means both "keeper" and "watching." Alternatively, this couplet could be translated as Cain's reply to God: "And is he who does not watch

אלוהים	נֵצֶר אִישׁוֹן
	לְלֹא עַיִן תְּשׁוּרֵינוּ
	וּלְאֵל נִסְתָּרוֹת
	לֹא שָׁת לְנֶגְדּוֹ
קין	נִין גּוֹנְבִים
	הוֹרָה רְצִיחָה
	וּפִיצַע צַדִּיק
	וְסִיקֵּל נָקִי
	נִיצַב לָרִיב
	נִשְׂגָּב בַּמָּרוֹם
	דָּרַשׁ הָרוּג
	מִיַּד רוֹצֵחַ
	נָעַן מִתְחַטֵּא
	וְהֵשִׁיב לַיּוֹצֵר
	"וְכִי שָׂכִיר אֲנִי
	לִשְׁמוֹר אָחִי"
	נֶחֱפוּ פָנָיו 355
	בְּהוֹכִיחוֹ אֵל
	"וּמִי לֹא שׁוֹמֵר
	מְזֻנָּב זָה מִמֶּנּוּ"
	"נָכוֹן תִּהְיֶה
	לִקְלָלַת מְאֵירָה
האדמה	עִם פָּצְתָה פִיהָ
דם הבל	לְחַלֵּק גְּנָבַיִךְ"
	נָע וָנָד
	נִכְנַע זְדוֹנוֹ
	וְהֵשִׁיב לְנִשְׂגָּב
	"מִנְּשׂוֹא גָּדוֹל עֲווֹנִי"

---

over a murderer more innocent?" That is, anyone who allows murder to take place is as guilty as the murderer. Cf. Tanḥuma Bereshit 9. Two couplets missing in this section may have completed this dialogue.

121. See Gen 4:11.

122. God is apparently answering Cain in this poetic dialogue. The idea here is that not only is Cain, who stole Abel's blood, cursed, but so is the earth, since it accepted Abel's blood by absorbing it.

He who bears guilt
was filled with mercy
and suspended the sentence
of **fading grass**.¹²³   humanity

As it is written: But He, being merciful, forgives iniquity (Ps 78:38).

[THE GENERATION OF ENOSH]

You dragged him away from seeing
Your glorious countenance,
and his parents were excluded
from **the great primordial dwelling**.   Eden

You increased the account of his generations¹²⁴
without limit,
and they were fruitful and multiplied
immeasurably.

You increased the abundance
of Your delicacies for rich pastures;
they ate what was Yours
but did not know You.

370   They luxuriated
on couches of licentiousness—
and because of that the divine beings
were called **those who fall about**.¹²⁵   Nephilim

They planned to proclaim
the Faithful One a false god
and called a **carving**¹²⁶   idol
by the name of **the One who dwells in shelter**.¹²⁷   God

The Rider,¹²⁸ to whom joyous praise is due,   God
was saddened in his heart,

---

123. Cf. Ps 103:15.

124. Lit., "book of generations" (Gen 8:1); the author is playing on the root *spr*, which can also refer to counting.

125. Playing on the Hebrew *nefilim* and the root *npl* "to fall"; see Gen 6:4.

AZ BE-ʾEN KOL

נוֹשֵׂא עָווֹן
רַחֲמִים נ[תְ]מַלָּא
וְתָלָה דִּין [צֶדֶק]
בני אדם   **לְחָצִיר עוֹבֵר**

ככ' והוא רחום (תה' עח, לח)

[דור אנוש]

סָחַבְתּוֹ מִלִּרְאוֹת
(עוֹד) פְּנֵי כְבוֹדֶךָ
עדן   **וְשָׁכֵן קֶדֶם טוֹב**
נִמְנְעוּ הוֹרָיו

סִפֵּר תּוֹלְדוֹתָיו
הָעֲצַמְתָּהּ בְּלִי חֵקֶר
וּפָרוּ וְרָבוּ
עַד אֵין מִסְפָּר

סָרַח מַעֲדַנֶּיהָ
הָעֲדַפְתָּהּ לְדַשְׁנָם
וְשָׁלָה אָכְלוּ
וּלְךָ לֹא יָדְעוּ

370   סְרוּחִים הָיוּ
בְּמִשְׁכְּבֵי זִמָּה
וּמִשָּׁם בְּנֵי אֱלֹהִים
נִקְרְאוּ נְפִילִים

סָרָה חָשְׁבוּ
לַעֲנוֹת בְּנֶאֱמָן
פסל   וְכִנּוּ מְסֻוָּרָד
האל   בְּשֵׁם יוֹשֵׁב סֵתֶר

האל   סוֹלוּ לָרֹכֵב
עַל לִבּוֹ נֶעֱצָב

---

126. Reading *mswrd* for *mswrr*. Cf. Isa 44:13.
127. Cf. Ps 91:1.
128. God rides the clouds, according to Ps 68:5.

for he had it set on[129]
creating an image on **dry ground**.   earth

Despising His work,
disgusted with[130] His creation,
He rejoiced in destroying,
as He had delighted in building.

There was **a fragrant spice**   Noah
among the rotten fruit—
balm in the wound,
and wine in the vinegar cellar.

380 You placed him as a watchman
for one hundred and twenty years
to warn the insolent
who knew no shame.

Before his ship
set sail,
he delayed for seven days
to allow for life.[131]

Their hope was lost,
their anticipation was extinguished,
their eyes darkened,
and sight ended.

As it is written in Your holy scriptures: But the eyes of the wicked pine away; escape is cut off from them; they have only their last breath to look forward to (Job 11:20).

[THE FLOOD]

Against them, the Merciful One
turned cruel,
locking up his compassion,
not listening to groaning.

---

129. Lit., "he had lifted it" (his heart).
130. Having had enough of; cf. Gen 27:46.

כִּי הוּא נְשָׂאוֹ
אֶרֶץ
לִבְרוֹת צֶלֶם בְּצִיָּיה

שָׁנֵא פָּעֳלוֹ
וְקָץ בְּמַעֲשָׂיו
וְשָׂשׂ לַהֲרוֹס בְּגִיל
כְּגִילוֹ לִבְנוֹת

שָׁם רֶקַח נִמְצָא
נֹחַ
בְּתוֹךְ צַחַן בְּאוּשִׁים
צֳרִי בְּתוֹךְ מַכָּה
וְיַיִן בְּמַרְתֵּף חוֹמֶץ

שַׂמְתּוֹ לְצוֹפֶה   380
שָׁנוֹת מֵאָה וְעֶשְׂרִים
לְהַזְהִיר זֵדִים
וְלֹא יָדְעוּ בֹשֶׁת

סְפִינָתוֹ
עַד לֹא הִפְרִישׁ
(עוֹד) שִׁבְעַת יָמִים אַחֵר
(רוּחַ) [רְוָחָה] לְחַיִּים

סִבְרָם אָבַד
וְתִקְוָותָם פָּחָה
וְעֵינֵיהֶם קָדְרוּ
[וּ]מְבָּטָם כָּל

ככ' בד' ק' ועיני רשעים (איוב יא, כ)

[הַמַּבּוּל]

עֲלֵיהֶם נֶהְפַּךְ
חַנּוּן לְאַכְזָר
וְנָעַל רַחֲמָיו
בְּלִי שְׁמֹעַ אֲנָק

131. According to a midrash (t. Sotah 10:3–5), God delayed the flood for seven days after the death of Methuselah to allow the sinful generation to repent and thus survive.

The Most High	
broke the edges of **the expanse**[132]	the earth
and opened the floodgates	
that he had closed with his word.	
The Mighty One burst open	
the fountains of the deep	
and smashed the heads	
of **the bolts of the seas.**	Leviathans
He punished them with rain	
for forty days and nights	
for they rebelled against Him	
who formed humankind in forty days.[133]	

395 He summoned and poured out
that which He holds in the hollow of His hand   water
and it rose up as fast as
that which cascades down.[134]   falling water

[   ]
to close up the sluices[135]—
they rose up in their strength,
but they fell like weaklings.

The **mighty** overcame   water of the flood
and swept away the fools;
the heathen were wiped out—
a people who lusted after theft.

[   ]
slaughtered the fools;
and every high mountain
was covered with **that which is cold.**   water

The sustenance of all existence   soil
was swept away with it,

---

132. That is, he ruptured the borders of the land by which it held back the water.
133. Their rebellion corrupted the form of the human embryo, which takes form in forty days. See Gen Rabbah 32.5 (ed. Theodor and Albeck, p. 292).

אדמה	עֶלְיוֹן נִיתַּק
	(עוֹל) עָבְרֵי **רְקוּעָה**
	וּפָתַח אֲרוּבּוֹת
	סָגֵר בְּמַאֲמָר
	עֵינוֹת תְּהוֹם
	עִיזוּז בִּיקַּע
לויתנים	וְשִׁיבֵּר רָאשֵׁי
	בְּרִיחֵי מְצוּלָה
	עָנַשׁ(ת)ם בִּגְשִׁימַת
	אַרְבָּעִים יוֹם וָלַיְלָה
	בְּבִגְדָם בְּיוֹצֵר
	אֱנוֹשׁ לְאַרְבָּעִים
מים	**עֲצוּרֵי שָׁעֲלוֹ** 395
	קָרָא וְשָׁפַךְ
	וּמִיהֲרוּ לַעֲלוֹת
נוזלים	כִּמְגוּרִים לֵירֵד
	⟨ע.. ..ג⟩ת
	לִסְתּוֹם אֲרוּבּוֹת
	וְגָאוּ בִּגְבוּרָתָם
	וְנָפְלוּ כְּחָלָשׁ
מי המבול	⟨עַזִּים גָּבְרוּ⟩
	וְטָאטְאוּ אֱוִילִים
	וְנִמְחוּ חֲנֵיפִים
	עַם גֶּזֶל חָשְׁקוּ
	⟨ע.. ...⟩
	⟨הִשְׁ⟩חִיתוּ אֱוִילִים
	וְכָל הַר גָּבוֹהַּ
מים	כִּסּוּ קָרִים
אדמה	**עוֹמֵד כָּל יְקוּם**
	עִימָּם הוּנַד

---

134. The meaning is that the waters rose as fast as rain falls; cf. Gen Rabbah 32:7 (ed. Theodor and Albeck, p. 294).

135. According to Gen Rabbah 31.12 (ed. Theodor and Albeck, p. 285), the giants of that generation tried to step on the sluices to stop the water from flowing.

for woe to the wicked
and woe to his neighbor!¹³⁶

405   On a boat of **the blameless man**   Noah
You floated life,
and in the midst of the storm
You led it on a straight path.

Who can tell
the abundance of Your wonders?
For with **the staff with which You strike**   water
You bind the wound.

Because of this **the strayer**¹³⁷   Habakkuk
was fearful and prayed,
when he saw that in Your anger
You remember compassion.

> As it is written: A prayer of the lowly man when he is faint and pours forth his plea before the Lord (Ps 102:1).
> As it is written by Your prophet: O Lord, I have learned of Your renown (Hab 3:2).

[THE TOWER OF BABEL]

The survivor of the universe   Noah
opened a porthole in his shelter,
and before he set out,
he sent forth two messengers.

415   You spoke to him,
"Go out in peace,
for **the scoffer** has been expelled,   Cain and his descendents
and the contention has ceased."

He offered young birds
and pieces of livestock

---

136. This phrase, apparently a popular saying found in m. Negaʿim 12:6, means that since the earth allowed the wicked generation to flourish, it too is cursed. See Gen Rabbah 31:7.

	כִּי אוֹי לָרָשָׁע
	וְאוֹי לִשְׁכֵינוֹ
נח	405 עַל אֲנִי תָמִים
	רוּחַ חַיִּים רִיחַפְתָּה
	וּבְתוֹךְ סְעָרָה
	בְּמִישׁוֹר הִילַכְתָּ ⟨ה⟩
	עוֹצֶם נִפְלְאוֹתֶיךָ
	מִי יוּכַל סִיחַ
מים	כִּי בְּשֵׁבֶט תַּכֶּה
	בּוֹ תַחֲבוֹשׁ מַחַץ
	⟨עַל ז⟩את חָרַד
חבקוק	שׁוֹגֵג וּפִיֵּל
	בְּשׁוּרוֹ רַחֲמֶיךָ
	כִּי בְרוֹגֶז תִּזְכְּרֵם

ככ׳ תפלה לעני כי וג׳ (תה׳ קב, א)

ככ׳ ע׳ י׳ נ׳ ⟨י״י⟩ שמעתי ⟨שמעך⟩ (חב׳ ג, ב)

[דור הפלגה]

נח	⟨פְּלִיט⟩ עוֹלָם
	פָּתַח צוֹהַר צְפוּנוֹ
	⟨וְ⟩טֶרֶם צֵאתוֹ
	שְׁנֵי צִירִים הֵרַץ
	415 פָּצְתָה לוֹ
	"צֵ⟨א⟩ בְּשָׁל⟨וֹ⟩ם
קין וצאצאיו	כִּי הַגְרֵשׁ לֵץ
	וְהָשְׁבַּ⟨ת⟩ מָדוֹן"
	פִּרְחֵי גּוֹזָלוֹת
	וּבִתְרֵי פְגָרִים

137. This epithet for Habakkuk is based on Hab 3:1, which would seem to mean "prayer of Habakkuk, prophet of errors." The idea is that Habakkuk erred in questioning God's mercy; see Midrash Tehillim 90:7.

in purity
on a pure altar.

You turned to smell
his sacrificial offering,
and You repented Your sadness
so that (the earth) not be cursed again.

You signaled the sight
of Your radiant glory in the clouds.
If again they are destroyed,
they will be drowned in the rivers.¹³⁸

A threefold thread　　　　　　　Shem, Ham, and Japheth
You fortified with blessings
and made the earth swarm
with sum of their descendents.

425　They unraveled Your moral teachings,
broke off Your yoke,
and trampled on **that which is rewarding**.　　　　Torah
[　　]

They opened their mouths to say "Come"¹³⁹
and were dispersed like corpses;
they wished to think Your thoughts
[　　]

They faced upward
but were cast downward,
for they rejected God,
[　　]

430　They founded a corner of plaster
and bound straw for a dome
[　　] to wage
war against **the Fire**.　　　　　　　　　God

---

138. God will no longer send a flood, but could in the future drown the wicked in the rivers if he desired.

עָרַךְ בְּטַהֲרָה
עַל מִזְבֵּחַ טָהוֹר

פָּנִיתָ וְהֵרַחְתָּ
מִנְחַת זְבָחָיו
וְשׁוֹבַבְתָּה עֲצָבְךָ
⟨לְלֹא⟩ עוֹד ⟨תִּקָּלַל⟩

פִּנּוּי זִיו כְּבוֹדְךָ
בֶּעָבִים רָמַזְתָּה
עוֹד אִם יַשְׁחִ⟨י⟩תוּ
⟨וּבַנְּהָרִים תִּשְׁטְפֵם⟩

שם, חם ויפת   פְּתִיל חוּט מְשׁוּלָּשׁ
בְּבִרְכוֹת אִמַּצְתָּ
וְהִרְחַשְׁתָּה תֵּבֵל
בְּ⟨חָק⟩ צֶאֱצָאֵיהֶם⟩

425 פִּיתְּחוּ מוֹסְרוֹתֶיךָ
וְנִתְּקוּ עוֹלָּךְ
התורה   וּבָעֲטוּ בִּמְשַׁלֵּם
אוֹי⟨..   ...⟩

פָּצוּ בְּפִיהֶם "הָבָה"
וְנוּפְּצוּ כְּמוֹ חָלָל
וְזָמְמוּ זְמָמָתָ⟨ךְ⟩
⟨...   ...⟩

⟨פָּ⟩נוּ כְּלַפֵּי מַעְלָה
וְהוּרְדוּ עַד מַטָּה
כִּי מָאֲסוּ ⟨אֵל⟩
⟨...   ....⟩

430 פִּנַּת טִיט יִסְּדוּ
וּבֵינָןֵ קַשׁ רִכְּסוּ
ע⟨..   לַ⟩עֲרוֹךְ
האל   קְרָב נֶגֶד אֵשׁ

139. Gen 11:4.

Suddenly You appeared
and dispersed their assembly;
their dialogue was distorted;
their speech was confused.

Shuddering seized them,
[   ]
Because of their love,
You did not destroy them.¹⁴⁰

As it is written: Hatred stirs up strife, but love covers up all faults (Prov 10:12).

[ABRAHAM]

[   ]
[   ] chickweed,¹⁴¹
a rose, a lily,
among mowed thorns.

440   A gazelle among wild asses,
upright among the crooked,
[   ]
the shade of a tree in the desert.

He was worried among the **worthless shapes**	idols
aggrieved among the graven images.¹⁴²	
He was appalled by **artifacts**,	idols
discarded that which is carried.¹⁴³	

His soul thirsted
for the Bundle of Life,
and the light of his eyes
was never extinguished.¹⁴⁴

He wrapped himself in a turban
of splendor and righteousness

---

140. Because they loved one another.
141. So the NJV translation of Prov 24:31.
142. The couplet engages in two plays on words: *ṣar* (troubled) and *ṣur* (shape) in the first stich, and *neʿeṣav* (sad) and *ʿaṣav* (idol) in the second.

⟨פֶּתַע הוֹפַ⟩עְתָּ
וְהִפְרַדְתָּה אֲגוּדָם
וְהוּתְמַר מַעֲנָם
וְהוּבַ⟨לַל⟩ מִילְלָם

פַּלָּצוּת אֲחָזָתַם
⟨...⟩
לְמַעַן אַהֲבָתָם
לֹא עֲשִׂיתָם כָּלָה

ככ׳ שינ⟨אה⟩ תעורר מדאנים וג׳ (מש׳ י, יב)

[אברהם המאמין]

⟨צ..⟩ ⟨...⟩
⟨..⟩קִי חֲרוּלִים
חֲבַצֶּלֶת שׁוֹשָׁן
בְּקִמְּסוֹנַי כְּסוּחִים

צְבִי בֵּין פְּרָאִים   440
יָשָׁר בֵּין מַעֲקָשִׁים
⟨...⟩
צֵל עֵץ בְּתוֹךְ חוֹרֶב

פסילים   צָר בְּצוּרֵי הֶבֶל
               וְנֶעֱצַב בַּעֲצַבִּים
אליל   וְתִיעַב מְתוֹאָר
               וּמָאַס בִּמְסֻבָּל

צָמְאָה נַפְשׁוֹ
בִּצְרוֹר הַחַיִּים
וְאוֹר עַפְעַפָּיו
הֵן לֹא נִדְעָכוּ

צָנִיף עָטָה
פְּאֵר וּצְדָקָה

---

143. Cf. Isa 46:7.
144. Based on an emendation; see Yahalom, *Az be-'En Kol*, 114.

and looked above and below
for You rule them all.

He spoke rightly,
abiding at the gates;
he was girded with faith
and relied on justice.

450 He looked over the earth and said,
"If no one spreads it out,[145]
from whom does it tremble,
and who keeps it steady?

"The luminaries of the sky—
if they are not called by name,
how is it that they do not change
their courses of day and night?

"The shadows of night—
if they are not spread out in time,
who holds back the sun,
detaining it until dawn?"[146]

He expounded the commandment:
"Who made the moon?[147]
Is there a house that is laid out,
built by itself?"

You soothed his heart,
for You are Lord of all,
and before You were revealed to him,
You tried him[148] and he prevailed.

460 You leapt toward him,[149]
like a lover his companion,
and by the power of Your light
he took his steps.

---

145. See Ps 136:6.
146. The idea here is that the sun must be held back in the tent of the night until day.
147. God commanded him (Gen 15:5) to look heavenward, and Abraham interpreted God's command according to Isa 40:26: "Who created these?"

וְהִבִּיט בְּמַעְלָה וּבְמַטָּה
כִּי אַתָּה מַנְהִיגָם

צֶדֶק הָגָה
וְשָׁקַד מְזוּזָה
וְנֶאֱזַר בָּאֱמוּנָה
וְנִשְׁעַן בְּמִשְׁפָּט

צָפָה עֲלֵי אֶרֶץ וְנָם 450
"אִם אֵין לָהּ רָקִיעַ
מִמִּי תִרְעַד
וּמִי מַעֲמִידָהּ"

"צַחְצוּחֵי שַׁחַק
אִם לֹא בְּשֵׁים קְרוּאִים
אֵיךְ לֹא יִשְׁנוּ
מִשְׁמְרוֹת יוֹם וָלַיְלָה"

"צִלְלֵי עֶרֶב
אִם לֹא בְּעִיתָם מְנוּטִים
מִי מַעֲמִיד חֶרֶס
וְעוֹצֵר עַד שַׁחַר"

צִיּוּוּי דָּרַשׁ
מִי לְבָנָה עָשָׂה
יֵשׁ בַּיִת נִרְתָּק
וְנִבְנֶה לְעַצְמוֹ

צָרֵי שַׁתָּ לְלִבּוֹ
כִּי אַתָּה אֲדוֹן כֹּל
וּבְטֶרֶם תִּמָּצֵא לוֹ
צָרְפַתּוֹ וְעָמַד

צָלְחָתָה עָלָיו 460
כְּאוֹהֵב עַל רֵעַ
וּלְתוֹקֶף נָו⟨וּ⟩גְהָ⟨הּ⟩
צָעֲדוּ אֲשׁ⟨וּ⟩רָיו

---

148. By commanding him to leave his home (Gen 12:1).
149. Following the suggestion of Bronznick, review of *Az be-ʾEn Kol*, 152, and idem, "Li-Meqoro u-le-Horato shel ha-Munaḥ Qefiṣat ha-Derekh," *Lešonénu* 37 (1972–73): 15–20.

As it is written by Your prophet: Who has roused a victor from the
east, summoned him to His service? (Isa 41:2).

[THE ELECTION OF ABRAHAM]

Bound as a seal on the heart,
like a bracelet for the arm,
like a belt for the loins,
like a turban for royalty,

465 You called him out
to gaze at the stars;
You augmented his faith
with reward and punishment.[150]

You cast darkness
and passed a torch through
and made a covenant of pieces
in which each piece was burned.

Before You took note of him
by making him **flourish** in old age,   have a son
You relieved him of a **trifle**   foreskin
and appeared in his honor.

The **rebels** were jealous of him   people of Sodom
as those who wanted no visitors,[151]
with the nature of the evil,
with the rage of sinners.

You let Your secret reach
the **father's**[152] ears   Abraham's
when their abominable outrage
went up before You.

475 He arose like a wise man
to appease the King's wrath,

---

150. Cf. Gen 15:8, 13–16.
151. Lit., "those who forgot the path"; cf. Job 28:4. In Gen 19:4–5 the Sodomites were inhospitable to the visitors.

ככ' ע' י' נ' מי העיר ממזרח צדק וג' (יש' מא, ב)

[בחירת אברהם]

קָושַׁר כְּחוֹתָם עַל לֵב
וּכְטַבַּעַת לִזְרוֹעַ
וּכְאֵזוֹר לְמָתְנַיִם
וּכְצָנִיף לִמְלוּכָה

465 קְרִיתוֹ לַחוּץ
וְשָׂר בַּכּוֹכָבִים
וְהוֹסִיף אֱמוּנָה
וְהֵשִׁיב וְנַעֲנַשׁ

קִידַּרְתָּה עֲלָטָה
וְהִבְעַרְתָּה לַפִּיד
וְכָרַתָּה בְּרִית נֶתַח
וְכָל פֶּגֶר נִיתַּךְ

קֶדֶם תִּפְקְדֶנּוּ
לָנוּב בְּשֵׂיבָה
ערלה   הִיתַּרְתָּה קַלּוּתוֹ
וְהוֹפַעְתָּה כַּבֵּדוֹ

אנשי סדום   קָמִים קִנְאוּ בוֹ
עַם נִשְׁכְּחֵי רֶגֶל
בְּמִידַּת רֵעִים
וּבְכַעַס חַטָּאִים

אברהם   קֶשֶׁב סוֹדְךָ
בְּאָזְנֵי אָב הִשְׁמַעְתָּה
בַּעֲלוֹת לְפָנֶיךָ
צַעֲקַת תּוֹעֲבָתָם

475 קָם כֶּחָכָם
לְכַפֵּר חֲמַת מֶלֶךְ

152. Gen 17:5.

to persuade, with discourse,
the Keeper of Faith: God

"If the yeast in still liquor
has begun to effervesce,[153]
recognize the contrite heart—
do not destroy all.

"If the impious[154]
have bared their necks,[155]
take heed to the humble—
do not commit extinction."

He offered his appeal,
and made his case;
he pleaded for the sake of fifty,
but not ten were found.

Easily and swiftly
You set Your hand against the flint[156]
and overturned the wicked;
they were decimated and were no more.

485 The ruthless slaughtered in the dark,
hiding their faces,
but their deeds were repaid;
they vanished like smoke.

> As it is written: Therefore, men of understanding, listen to me; wickedness be far from God, wrongdoing, from Shaddai (Job 34:10).
> And it is said: For He pays a man according to his actions, and provides for him according to his conduct (Job 34:11).

---

153. "If the people of Sodom have begun to repent." The reference is to a fermented beverage whose fermenting agents (i.e., the few righteous people) have just begun to take action but have not yet caused fermentation.

האל

לִפְתּוֹת בְּשִׂיחַ
לְשׁוֹמֵר אֱמוּנִים

"קְפוּאִים אִם חָלוּ
לְחַלְחֵל שְׁמָרֵיהֶם
בֵּין בְּדַכּוּת לֵב
וְאַל תַּשְׁחִית הַכֹּל"

"קַלֵּי רֹאשׁ
אִם עוֹרֶף הִפְנוּ
שׁוּר בְּשִׁפְלֵי רוּחַ
וְאַל תַּעַשׂ כָּלָה"

קֵירַב עֲצוּמוֹת
וְהִגִּישׁ צְדָקוֹת
וּבִיקֵּשׁ עַל חֲמִשִּׁים
וַעֲשָׂרָה לֹא ‹נִמְצָאוּ›

קַל מְהֵירָה
יָד בְּחַלָּמִישׁ שִׁילַּחְתָּה
וְהָפַכְתָּה רְשָׁעִים
וְהוּבְקְעוּ וְאֵינָם

קָשִׁים בַּחוֹשֶׁךְ הִישְׁחִיתוּ 485
וְסֵיתָר פָּנִים שָׂמוּ
וְהוּמְחָה לָמוֹ פָּעֳלָם
כְּקִיטוֹר נִידְעָכוּ

כ"כ' לכן אנשי לבב שמעו לי וג' (איוב לד, י)

ו"נ' כי פועל אדם ישל' לו וג' (שם, שם יא)

---

154. Lit., "light-headed."
155. A sign of contrition.
156. Cf. Job 28:9.

[THE BINDING OF ISAAC]

You fulfilled faithfully
the essence of Your word
and made the withered tree flourish,
yielding rich fruit.

The laughing woman was refreshed with shade,[157]   Sarah
and she said, "Everyone will laugh at me."
The one who laughed was expelled,   Ishmael
to be free as a wild animal.

You resolved to prove
Your **friend's** devotion   Abraham's
to glorify Your name
before **those who said "what is humanity?"**[158]   the angels

495 The father was tested greatly
with a son who was born to him at one hundred,
a son tender to his mother
and unique before his father.

"Take the [beloved, from your loins,]
away to Mount Moriah,
for I desire him
to take back My gift."

His insides were in turmoil,
and his thoughts articulated:
"Who is dearer to a man—
his flesh or his Creator?

"I have gone down to fire and hot coals,
and I react with dismissal;[159]
now, what He has entrusted me—
shall I not return it gladly?"

He stirred and exulted
gladly

---

157. That is, she was blessed with the cool refreshment of a son.
158. Ps 8:5, often used in Midrash by angels disparaging humanity.

[יצחק והעקדה]

רֹאשׁ דְּבָרְךָ
כְּנֶאֱמָן הֶאֱמַנְתָּהּ
וְהִפְרַחְתָּהּ יָבֵישׁ
לִיתֵּן פְּרִי מֶגֶד

שרה │ רוֹעֲנַנָּה צֵל מְצַחֶקֶת
│ וְשָׂחֲ⟨ה⟩ "לִי כֹּל יִצְחָק"
ישמעאל │ וְהוּגְרַשׁ מְצַחֵק
│ לְחוּפְשַׁת פְּרָאִ⟨י⟩ם

אברהם │ רֵעוּת אוֹהַבְךָ
│ שָׁקַדְתָּהּ לְהַרְאוֹת
│ לְהַאֲדִיר שִׁימְךָ
המלאכים │ בְּאָמְרֵי "מָה אֱנוֹשׁ"

495 רַב מְנֻסֶּה אָב
בְּבֵן נוֹלַד לְמֵאָה
בֵּן רַךְ לְאֵם
וְיָחִיד לִפְנֵי אָב

"רַחֲמֵי מֵעֶיךָ
מְשׁוֹךְ לְהַר הַמּוֹרִיָּה
כִּי בָ⟨ו⟩וִּיתִי
קַחַת מַתְּנָתִי"

רָחֲשׁוּ קְרָבָיו
וְהָגוּ שַׂרְעַפָּיו
"מִי מוּטָב לְאִישׁ
שְׁאֵרוֹ אוֹ יוֹצְרוֹ"

"רַדְתִּי לָאֵשׁ וְּלַגַּחַל
וְלֹא אָמַרְתִּי בְּחֶבֶל
וּפִקְדוֹנוֹ
לֹא אָשִׁיב בְּשִׂמְחָה"

רָגַשׁ וְצָהַל
בְּשִׂמְחָה ⟨...⟩

---

159. That is, I spurn my fate, as if to say "to hell with it."

505 He ran quickly to do His desire,
though the way was concealed from him;
he did not shirk from doing it
and believed in the Rescuer.[160]

He discovered at Ariel
the crouching of the lion[161]   the divine presence
and arranged at Moriah
a pure offering.

The angels quaked
and the heroes grew weak
when they saw the enthusiastic sacrificer
and the eager offering.

You made known Your presence[162]
among **a great company**   of angels
when You showed that not in vain
was humankind created.

As it is written: O Lord, our Lord, how majestic is Your name throughout the earth (Ps 8:2).

[JACOB]

515 [   ]
[   ]
He joined with him when he fled[163]
he was taken as a tithe[164]

[   ]
[   ]
[   ]
[   ]

---

160. The spelling, *mšh*, may reflect a play on the name Moses (Moshe), from Exod 14:31.
161. Heb. *arieh*.
162. Lit., "his crouching"; see above, line 507.

⟨... ...⟩
⟨... ...⟩

505 רָץ לְמַהֵר חֵיפֶץ
וְדַרְכּוֹ מֶינּוּ הָעוֹלָמָה
וְלוֹ קָץ בַּדָּבָר
וְהֶאֱמִין בְּמֹשֶׁה

השכינה **רְבִיצַת אַרְיֵה**
מָצָה עַל אֲרִיאֵל
וְעָרַךְ בְּמוֹרִיָּה
מִנְחָה טְהוֹרָה

רָעֲשׁוּ אֵלִים
וְרָפוּ אֶרְאֵלִים
בְּשׁוּרָם זוֹבֵיחַ דָּץ
וְנִזְבָּח שָׂמֵיחַ

של מלאכים רו⟨ב⟩צוֹ בְּסוֹד
רַבָּה הוֹדַעְתָּה
בְּהַרְאֲךָ לְלוֹ רִיק
יְצַרְתָּהּ אָדָם

ככ' יְיָ אֲדוֹנֵינוּ וג' (תה' ח, ב; י)

[יעקב]

515 ⟨ת.. ...⟩
⟨... ...⟩
⟨נ⟩לְוָוה לוֹ בְּבָרְחוֹ
⟨... ע⟩וּשֶׁר

⟨ת.. ...⟩
⟨... ...⟩
⟨עַל⟩ שֶׁלָּךְ הִיגְדַּלְתָּה
וְל⟨ר.. ת⟩וֹךְ שֶׁלָּךְ

163. The word "joined" (*nilvah*) may be an allusion to Levi. See the following note; cf. Jubilees 31:16.

164. Probably referring to Levi, who according to Pirqe de-Rabbi Eliezer ch. 37 was pledged to God's service by Jacob at Jabbock to fulfill his promise in Gen 28:22.

[   ]
[   ]
[   ]
[   ]

[As it is written:]

[THE CHOSEN CLAN]

[   ]
[   ]
[   ]
[   ]

[   ]
[   ]
[   ]
[   ]

[   ]
[   ]
[   ]
[   ]

[   ]
[   ]
sprouting almonds
and putting complaints to rest.[165]

530 [   ]
giving honor
to warn [against violating the proscription],
You punished Achan.[166]

[   ]
Your staff [   ] peoples
[   ]
to strike the rebels.[167]

165. See Num 17:21–23.
166. Probably referring to Josh 7, in which Achan violates the ban against taking the spoils of Jericho.

⟨ת.. ⟩
⟨... ...⟩
⟨... ...⟩
⟨... ...⟩

⟨ככתוב ...⟩

[המשפחה הנבחרת]

⟨ת.. ...⟩
⟨... ...⟩
⟨... ...⟩
⟨... ...⟩

⟨ת.. ...⟩
⟨... ...⟩
⟨... ...⟩
בְּיוֹפִי סַנְסִנִּים

⟨ת.. ...⟩
⟨... ...⟩
⟨... ...⟩
בִּמְלִיצֵי צֶדֶק

⟨ת.. ...⟩
⟨... ...⟩
⟨לִגְמוֹ⟩ל שְׁקֵדִים
וּלְהַשְׁבִּ⟨ית⟩ תְּ⟨לֻ⟩נּוֹת

⟨ש..⟩ עָר   530
⟨לְשַׁ⟩מְתָּ כָּבוֹ⟨ד⟩
לְהַזְהִיר ⟨... ⟩ מֵחֶרֶם
עָקָן תְּ⟨יַ⟩סֵּר

⟨ש.. ...⟩
⟨שבטך ...⟩ עַ⟨מִּ⟩ים
בִּ⟨ר ...⟩
לְהַכּ⟨וֹ⟩ת הַמְּ⟨אוֹ⟩רִים

---

167. Cf. Num 20:10, in which Moses strikes the rock to silence the people's rebellion.

He executed judgment	
against **Zoan** and its idols	Egypt
and tore, like a garment,	
that which is measured in His hollow[168] into footpaths.	water

[ ] approached	
the one with whom He plays[169]	wisdom
when he would speak	
and You would answer.[170]	

[   ] peace
on the neck [   ]
when his lips produce
genuine knowledge.[171]

540   You raised his stature
from all the people of [   ]
[for there is none so] great;[172]
he served like an angel.

They perfumed his beard	
with the aroma of spices	
to mix for **the mixer**[173]	Aaron
of the fragrance of myrtle.	

He hurried in the place of Ariel
for seven days
to fulfill his installation[174]
for Him (whose glory) fills the world.

As it is written in Your Torah: Everything done today, the Lord has commanded to be done to make expiation for you (Lev 8:34).

---

168. Isa 40:12.
169. See Prov 8:30.
170. An apparent reference to Exod 19:19, in which Moses spoke on Mount Sinai and God answered him in thunder.
171. Cf. Mal 2:7; the stanza refers to the priest.

⟨שְׁפָטִים⟩ עָשָׂה
בְּצִ⟨וֹעַ⟩ן ⟨וּבְ⟩אֱלִילֶיהָ מצרים
וְקָרַע כְּשַׂמְ⟨לָ⟩ה
⟨שָׁ⟩בִיל רֶגֶל בְּתוֹךְ שׁוֹעַ⟨ל⟩ מים

⟨שׁ..⟩ נִ⟨י..גָ..⟩שׁ
⟨...⟩ לְלוֹ מְשַׂחֶקֶת חכמה
בִּ⟨הְיוֹ⟩תוֹ מְדַ⟨בֵּ⟩ר
וְאַתָּה עוֹנֶה

⟨ר.. ..ר⟩ שָׁלוֹם
⟨בְּ⟩צַוָּאר ⟨... ..תה⟩
בְּהָפִיק שְׂפָתָיו
דַּעַת נְכוֹחִים

רוֹמַמְתָּה גַדְלוֹ   540
מִכָּל בְּנֵי ר⟨.ב.⟩
⟨כִי..⟩ בִּלְתּוֹ גָּדוֹל
כְּמַלְאַךְ מְשָׁרֵת

רֵיקַח מֶרְקָחִים
עַל זְקָנוֹ רוֹ⟨קְקָחִים⟩
לִרְ⟨קוֹחַ⟩ לִרְקַח
מֶרְקָחוֹת הֲדַסִּים

רָץ בִּמְקוֹם אֲרִיאֵל
שִׁבְעַת ⟨יָמִ⟩ים
מִמַּלֵּא ⟨יָדָיו⟩
לְמַלֵּא עוֹלָם   האל

ככ' בת' כאשר עשה (ויק' ח, לד)

---

172. This restoration is tentative.
173. Aaron mixes the incense.
174. Heb. *le-male yadav*. Cf. Exod 28:41. The biblical meaning is "commissioning" or "ordaining"; the rabbinic sense is "instruction" (cf. Rashi to Exod 28:14).

[IN PRAISE OF THE PRIESTHOOD]

Before he approached
to present a gift of sacrifices,
they adorned him
in eight garments.

Holiness struck him,[175]
purity tempered him,
before he wrapped linen
around his flesh.[176]

His stature
rose to the height of a cedar
when he was fit with embroidered garments
to ornament his body.

The pact of brothers	
over a brother in a tunic	Joseph
he atoned for with his tunic	
for **her who takes off her tunic**[177]	Israel

555 The shape of the robe is like a paenula,[178]
woven at its narrow and wide parts,
to swaddle his chest
and to make way for wide steps.

The shape of the neck opening
reinforces its hem
lest it tear
when he attacks the malevolent one.

He set golden bells
and wove them into his hem
to recall (God's) love
of (the one of whom it is said): "How beautiful are your steps."[179]

---

175. Perhaps referring to the young priests' beating him to keep him awake.

176. Lit., "neck." Perhaps an allusion to his private parts, which he covers with the breeches. The reading is from ms ה.

177. Song 5:3. Note the echo of a form found in Midrash and early piyyut in which a keyword is repeated three or four times; on this form, see Joseph Heinemann, "ʿAl Defus Piyyuti Qadum," *Bar Ilan* 4–5 (1977): 132–37; Ze'ev Yavetz, "Ha-Piyyutim ha-Rishonim," in *Festschrift zum siebzigsten*

[שבח כהונה]

קֶדֶם גָּשׁ
לַעֲרוֹךְ שַׁי קָרְבָּנוֹת
בִּבְגָדִים שְׁמוֹנָה
אָז הֶאֱדִירוּהוּ

קְדוּשָׁה פִּעֲמַתְהוּ
טׇהֳרָה בֵּירְרַתְהוּ
וַחֲרִיזַת בַּד
עַל צַוָּארוֹ

קוֹמָתוֹ
כְּאֶרֶז נִתְעַלָּת
בְּהַתְאִים לוֹ מִשְׁבְּצוֹת
לְהַדֵּר גֵּוִיו

קֶשֶׁר אַחִים
יוסף **עַל ⟨אָח בְּ⟩כְתוֹנֶת**
יָרְצָה בְּכָתְנָתוֹ
ישראל **לְפוֹשְׁטֵי כְתוֹנֶת**

צוּרַת מְעִיל כְּפֶל⟨נֵ⟩ס   555
אֲרִיגַת צַר וְרָחַב
לְ⟨הַח⟩שִׁיק חָזֵהוּ
וּלְהַסְרִיחַ פְּעָמָיו

צוּרַת בֵּית צַוָּאר
יַתְחִיל שְׂפָתוֹ
פֶּן יִקָּרֵעַ
בְּפִגְעוֹ בְּמַסְטִין

צָג פַּעֲמוֹנֵי פָז
וְשִׁילְשִׁי⟨לָ⟩ם בְּשׁוּלָיו
לְהַזְכִּיר חֶשְׁקַת
⟨מַה יָּפוּ⟩ פְּעָמַ⟨יִךְ⟩

Geburtstage David Hoffman's, ed. Simon Eppenstein, Meier Hildesheimer, and Joseph Wohlgemuth (Berlin: Lamm, 1914), 69–70 [Hebrew section]; Swartz, *Mystical Prayer*, 197–98; and Yahalom, *Piyut u-Meṣi'ut*, 137–43.

178. A long sleeveless cloak worn on the upper body, narrow at the top and wide at the bottom.
179. Song 7:2.

Alongside of them he placed
pomegranates of majesty
made of three (colors)
to recall our faithful deeds:

A blue-green thread for the fringes,
and purple for the locks of the head,[180]
a silken strand
like the thread of her lips.[181]

565 A paenula [   ]
and struck one another
so that the Beloved would listen
to the pomegranates of his steps.[182]

When his soles moved,
they gave voice,
like **him who called in the wilderness**   Aaron
to make a path straight.

The servants of the Shekhinah
were fearful of him,
for the robe was named
after the One who wears justice.[183]

Over his heart there was
an open place
so that **that which searches hearts** could be redeemed   the soul
by the One who unravels the heart.[184]

It measured
a span by a span
to glorify the One who measures
the heavens with his span.

575 Its work was like that of a craftsman
for the One who crafted all by His design

---

180. That is, to recall Israel: Song 7:6.
181. See Song 4:3.
182. Here the poet relates Isa 40:3 to Aaron's intervention in Num 17. See Yahalom, *Az be-'En Kol*, 32.

צִדָּם שָׁת
רִמּוֹנֵי הוֹד
פְּעוּלִים מְשֻׁלָּשָׁה
לְהַזְכִּיר חֲסָדֵינוּ

פְּתִיל תְּכֵלֶת לְצִיצִית
וְאַרְגָּמָן לְדַלַּת רֹאשׁ
וְתוֹלַעַת שָׁנִי
כְּחוּט שְׂפָתוֹתֶיהָ

פֶּלֶ‹נָ›ס כג‹..›נוּ 565
וְהִקִּישׁ[וּ] זֶה לָזֶה
לְמַעַן יַאֲזִין דּוֹד
לְרִמּוֹנֵי שְׁלָחָיו

פְּעָמָיו יָנִיעַ
וְהֵם יִתְּנוּ קוֹל
כְּקוֹרֵא בַּמִּדְבָּר   אהרון
לְיַשֵּׁר מְסִלּוֹת

פֶּ[וּ]חֲדָדִים מִמֶּנּוּ
מְ‹שָׁ›רְתֵי שְׁכִינָה
כִּי מְעִיל נִקְרָא
לְשֵׁם לוֹבֵשׁ צְדָקָה

עַל לִבּוֹ הָיָה
בְּמָקוֹם קָרוּעַ
לִ‹פְדּ›וֹת **לְחוֹפֵס לֵב**   הנשמה
אֵצֶל קַרְ‹קַשׁ› לֵב

עַל זֶרֶת וָזֶרֶת
הָיָה מְמֻדָּד
לְהַאֲדִיר לִמְתַכֵּן
שָׁמַיִם בַּזֶּרֶת

עֲשִׂיָּתוֹ כִּמְלֶאכֶת חוֹשֵׁב 575
לְעַשׂ כֹּל בְּמַחְשָׁבֶת

---

183. Isa 59:17.
184. God, who opens the heart to discover its secrets.

and who calculates
[   ] a penalty.

Because of that it was called
the Breastpiece of Judgment
for the One who judges in secret
and so that offense could be covered.

He placed it on his heart,
like a seal on the heart,
as a remembrance of placing
a seal on the heart.

He encircled it
with corded chains
to arouse feelings of
the drawing of cords.[185]   God's love

He arranged in it
twelve stones
to remove the heart of stone
from the remnant of **the mild man.**[186]   Israel

585 Sheathed in gold,
like the wings of a dove,[187]
engraved with the names
of the twelve tribes.

They were arranged in rows,
three by three,
to remind the people
of the righteousness of **their three ancestors.**   the patriarchs

They were set and bordered
into four rows
to propitiate the One who deposes the four (empires)[188]
and gathers the exiles from the four (corners of the earth).

---

185. In Hos 11:4 God draws Israel with ties of love.
186. Cf. Gen 25:27.

וּמְחַשֵּׁב
‹..›‹אל› ‹כ׳›פֶר

עַל כֵּן נִקְרָא
חוֹשֶׁן הַמִּשְׁפָּט
לְשׁוֹפֵט כֹּל בַּחֲשַׁי
וּלְמַעַן [יְכַסֶּה פֶּשַׁע]

שָׂמוֹ עַל לִבּוֹ
כְּחוֹתָם עַל לֵב
זִכְרוֹן (שׁ)[א]ֵימַת
חוֹתָם עַל לֵב

סִבֵּב לוֹ
שַׁרְשְׁרוֹת עֲבוֹתוֹת
לְעוֹרֵר חִישַׁת
מְשִׁיכַת עֲבוֹתוֹת

אהבת האל

סִידֵּר ‹בְּ›תוֹכוֹ
שְׁתֵּים עֶשְׂרֵה אֶבֶן
לְהָסִיר לֵב אֶבֶן
מִשְׂאֵרִי(ם)[ת] **(אבן)[תָּם]**

ישראל

585　סְכֻכוֹת יְרַקְרַק
בְּכַנְפֵי יוֹנָה
מְפֻתָּחוֹת שֵׁמוֹת
שְׁנֵים עָשָׂר שָׁבֶט

נְתוּנִים בְּטוּרִים
שְׁלֹשָׁה שְׁלֹשָׁה
לְהַזְכִּיר לְכוּלָם
[צֶדֶק] **שְׁלוֹשֶׁת הוֹרֵיהֶם**

האבות

נְכוֹנִים וּמְוּגְבָּלִים
לְאַרְבָּעָה טוּרִים
לְחַלּוֹת לְמַפִּיל אַרְבַּע
וּמְקַבֵּץ מֵאַרְבַּע

---

187. Lit., "in the wings of a dove"; cf. Ps 68:14.
188. See Dan 8:22.

To **the first** was given (the color) red	Reuben
for the first fruit of his vigor[189]	
to make scarlet white[190]	
and so that he may sit at the head of his tribes.	
The second was stamped	Simeon
with the impression of topaz	
to absolve the tribe of Simeon	
from the sin of Shittim.	
595 **The third one** gave off	Levi
light like the morning star	
as he hurried in his camp	
to do his mission like lightning.	
The fourth caused	Judah
an uproar against his foes,	
and he shall not bare his neck,[191]	
for there is an emerald at hand.[192]	
The fifth is provided	Issachar
with a sapphire among the sheepfolds.[193]	
For he understood **Comfort**	Torah
and inclined his shoulder to bear the burden.	
The inscription of **the sixth**	Zebulun
he placed inside a diamond,	
for he nursed	
from the hidden hoards of **the countless**.[194]	grains of sand
Leshem, **the seventh**,[195]	Dan
You chiseled into a jacinth,	
for in it **the mild man**[196]	Jacob
waited for redemption of the great name.[197]	

---

189. Gen 49:3.
190. See Isa 1:18.
191. In submission.
192. The word for emerald, *nofekh*, plays on the sound of *yafneh*, "bares."
193. Gen 49:14. NJV: saddlebags; KJV: sheepfolds. Gen Rabbah 99:10 (ed. Theodor and Albeck, p. 1282) and 98:12 (ibid., p. 1262) interpret this to be the rows of students learning Torah from the lips

ראובן	נִיתַּן **רִאשׁוֹן** אוֹדֶם
	⟨לְשֵׁ⟩ם (אל) [אוֹן]
	לְהַלְבִּין אֲ⟨וֹדֶם⟩
	וְלֵ⟨י⟩שֵׁיב בְּרֹאשׁ מְתָיו
שמעון	נִטְבַּע **שֵׁינִי**
	בְּמַטְבֵּעַ פִּטְדָה
	לִפְטוֹר שֶׁבֶט שִׁמְעוֹן
	מֵעֲוֹן שִׁטִּים
	מְאוֹר הִבְהִיק 595
לוי	**שְׁלִישִׁי** כִּבְרָקֶת
	כְּמַהֲרוֹ בַּמַּחֲנֶה
	לִהְיוֹת צִיר כִּבְרָק
	מְהוּמָה עָשָׂה
יהודה	**רְבִיעִי** בְּצָרָיו
	וְעוֹרֶף אֵל יַפְנֶה
	כִּי בְנוֹפֶךְ סָמוּךְ
יששכר	מוּכָן **חֲמִישִׁי**
	בְּסַפִּיר בְּמִשְׁפְּתַיִם
התורה	כִּי הֵבִין **מְנוּחָה**
	וְהִטָּה שְׁכֶם לִסְבֹּל
זבולון	מִכְתָּב **שִׁשִּׁי**
	שָׂם בְּתוֹךְ יַהֲלוֹם
	כִּי הוּא יוֹנֵק
גרגרי חול	סְפוּנֵי מְדוּדִים
דן	לְשֵׁם **הַשְּׁבִיעִי**
	חָרַטְתָּה בְלֶשֶׁם
יעקב	כִּי בוֹ חִיקָּה **תָם**
	לִישׁוּעַת שֵׁם גָּדוֹל

---

of the rabbis; the Sanhedrin, which sat in rows, consisted mostly of Issacharites. Jastrow, *Dictionary*, renders *shefatayim* as "border-mounds."

    194. See Deut 33:19.
    195. See Josh 19:47.
    196. Gen 25:27; cf. line 584 above.
    197. Heb. *shem*. The divine name engraved on the frontlet.

605	For **the one full of blessing**[198] he engraved the eighth with agate, for he returned[199] to inherit the west and south.	Naftali
	The one who raids at the heel[200] (was inscribed) on the ninth, amethyst, for as a lion he tears off arm and scalp.	Gad
	The one whose bread is rich[201] (was) on the tenth, beryl, for it yielded royal delicacies.	Asher
	He placed the glory of onyx on the head of **the elect of his brothers**[202] when he sanctified the Name in secret[203] and El Shaddai helped him.	Joseph
	A diadem of jasper became the crown of **the beloved one**,[204] for (the One who says) "I will dwell here" rests between his shoulders.	Benjamin
615	Each one was placed in its station like **mighty forces**[205] going out by number.	stars
	It was set into the ephod, held in place with rings, and chained with thread.	

---

198. Deut 33:23.
199. Heb. *šb*; a play on *šbw*.
200. Gen 49:19.
201. Gen 49:20.
202. Gen 49:26.

לְמַלֵּא בְרָכָה 605	נפתלי
חָקַק שְׁמִינִי בְּשִׁבְטוֹ	
כִּי שָׁב לִירַשׁ	
יָם וּבְדָרוֹם	
לִגְגוֹד עָקֵב	גד
בַּאֲחַלְמָה הַתְּשִׁיעִי	
כִּי כְלָבִיא טָרַף	
זְרוֹעַ אַף קָדְקֹד	
לְלַחְמוֹ שְׁמֵנָה	אשר
בְּתַרְשִׁישׁ הָעֲשִׂירִי	
כִּי הוּא נוֹתֵן	
מַעֲדַנֵּי מֶלֶךְ	
כְּבוֹד שׁוֹהַם שָׁם	
בְּרֹאשׁ נְזִיר אַחִים	יוסף
בְּקַדְּשׁוֹ שֵׁם בַּסֵּתֶר	
וְאֵל שַׁדַּי עֲזָרוֹ	
כְּלִיל יָשְׁפֶה	
הוּכְתַּר לִידִיד	בנימן
כִּי פֹה אֵשֵׁב	
נָח בֵּין כְּתֵפָיו	
כֻּלָּם נְכוֹנִים 615	
אִישׁ בְּמִשְׁמָרוֹ	
כְּצִבְאוֹת אוֹנִים	כוכבים
יוֹצְאִים בְּמִסְפָּר	
כָּנוּס הָיָה	
בְּתוֹךְ הָאֵפוֹד	
מְרֻכָּס בְּטַבָּעוֹת	
וְשָׁלוּל בִּפְתִיל	

---

203. By resisting Potiphar's wife. See Gen Rabbah 98:20 (ed. Theodor and Albeck, p. 1270) and b. Sotah 36b: An image of his father appeared to him and said: In the future your name will be placed among those of your brothers on the ephod. Do you want it to be erased?

204. Deut 33:12.

205. See Isa 40:26.

He placed his beautiful ephod
between his shoulders
girded with frames
like the work of the breastpiece.

He placed on it
two onyx stones
engraved
for the twelve tribes:

On the right he engraved
Exceeding in Rank and Weapons　　　　Reuben, Simon and Levi
Lion Cub　　　　　　　　　　　　　　　　　　Judah
Snake and Hind;　　　　　　　　　　Dan and Naftali

625　he indicated on the left
Ass and Sailor　　　　　　　　　Issachar and Zebulun
Delicacy and Tearer　　　　　　　　　Asher and Gad
Ox and Wolf.　　　　　　　　　Joseph and Benjamin

He set the two
on his two shoulders
so that when he went forth before the holy shrine,
we would be remembered for good.

He whose eyes are pure
would look at them
to arouse feelings of
{the drawing of cords}.[206]　　　　　　　　　God's love

The hewing of the stone
was done without hands
to smash **plaster**　　　　　　　　　　　the nations
and to shatter **iron**.[207]　　　　　　the fourth kingdom

The second (stone),
which was engraved by hand,
was hewn to injure our injurers
and to tear out **those who tear us out**.　　the enemies of Israel

---

206. Cf. line 582 above.

יָפְיִ אֲפוּדָתוֹ
שָׁת בֵּין כְּתֵפָיו
חֲרוּזָה בְּמִשְׁבְּצוֹת
כְּמַחְשֶׁבֶת הַחֹשֶׁן

יֵישֵׁב עָלָיו
שְׁתֵּי אַבְנֵי שֹׁהַם
מְפֻתָּחוֹת
לִשְׁנַיִם עָשָׂר שֶׁבֶט

יְמִינִי חָקַק
שְׂאֵת וּכְלֵי חָמָס   ראובן, שמעון ולוי
גּוּר אַרְיֵה   יהודה
נָחָשׁ וְאַיָּלָה   דן ונפתלי

יֵידַע בַּשְּׂמָאלִית   625
גֶּרֶם וּמַלָּח   יששכר וזבולון
מַעֲדָן וְטוֹרֵף   אשר וגד
שׁוֹר וּזְאֵב   יוסף ובנימן

טוֹפְסוּ שְׁנֵיהֶם
עַל שְׁתֵּי כְתֵפוֹתָיו
בְּבוֹאוֹ לִפְנֵי קוֹדֶשׁ
יַזְכִּרֵנוּ לְטוֹבָה

טְהוֹר עֵינַיִם
בָּהֶם יַבִּיט
וִיעוֹרֵר חִישַׁת
⟨מְשִׁיכַת אַהֲבָתֵינוּ⟩   אהבת־אל

טִיעַת אֶבֶן
חֲצוּבָה בְּלֹא יָדַיִם
לִידוֹק **טִיט**   האומות
וְלֵ(י)רוֹעַ **בַּרְזֶל**   המלכות הרביעית

טִירַת שְׁנִיָּה
חֲקוּקָה בְכַפַּיִם
לְשָׂרוֹת שׂוֹרְטֵינוּ
וְלִמְרוֹט מוֹרְטֵינוּ   אויבי ישראל

---

207. See Dan 7:19.

635 He put on the sash,
like a belt on his loins,
to cleave **the place of fire**   Israel
to the **Fire Consuming Fire**.   God

He wore it on top of it,
like a dressing for a wound,
to wear over **a ruin**
as vast as the sea.[208]   Jerusalem

It was hollow
and made of embroidered work
to revive our hollow corpses
and to stop our slaying.

He girded himself
and concealed its end inside,
like the rivers that go around,
ending at the sea.

He placed on his head
the radiant royal headdress,
like a hairnet
and like large twisted chains.

645 Sparks of the seraphim
recoiled from it,
for its image
is like that of a helmet of redemption.

Rage,[209] when he saw it,
could not open his mouth,
for on the day of vengeance
he will be swallowed up.

He tied his head
with a sky blue thread
and tied it to his neck
like the bonds of a cow.

---

208. Lam 2:13.

ישראל	
האל	

חָגַר אַבְנֵט 635
כְּאֵזוֹר לְמָתְנַיִּים
לְהַדְבִּיק **לְבֵית אֵשׁ**
לְאֵשׁ אוֹכְלָה אֵשׁ

חָבְשׁוּ עָלָיו
כְּחִיתּוּל לְמַכָּה
לַחֲבוֹשׁ שֶׁבֶר
גָּדוֹל כַּיָּם

חָלוּל הָיָה
וּמַעֲשֵׂיהוּ כְּחוֹשֵׁב
לְהַחֲיוֹת חֲלָלֵינוּ
וּלְהַשְׁבִּית הֲרוּגֵינוּ

חֲגָרוֹ לוֹ
וְהֶחְבִּיא רֹאשׁוֹ בּוֹ
כִּנְחָלִים סוֹבְבִים
וְסוֹפָם לַיָּם

זִיו הוֹד מִצְנֶפֶת
נָתַן בְּרֹאשׁוֹ
כְּמַעֲשֵׂה שְׂבָכָה
וּכְשַׁרְשְׁרוֹת גְּדִילִים

זָחֲלוּ מִמֶּנָּה 645
זִיקֵי שְׂרָפִים
כִּי דְּמוּתָהּ
כְּכוֹבַע יְשׁוּעָה

זַעַף בְּשׂוֹרוֹ בָּהּ
פֶּה לֹא יִפְצֶה
כִּי בְּעֵת נְקָמָה
הוּא מִתְבַּלֵּעַ

זֵרְזָהּ בְּרֹאשׁוֹ
בְּחוּטֵי תְּכֵלֶת
וּקְשָׁרָהּ לְעָרְפּוֹ
כְּמוֹסֵרַת פָּרָה

---

209. This is probably the name of a destructive power.

And[210] he placed on his forehead
the frontlet, the holy diadem,
and his eyes
shone like the heavens.

And on it was written
the letters of the Great Name,
"YY" above[211]
and "Holy" below.

655   And the supernal demigods
made room for him
lest their eyes be filled with (the sight of him)
and grow dim.

And at his right
walked **grass**;[212]   humankind
he communed with fire
and was not burnt.

They brought him
the holy linen breeches,
like a kind of leggings[213]
that horsemen wear.

He attached them to his loins
and draped them over his thighs
in order not to be revealed
because of the One who covers up our sins.[214]

It hid the shameful place
when he stood in the place of glory,
for the covering of our shame
would be opened there.

---

210. The conjunction *vav* is used here for the acrostic.
211. The Tetragrammaton.
212. Cf. Isa 40:6.

וְשָׂם עַל מִצְחוֹ
צִיץ נֵזֶר הָדָר
וְעַפְעַפָּיו
הִבְהִיקוּ כָּרָקִיעַ

וְכָתוּב עָלָיו
אוֹתוֹת שֵׁם גָּדוֹל
"יי" לְמַעְלָן
וְ"קָדוֹשׁ" לְמַטָּן

וְאֵילֵי מָרוֹם 655
מָקוֹם יִתְּנוּ לוֹ
פֶּן יִמָּלְאוּ מִמֶּנּוּ
עֵינַיִם וְיִכְהוּ

וּמִימִינוֹ שַׁדַּי
מִתְהַלֵּךְ חָצִיר   בן אנוש
מִתְיַיחֵד עִם אֵשׁ
וְלֹא נִשְׂרָף

הֱבִיאוּ לוֹ
מִכְנְסֵי בַד קוֹדֶשׁ
כְּמִין פָּמַלְיָא
לְבוּשׁ פָּרָשִׁים

הִדְבִּיקָם לְמָתְנָיו
וְהִסְרִיחָם לִירֵכָיו
בְּלִי יֶעֱרֶה
עַל מְכַסֶּה פְּשָׁעֵינוּ

הִסְתִּיר בֵּית בּוֹשֶׁת
בְּעָמְדוֹ לְבֵית כָּבוֹד
כִּי כִסּוּי בָּשְׁתֵּינוּ
שָׁם יִיקָּרֵיעַ

---

213. Gk. *feminalia*: see Daniel Sperber, "Meḥqarim be-Milim ve-Girsaʾotehen," *Teʿudah* 7 (1991): 149–51.

214. That is, so as not to expose him before God.

665 He put on the Urim
and strapped on the Thummim,
which is consulted and replies—
a sign of testimony.

He mortified his soul
and humbled his spirit,
for contrite hearts
and the downcast shall live.

He would reply
in soft language,
for a soft reply
turns away anger.

He would make
the rough places plain
and return many
from pursuit of **the abyss**.[215]   the mouth of Sheol

He would cast down
the doors of his eyes
lest he look at the Glory
and his pupil dissolve.[216]

675 His throat would
express peace,[217]
for he served
Him who makes peace.

Nor would he plan treachery
in his inmost parts,
for he must open discourse
with Him who searches hearts.

(Though) great in his glory,
he would not be too proud,
for pride and presumption
are loathsome to high God.

---

215. See Isa 5:14. By leveling the ground, God will bring the abyss to the same level as the plains.
216. Heb. *dwqw*. Usually "cataract"; here, most likely, "pupil."

665 הִתְלַבֵּשׁ בְּאוּרִים
וְנִתְאַזֵּר בְּתֻמִּים
וְנִשְׁאָל וּמֵשִׁיב
אוֹת מִתְעוּדָה

דִּכֵּא נַפְשׁוֹ
וְהִשְׁפִּיל רוּחוֹ
כִּי לֵב שְׁפָלִים
וְנִדְכָּאִים תְּחַיֶּה

דְּבַר לָשׁוֹן רַכָּה
הָיָה מֵשִׁיב
כִּי מַעֲנֶה רָךְ
מֵשִׁיב חֵמָה

דֶּרֶךְ מַעֲקַשִּׁים
הָיָה מְי(ַ)שֵּׁר
וּמֵשִׁיב רַבִּים
מֵרֶדֶף **פּוֹעֵידָה** פי שאול

דַּלְתֵי עֵינָיו
יַרְכִּין לְמַטָּן
פֶּן יַבִּיט בַּכָּבוֹד
יִדְלוֹף דּוֹקוֹ

675 גְּרוֹנוֹ הָיָה
מַבִּיעַ שָׁלוֹם
כִּי לְעוֹשֵׂה שָׁלוֹם
הָיָה מְ⟨שָׁרֵת⟩

גַּם בְּקִרְבָּיו
לֹא תֶאֱרוֹב אֵיבָה
כִּי לְחוֹקֵר לֵב
יָפִיק שִׂיחָה

גָּדוֹל בִּכְבוֹדוֹ
לֹא יִתְגָּאֶה
כִּי גֵּאָה וְגָאוֹן
יְגָעַל אֵל רָם

217. That is, give greeting.

No stranger could cross
the border of his place,
for he was exalted
by twenty-four **gifts**.²¹⁸   contributions to the priesthood

Generally and specifically
they were all inscribed
to silence the mouth
of one who would find fault with him.²¹⁹

685   {You made with him}
a covenant of salt,
for You drew him near,
and no one can distance him.

He had no inheritance
in **the favored legacy**,²²⁰   the land of Israel
for his allotted share
and portion²²¹ are in heaven.

He did not expend his energy
on working the soil,
for he feasted on
bread from Your table.

Happy are those who fear You!
What is stored up for them:
Your good actions
in the presence of human beings.²²²

How happy indeed,
were Moses and Aaron,
for the glory they inherited
cannot be conceived.

695   Happy are our fathers—
what their eyes saw!

---

218. See Num 18.
219. According to Sifre Num pisqa 119 (ed. Horovitz, p. 143), the proximity of Num 18 to Num 17 indicates that the priestly gifts were given to Aaron to silence Korah.

גְּבוּל מְקוֹמוֹ
אֵין זָר לְהַשִּׂיג
כִּי בְּעֶ‹שְׂרִים וְאַרְבַּע
מַ‹תָּנ›וֹת מְעוּלָּה

בִּכְלָל וּפְרָט
יַחַד כֻּלָּם חֲקוּקוֹת
לְהַדְמִים פֶּה
‹נ›וֹתֵן בּוֹ דּוֹפִי

בְּרִית מֶלַח 685
‹אִתּוֹ כָרַתָּה›
כִּי אַתָּה קֵירַבְתָּהּ
וְאֵין מִי לְהַרְחִיק

ארץ ישראל

בְּנַחֲלַת צְבִי
יְרוּשָּׁה אֵין ל‹וֹ›
כִּי מְנָת חֶלְקוֹ
וְ‹כוֹסוֹ› בַּשָּׁמַיִם

בַּעֲבוֹדַת אֲדָמָה
כּוֹחוֹ לֹא יְבַלֶּה
כִּי בְלֶחֶם
שׁוּלְחָנְךָ יִסְעָד

אַשְׁרֵי יְרֵאֶיךָ
מַה גִּצְפַּן לָמוֹ
פְּעוּלַּת טוֹבָתְךָ
נֶגֶד בְּנֵי אָדָם

אַשְׁרֵיהֶם מְאֹד
מֹשֶׁה וְאַהֲרֹן
כִּי אֵין לַחְקוֹר
כָּבוֹד נָחָלוּ

אַשְׁרֵי אֲבוֹתֵינוּ 695
מַה חָזוּ עֵינֵיהֶם

---

220. Specifically, the portions accorded to the tribes; see Deut 18:2.
221. Lit., "cup": Ps 16:5.
222. That is, God stores up good deeds for his worshipers to perform in the presence of other people.

Happy are their children
for **whom** they can expect!   the Messiah

As it is written, Happy the people who have it so; happy the people
    whose God is the Lord (Ps 144:16).

[THE AVODAH]

Then, every year[223]
a faithful man
was distinguished
from the seed of Aaron.

700   Chief of his brothers,
valiant in deeds,
a harvest of wisdom,
a treasury of understanding.

In the dwelling of the counselors
he would abide
for seven days
before **the Tenth**.[224]   Yom Kippur

They would select
a select one instead of him
in case he became repugnant by emission
and his service be interrupted.

He would betroth
a second **one who was shaped from a bone**   a wife
lest **his rib be broken**   his present wife die
and (his prayer) "for his household" become invalid.

In a circular court,
like the shores of the sea, they would surround him
lest he become distracted[225]
and he be defective for service.

---

223. The first word in this section is *Az*, which began the entire poem.
224. Yom Kippur occurs on the tenth day of the month.

וְאַשְׁרֵי בְּנֵיהֶם
לְמִי הֵם מְצַפִּים

המשיח

ככ' אשרי העם שככה לו אשרי וג'> (תה' קמד, טו)

[העבודה]

אָז בְּכָל שָׁנָה
הָיָה מוּבְדָּל
אִישׁ אֱמֶת
מִזֶּרַע אַהֲרֹן

אַלּוּף אַחִים 700
אַבִּיר מַעֲשִׂים
אָגוּר חָכְמָה
אָסוּם בִּינָה

בְּדִירַת פַּלְהֶדְרִין
הָיָה מִתְלוֹנֵן
שִׁבְעַת יָמִים
קוֹדֶם לֶעָשׂוֹר

יום הכיפורים

בּוֹרְרִים הָיוּ
בָּרוּר לְעוּמָּתוֹ
שֶׁאִם יוּגְעַל בְּקֶרִי
וְתוּגְרַע עֲבוֹדָה

אישה

גְּלוּפָה מֵעֶצֶם
שְׁנִיָּה יְאָרֵס
פֶּן תִּשָּׁבֵר צַלְעוֹ
"וּבְעַד בֵּיתוֹ" יְעוֹכַב

תמות אשתו

גּוֹרֶן עֲגוּלָה
כִּגְבוּל יָם יְסוֹבְבוּהוּ
פֶּן יֻלְפַּת
וְיִפָּגֵל מִן הָעֲבֹדָה

225. That is, lest he become aroused. Cf. *Sanh.* 19b.

710   He could not stray in his way
from the platform of **the Prominent One**,²²⁶   **God**
offering fatlings continually
and not to his liking as otherwise.

Rich foods
and sweet delicacies
were served at his table
for six and a half days.

They woke up early to hand him over
to the ministers of the priesthood.
Then they warned him not to change (the order)
and turned aside and wept.

They directed his steps
to the eastern gates
to acquaint him with his sacrifices
so that he would be adept.

And in the spice-maker's loft
he would dine in the evening
but would not taste after that,
for food brings sleep.

720   And scholars taught him
from four books;²²⁷
if he was not wise
they would entertain him with tales of kings.

Youthful Levites
would wake him up with the middle finger,
and if sleep was weighing him down,
they would drive it away on the floor.

The time came
to clear the altar;
those hoping for forgiveness
hurried to the court.

---

226. See Song 5:10.

האל

710 דֶּרֶךְ אֵל יָנִיא
מַדְבִּיר **דָּגוּל**
לְהַתְמִיד מֵחִים
וְלֹא כְּאָז חֲפָצוֹ

דִּשְּׁנֵי מַאֲכָל
וּמְתֻקֵּי עִידּוּנִין
שֵׁשֶׁת יָמִים וּמֶחֱצָה
שָׁלְחָנוּ יְעוֹדֵן

הִשְׁכִּימוּ לְמָסְרוֹ
לְשָׂרֵי כְהוּנָּה
וּבִיטוּהוּ לְלֹא יְשַׁנֶּה
וּפָרְשׁוּ וּבָכוּ

הֵם הִצְעִידוּהוּ
לְדַלְתֵי מִזְרָח
לְבַקְּרוֹ בְקָרְבְּנוֹתָיו
לְמַעַן יְהִי בָקִי

וּבַעֲלִיַּית רְקָחִים
כְּעֵת עֶרֶב יִסְעָד
וְעוֹד לֹא יִטְעַם
כִּי אוֹכֵל מַרְדִּים

720 וּבְאַרְבַּעַת סְפָרִים
חוֹקְרִים לִימ[וּ]דוֹ
אִם לֹא יֶחְכַּם
בְּסִיחַ מְלָכִים יְשַׁעֲשְׁעָהוּ

⟨ז⟩כֵּי לִוְיָה
בְּצָרְדָּה יְעוֹרְר[וּ]הוּ
⟨וְאִם⟩ כָּבֵד נוּם
עַל רֹ[ו]צְפָּה יְפִיגוּהוּ

⟨ז⟩מָן הִגִּיעַ
עֵת לִתְרוֹם מִזְבֵּחַ
מְיַחֲלֵי סְלִיחָה
הִרְגִּישׁוּ לָעֲזָרָה

227. See m. Yoma 1:6.

When the cock began to call,
the doorkeepers hastened
to open the gate
before **that which glides** emerged from its canopy.[228]   the sun

They held and sounded
two trumpets
to entreat the **One who gives
songs in the night.**[229]   God

730 Before the sun
stepped out from the east,
he declared, "Determine
if the time for slaughtering has come."

They answered him aloud
and gave him a sign;[230]
then the true emissary
began to serve.

They made a partition
between him and the people;
then he washed and immersed
and went up and dried himself.

He adorned his limbs
in golden clothing;
then again he washed
his hands and his feet.

He began to perform (the sacrifice)
of the lamb for the Tamid,
offering it entirely
over **that which is entirely beautiful.**[231]   Zion

740 As required, he made the incision,
and they finished slaughtering it

---

228. See Eccl 1:5 and Ps 19:6.
229. Job 35:10. Cf. b. Erubin 18b: a house in which words of Torah are spoken in the night will never be destroyed.

חָשׁ גֶּבֶר לִקְרוֹת	
וְחָשׁוּ שׁ[וֹ]עֲרִים	
לִפְתּוֹחַ פֶּתַח	
לִפְנֵי חוּפַת שׁוֹאֵיף	השמש
חֲצוֹצְרוֹת שְׁתַּיִם	
אָחֲזוּ וְתָקְעוּ	
לַחֲלוֹת לְנוֹתֵן	
זְמִירוֹת בַּלַּיְלָה	הָאֵל
730 טֶרֶם יִצְעַד	
חֶרֶס מִמִּזְרָח	
מֵפִיק "בִּינוּ	
אִם בָּאַת עוֹנַת שְׁחִיטָה"	
טַעַם הֱשִׁיבוּהוּ	
וְגַם אוֹת נָתְנוּ לוֹ	
וְאָז הִתְחִיל	
צִיר אֱמֶת לְשָׁרֵת	
יַעֲשׂוּ מְחִיצָה	
בֵּינוֹ לְבֵין עָם	
וְקִדֵּשׁ וְטָבַל	
וְעָלָה וְנִסְתַּפַּג	
יָפָּה פְדָרוֹ	
בִּלְבוּשׁ פָּז	
וְעוֹד קִדֵּשׁ	
יָדָיו וְרַגְלָיו	
כֶּבֶשׂ הַתָּמִיד	
הִתְחִיל לַעֲשׂוֹת	
לְקָרְבוֹ כָּלִיל	
עַל מִכְלַל יֹפִי	צִיּוֹן
740 בְּמִשְׁפָּט קְרָצוֹ	
וְהֵם יַמְרִיקוּהוּ	

---

230. They gave him an answer both verbally and by indicating the light over Hebron (m. Yoma 3:1).
231. According to Ps 50:2. Alternatively, according to a midrash in t. Kippurim 2:14, "that on which (is founded the) entire (world's) beauty."

and collected its blood
in a bowl to be tossed.

He cut it to pieces,
dividing it according to its limbs
to ten (priests),
with the recitation of the Shema.

To the Mountain-of-God[232]
he ascended like a lion
to present the aroma
in the chambers of Lebanon.

They supplied him
with wine[233] for libation,
with the blood of the grape,
and with that which reddens the eyes.

Immediately he bowed
and waved a towel,
and with cymbals of thanksgiving
the singers extolled.

750 He entered and repaired
the lamps in order
and offered the incense
for the morning service.

He quickly came
to the house of Parvah,
and they spread out a curtain,
respecting his privacy.

The pourers would pour
from bowls of gold of Parvaim;
then he washed his hands
and his feet and immersed.

---

232. Heb. *le-Har'el*; cf. Pesiqta de-Rav Kahana pisqa 13 (ed. Mandelbaum, p. 239), which plays on the term *Ariel* for Zion and *arieh*, "lion," as a term for God.

וְקִיבֵּל דָּמוֹ
בְּמִזְרָק לְזָרְקוֹ

לִנְתָחָיו נְתָחוֹ
כְּפִי אֵיבָרָיו בִּיתְּרוּהוּ
עַל יְדֵי עֲשָׂרָה
עִם קְרִיַּת שְׁמַע

לְהַהַרְאֵל
כְּאַרְיֵה עָלָה
לִיתֵּן רֵיחַ
בְּחַדְרֵי לְבָנוֹן

מַמְצִיאִים לוֹ
עָסִיס לְנַסֵּךְ
מִדַּם עֵינָב
וְחַכְלִילִי עֵינָיִם

מִיָּד שָׁחָה
וְהֵנִיף בַּסּוּדָרִים
וּבְנִבְלֵי תוֹדוֹת
מְשׁוֹרְרִים רוֹמֵמוּ

נִכְנַס וְהֵיטִיב   750
נֵירוֹת כְּעָרְכָּם
וְהִקְטִיר קְטֹרֶת
עֲבוֹדַת שַׁחֲרִית

נִמְהַר לָבוֹא
לְבֵית הַפַּרְוָוה
וּפָרְשׂוּ מָסָךְ
לְיַחֲדוֹ בְּכָבוֹד

סָף זָהָב פַּרְוָויִים
פּוֹשְׁטִים יָרִיקוּ
וְקִדֵּשׁ יָדָיו
וְרַגְלָיו וְטָבַל

---

233. Heb. *asis*, possibly referring to must.

He dried himself and was adorned
in white garments;
then again he washed
his hands and his feet.

His bull was placed
between the portico and the altar—
the place where they say,
"Spare Your people, O Lord."[234]

760 His eyes[235] faced the west,
and his head faced the south,
before **the One who comes from Teman**—[236]   God
and he is a servant to Him.

He opened the Gate
of Justice for himself,
for an offender cannot
make atonement for (others') offenses.

"Forgive my offenses—
I am a messenger of Your redeemed;
pull me out of the pit
lest those who wait for You be accused!

"I am an emissary of the faithful
(sent) to implore my God:
Save, I pray, Your servant;
restore my soul, as You have promised."

Excitedly, he placed
his hands on his ox
and asked balm for his wound,
and well-being for his mate.[237]

770 Thus he would say: ["O Lord, I have sinned, I have done wrong, I have transgressed before You, I and my household. O Lord, forgive the sins and iniquities and transgressions that I have committed against you, I and my household, as it is written in the Torah of

---

234. Joel 2:17.
235. Lit., "eyelids."

סִיֵּג וְהוֹהַדָּר
בְּבִגְדֵי לָבָן
וְעוֹד קִידַּשׁ
יָדָיו וְרַגְלָיו

עֲמִידַת פָּרוֹ
בֵּין אוּלָם לַמִּזְבֵּחַ
מָקוֹם אוֹמְרִים
"חוּסָה יְיָ עַל עַמְּךָ"

עַפְעַפָּיו לַמַּעֲרָב   760
וְרֹאשׁוֹ לַדָּרוֹם
לִפְנֵי **בָּא מִתֵּימָן**
וְלֹא מְשַׁמֵּשׁ

אלוהים

פָּתַח צְדָקָה
לְעַצְמוֹ יִפְתַּח
שֶׁאֵין פּוֹשֵׁעַ
מְכַפֵּר עַל פּוֹשְׁעִים

"פְּשָׁעַתִי סְלַח
שָׁלוֹחַ פְּדוּיֶיךָ אָנִי
פְּצֵה נַפְשִׁי מִשַּׁחַת
פֶּן יֶאְשְׁמוּ מְצַפֶּיךָ"

"צִיר אֱמוּנִים אָנִי
לְחַלּוֹתְךָ אֵלִי
הַצְלִיחָה נָא לְעַבְדֶּךָ
וְהָשִׁיבָה נַפְשִׁי בְנוֹאֲמֶךָ"

צָהַל לָתֵת
יָדָיו עַל שׁוֹרוֹ
וּבִיקֵּשׁ צֳרִי לְמַחֲצוֹ
וְרִפְאוּת לְצַלְעוֹ

וְכָךְ הָיָה אוֹמֵ' ‹אָנָּא הַשֵּׁם›. חָטָאתִי, עָוִיתִי, פָּשַׁעְתִּי לְפָנֶיךָ אֲנִי וּבֵיתִי: אָנָּא בַשֵּׁם,   770
כַּפֶּר נָא לַחֲטָאִים וְלַעֲוֹנוֹת וְלַפְּשָׁעִים. שֶׁחָטָאתִי וְשֶׁעָוִיתִי וְשֶׁפָּשַׁעְתִּי לְפָנֶיךָ אֲנִי
וּבֵיתִי. כַּכָּתוּב בְּתוֹרַת מֹשֶׁה עַבְדֶּךָ מִפִּי כְבוֹדֶךָ. כִּי בַיּוֹם הַזֶּה יְכַפֵּר עֲלֵיכֶם לְטַהֵר
אֶתְכֶם מִכֹּל חַטֹּאתֵיכֶם לִפְנֵי יְהֹוָה: וְהַכֹּהֲנִים וְהָעָם הָעוֹמְדִים בָּעֲזָרָה כְּשֶׁהָיוּ

---

236. According to Hab 3:3.
237. Lit., "rib."

Moses, Your servant: 'For on this day atonement shall be made for you to cleanse you of all your sins; before the Lord—' " (Lev. 16:30). And when the priests and the people standing in the court and serving in the Sanctuary heard the glorious explicit name coming forth from the mouth of the high priest in holiness and purity, they would kneel, prostrate themselves, and fall to their faces and say: "Blessed is the name of His Majesty's glory for ever and ever." He would also intend to finish the name while facing those saying the blessing and say to them, "You shall be pure."]

His feet hastened[238]
to the two goats
standing like a palm frond[239]
between the myrtle and the willow.

The officer of the priest's division on the left
and the prefect on the right
planted in Your abode
to flourish in Your courts.

775 He cast the lot
and shook the urn,
and the first came up for the Lord,
and the second for Azazel.

He drew near to (the goat)
that bore a crimson strand
to give a sign
that our scarlet has been turned to white.[240]

He turned (the goat)
to face the precipice;
he handed it over to the designated man
until the time that it was to be sent.

His steps were aligned   the feet of the goat
with the slaughtering place,

---

238. Lit., "his ankles came early."
239. In the lulav, used in the holiday of Sukkot.

שׁוֹמְעִים אֶת הַשֵּׁם הַנִּכְבָּד וְהַנּוֹרָא מְפֹרָשׁ יוֹצֵא מִפִּי כֹהֵן גָּדוֹל בִּקְדֻשָּׁה וּבְטָהֳרָה הָיוּ
כּוֹרְעִים וּמִשְׁתַּחֲוִים וְנוֹפְלִים עַל פְּנֵיהֶם וְאוֹמְרִים: בָּרוּךְ שֵׁם כְּבוֹד מַלְכוּתוֹ לְעוֹלָם
וָעֶד: וְאַף הוּא הָיָה מִתְכַּוֵּן כְּנֶגֶד הַמְבָרְכִים לִגְמֹר אֶת הַשֵּׁם, וְאוֹמֵר לָהֶם תִּטְהָרוּ〉

קִדְּמוּ קַרְסֻלָּיו
אֵצֶל שְׁנֵי [הַ]שְּׂעִירִים
מֵי⟨תָ⟩יו כְּלוּלָב
בַּהֲדַס בַּעֲרָבָה

קְצִין בֵּית אָב מִשְׂמֹאל
וּסְגָן מִיָּמִין
שְׁתוּלִים בְּנָוֶיךָ
לְהַפְרִיחַ בְּחַצְרוֹתֶיךָ

רָמָה חֲבָלִים 775
וְטָרַף בַּקַּלְפֵּי
וְעָלָה הָרֹאשׁ לַשֵּׁם
וְהַשֵּׁנִי לַעֲזָאזֵל

רִיתֵּק בְּנוֹשֵׂא
דַּלַּת שָׁנִי
לָתֵת אוֹת
לְלַבֵּן אֲדַמְנוּ

שָׂם פָּנָיו
כְּנֶגֶד גְּזֵירָה
מְסָרוֹ לְעִתִּי
עַד עֵת יְשַׁלְּחֶנּוּ

רַגְלֵי שָׂעִיר הַחַטָּאת   **שָׁלְחָיו יַיְשֵׁר**
לְבֵית הַשְּׁחִיטָה

240. Isa 1:18.

for they were fated as fragrant (offering)
for **Him who does not eat or drink.** God

He proceeded, returning
to the second bull,
and lay his dear hands[241]
to rest between its horns.

785 Errors and unperceived guilt,[242]
and flaws in guilt offerings—
his own and his clan's—
over these he confessed.

And thus he would say: [O Lord, I have sinned, I have done wrong, I have transgressed before You, I and my household and the children of Aaron, Your holy people. O Lord, forgive the sins and iniquities and transgressions that I have committed against you, I and my household and the children of Aaron, Your holy people, as it is written in the Torah of Moses, Your servant: 'For on this day atonement shall be made for you to cleanse you of all your sins; before the Lord—'" (Lev. 16:30). And when the priests and the people standing in the court and serving in the Sanctuary heard the explicit name coming forth from the mouth of the high priest in holiness and purity, they would kneel, prostrate themselves, and fall to their faces and say: "Blessed is the name of His Majesty's glory for ever and ever." He would also intend to finish the name while facing those saying the blessing and say to them, "You shall be pure."]

He held up the knife
and passed it through its neck
and collected in a basin
the outpouring of his slaughtering.

790 He gave it to another
to stir while it was bubbling
so that it would not coagulate,
as it was needed for the Ḥaṭṭa't.

---

241. Cf. Jer 12:7.

הָאֵל	כִּי לְלֹא אוֹכַל
	הוּגְרַל לְנִיחוֹחַ
	תָּר לָשׁוּב
	אֵצֶל פָּרוֹ שְׁנִיָּיה
	וְהִשְׁכִּין בֵּין קַרְנָיו
	יְדִידוּת כַּפָּיו
	תָּעוֹת וְנִסְתָּרוֹת 785
	וּמַחֲצֵי אֲשָׁמוֹת
	שָׁלוֹ וְשֶׁלְשִׁבְטוֹ
	עָלָיו הִתְוַדָּה

וְכָךְ הָיָה אוֹמֵ' ‹אָנָּא הַשֵּׁם. חָטָאתִי, עָוִיתִי, פָּשַׁעְתִּי לְפָנֶיךָ אֲנִי וּבֵיתִי: אָנָּא בַשֵּׁם, כַּפֶּר נָא לַחֲטָאִים וְלַעֲוֹנוֹת וְלַפְּשָׁעִים. שֶׁחָטָאתִי וְשֶׁעָוִיתִי וְשֶׁפָּשַׁעְתִּי לְפָנֶיךָ אֲנִי וּבֵיתִי. כַּכָּתוּב בְּתוֹרַת מֹשֶׁה עַבְדֶּךָ מִפִּי כְבוֹדֶךָ. כִּי בַיּוֹם הַזֶּה יְכַפֵּר עֲלֵיכֶם לְטַהֵר אֶתְכֶם מִכֹּל חַטֹּאתֵיכֶם לִפְנֵי יְהֹוָה: וְהַכֹּהֲנִים וְהָעָם הָעוֹמְדִים בָּעֲזָרָה כְּשֶׁהָיוּ שׁוֹמְעִים אֶת הַשֵּׁם הַנִּכְבָּד וְהַנּוֹרָא מְפֹרָשׁ יוֹצֵא מִפִּי כֹהֵן גָּדוֹל בִּקְדֻשָּׁה וּבְטָהֳרָה הָיוּ כּוֹרְעִים וּמִשְׁתַּחֲוִים וְנוֹפְלִים עַל פְּנֵיהֶם וְאוֹמְרִים: בָּרוּךְ שֵׁם כְּבוֹד מַלְכוּתוֹ לְעוֹלָם וָעֶד: וְאַף הוּא הָיָה מִתְכַּוֵּן כְּנֶגֶד הַמְבָרְכִים לִגְמֹר אֶת הַשֵּׁם, וְאוֹמֵר לָהֶם תִּטְהָרוּ›

	תָּמַךְ מַאֲכֶלֶת
	וְהִילְּכָהּ בְּצַוָּארוֹ
	וְקִיבֵּל בְּמִזְרָק
	שְׁפִיכַת שָׁחֲטוֹ
	תְּנָהוּ לְאַחֵר 790
	לְמָרְסוֹ רוֹתֵחַ
	שֶׁלֹּא יִקְרֹשׁ
	וְצֹרֶךְ בּוֹ לַחַטָּא

---

242. Heb. *nistarot*, "hidden things"; following the NJV translation of Ps 19:13.

[Note: This is where the extant fragments end. The acrostic of this section has reached the letter *shin*.]

[AROMEM LA-ʾEL]

[   ]
[   ]
to go quickly
up to the altar.

He extended his hand
and took the fire-pan
and took a handful of the **burning**   incense
according to his strength;

he returned, and they gave him
the fire-pan with a shovel.
Then he poured into the pans
fire from the censer.

When he carried them both,
his appearance glowed.
The fire-pan in his right hand
and the shovel in his left,

he approached diligently
between the curtains.
Displaying his great strength,
he passed, pushing them aside

that one does not dominate
the image [   ]
while he importuned
(with) a brief prayer.

He put the fire-pan
between the poles
and prepared below
for the image of His presence.[243]

---

243. These lines are obscure.

[ארומם לאל]

⟨ש.. ...⟩
⟨... ...⟩
לַעֲלוֹת מְהֵרָה
אֵ⟨צֶ⟩ל הַמִּזְבֵּחַ

שָׁלַח יָדָיו
וְלָקַח מַחְתָּה
וְחָפַן **בּוֹעֶרֶת**
לְפִי גְּבוּרָתוֹ

קטורת

שָׁב וְנָתְנוּ לוֹ
מַחְתָּה עִם כַּף
וְעֵרָה בְּמַחְתּוֹת
אֵשׁ מִן הַבַּזָּךְ

שְׁתֵּיהֶם בְּנָשְׂאוֹ
יַבְהִיק מַרְאֵהוּ
מַחְתָּה בְיָמִין
וְהַכַּף בִּשְׂמֹאל

שָׁקַד לָבוֹא
בֵּין הַפָּרוֹכ⟨וֹת⟩
לְהוֹדִיעַ רוֹב כֹּחַ
יַעֲבוֹר לְדָחֳתָם שָׁם

שֶׁלֹּא יָשׁוּר
דְּמוּת ⟨ה..⟩
בְּהַפְגִּיעוֹ
תְּפִילָּה קְצָרָה

שָׁם מַחְתָּה
בֵּין הַבַּ⟨דִּ⟩ים
וְהֵכִין לְמַטָּה
דְּמוּת צוּרַת פָּנָיו

The Shekhinah could be seen
[over the smoke of][244] the incense;
then he turned to depart
the way he entered.

He hurried to [   ].
[   ]
blood in the bowl
and entered inside

[   ]
He sprinkled once upward
[   ]
and seven times downward.

He set his steps
to go out [   ]
to slaughter the goat of the people
and to collect its blood.

He directed (his steps) a second time,
entering, [   ]
to do with (the goat's) blood
as he did with the bull's blood.

He made a mixture
a second time;
with it he would purge
the inner altar.

He set forth and sprinkled
on the curtain,
facing the ark
for the times[245] he sprinkled.

He raised his hands
and sprinkled the altar,
four around
and seven [on the top.]

---

244. Conjectural restoration.

שְׁכִינָה נִרְאֵית
עַ‹..›הַקְּטֹרֶת
וְאָז יִיפֶן וְיֵצֵא
דֶּרֶךְ כְּנִיסָתוֹ

תָּקַף לִ‹..›
‹... ...›
דָּם בַּמִּזְרָק
וְנִכְנַס לִפְנִים

‹ת.. ...›
אַחַת לְמַ‹עְלָ‹ה יַזֶּה
א‹.. ..›ךְ
שֶׁבַע לְמַטָּה בְּמִסְפָּר

תִּכֵּן פְּעָמָיו
צֵאת א‹..›
לִשְׁ‹חוֹ›ט שְׂעִיר עַם
דָּמוֹ לְקַבֵּל

תִּרְגֵּל שְׁנִיָּה
לְהִיכָּנֵס ‹נ..›
לַעֲשׂוֹת דָּמוֹ
כְּעָשָׂה לְדַם הַפָּר

תַּעֲרוֹבוֹת עָשׂ
שֵׁנִי‹ת ...›
יְחַטֵּא מִמֶּנּוּ
מִזְבֵּחַ הַפְּנִימִי

תִּיכֵּן וְהִזָּה
עַל הַפָּרוֹכֶת
‹נ›וֹכַח הָאָרוֹן
כְּתוֹכֶן הַזָּיוֹת

תָּלָה יָדָיו
וְהִזָּה מִזְבֵּחַ
אַרְבַּע סָבִיב
וְשֶׁ‹בַ›ע עַ‹ל טָהֳרוֹ›

---

245. That is, corresponding to the number of times he sprinkles the blood.

When the sprinkling was completed,
he went out and poured
the rest of the blood
on the foundation of the altar.

The service of the Day
of Atonement was completed
according to its order and custom,
every year.

He turned and came close[246]
to the scapegoat,
then laid his hands on it
firmly and confessed.

Thus he would say: "O Lord, they have sinned, they have done wrong, they have transgressed before You, Your people, the house of Israel. O Lord, forgive and pardon the sins and iniquities and transgressions that they have committed against You, Your people, the house of Israel, as it is written in the Torah of Moses, Your servant: 'For on this day atonement shall be made for you to cleanse you of all your sins; before the Lord—'" (Lev. 16:30). And when the priests and the people standing in the court and serving in the Sanctuary heard the explicit name coming forth from the mouth of the high priest in holiness and purity, they would kneel, prostrate themselves, and fall to their faces and say: "Blessed is the name of His Majesty's glory for ever and ever." He would also intend to finish the name while facing those saying the blessing and say to them, "You shall be pure." And You, in Your great beneficence, aroused Your mercy and [pardoned the community of Jeshurun] for the sake of Your holy name.

The assistants of the priesthood
would always do it this way:
leading the goat
in the hands of a designated man.

---

246. From here to the end the text is from Yahalom's edition in *Az be-'En Kol*, 186–88, lines 439–60.

תַּמּוּ הַזִּיּוֹת
וְיָצָא וְשָׁפַךְ
שִׁיּוּר דָּמִים
יְסוֹד ⟨הַמִּזְבֵּחַ⟩

תַּמָּה עֲבוֹדַת
יוֹם כַּפָּרָה
תְּכוּנָה כְּדִבְרָהּ
בְּכָל שָׁ⟨נָה וְשָׁנָה⟩

תָּבַע וְנִצְמַד
שָׂעִיר הַמִּשְׁתַּלֵּחַ
סָמַךְ יָדָיו עָלָיו
בְּכוֹבֶד וְהִתְוַדָּה

תָּבַע וְנִצְמַד
שָׂעִיר הַמִּשְׁתַּלֵּחַ
סָמַךְ יָדָיו
בְּכוֹבֶד עָלָיו וְנִתְוַ⟨דָּה⟩

וְכָךְ הָיָה אוֹמֵר. אָנָּא הַשֵּׁם חָטְאוּ ⟨עָוּ⟩ ⟨פָּ⟩שְׁעוּ לְפָנֶיךָ עַמְּךָ בֵּית יִשְׂרָאֵל: אָנָּא בַשֵּׁם. כַּפֶּר נָא עַל הַחֲטָאִים עַל הָעֲוֹ' עַל הַפְּשָׁעִים. שֶׁחָטְאוּ שֶׁעָווּ ⟨וְשֶׁפָּשְׁעוּ לְפָנֶיךָ עַמְּךָ בֵּית יִשְׂרָאֵל. כַּכָּתוּב בְּתוֹרַת מֹשֶׁה עַבְדֶּךָ מִפִּי כְבוֹדֶךָ. כִּי בַיּוֹם הַזֶּה יְכַפֵּר עֲלֵיכֶם לְטַהֵר אֶתְכֶם מִכֹּל חַטֹּאתֵיכֶם לִפְנֵי יְהֹוָה: וְהַכֹּהֲנִים וְהָעָם הָעוֹמְדִים בָּעֲזָרָה כְּשֶׁהָיוּ שׁוֹמְעִים אֶת הַשֵּׁם הַנִּכְבָּד וְהַנּוֹרָא מְפֹרָשׁ יוֹצֵא מִפִּי כֹהֵן גָּדוֹל בִּקְדֻשָּׁה וּבְטָהֳרָה הָיוּ כּוֹרְעִים וּמִשְׁתַּחֲוִים וְנוֹפְלִים עַל פְּנֵיהֶם וְאוֹמְרִים: בָּרוּךְ שֵׁם כְּבוֹד מַלְכוּתוֹ לְעוֹלָם וָעֶד: וְאַף הוּא הָיָה מִתְכַּוֵּן כְּנֶגֶד הַמְבָרְכִים לִגְמֹר אֶת הַשֵּׁם וְאוֹמֵר לָהֶם תִּטְהָרוּ. וְאַתָּה בְּטוּבְךָ מְעוֹרֵר רַחֲמֶיךָ וְסוֹלֵחַ לַעֲדַת יְשֻׁרוּן⟩

תְּמוּכֵי כְהֻנָּה
בְּכֵן יָעֲשׂוּ קֶבַע
לְהוֹלִיךְ שָׂעִיר
בְּיַד אִישׁ עִתִּי

A company of elders
would accompany it,
for there were ten tents
between Jerusalem and Ṣoq.

445 They set forth to **the emissary**,   high priest
and he divided the scarlet thread;
half of it he tied to its horns,
and half to the rock.

Those who insisted on being observers[247]
while he was reciting eight blessings
were not allowed to see
the burning of the bulls.

He took off his garment
of linen when he was finished;
five immersions
and ten washings.

As is customary, he performed
the evening Tamids.
He returned the incense utensil
and maintained the lamps.

A quick immersion,
then he washed and undressed,
and he wrapped himself in his own covering[248]
and went out backward.

455 **His perfect one**[249] would rejoice   the priest's people
when they saw the silken thread,
which had turned as white
as lye and snow.

He stepped like a deer,
going out of the sanctuary,
and the nobles of the people
accompanied him to his home.

---

247. See m. Yoma 7:1.
248. A garment that belonged to him; see m. Yoma 7:4.

תַּחְבּוּרַת יְשִׁישַׁת
עִמּוֹ יְשׁוּלָחוּ
כִּי עֶשֶׂר סֻכּוֹת
מֵעִיר וְעַד צוּק

445 תְּרַגְּלוּ לַצִּיר
וְחָלָק לָשׁוֹן שֶׁלְּזְהוֹרִית
בְּקַרְנָיו קָשַׁר חֶצְיוֹ
וְחֶצְיוֹ בַּסֶּלַע

תּוֹקְפֵי לַחֲזוֹת
מְבָרֵךְ שְׁמוֹנֶה
יוּבְטְלוּ מֶרְ⟨אוֹ⟩ת
שְׂרֵיפַת פָּרִים

תִּלְבּוֹשֶׁת בּוּץ
יִפְשׁוֹט בְּגָמְרוֹ
חָמֵשׁ טְבִילוֹת
וְעֶשֶׂר קְדוּשׁוֹת

תְּמִידֵי עַרְבַּיִם
יַעֲשֶׂה כִּדְבָרוֹ
יָשׁוּבֵב כְּלֵי קְטֹרֶת
וְיֵיטִיב נֵירוֹת

תָּכַף טְבִילָה
קִדֵּשׁ וּפָשַׁט
וְעָט כְּסוּת הוֹנוֹ
וְיוֹצֵא לַאֲחוֹרָיו

455 תַּמָּתוֹ תָרֹן
בְּשׁוּר חוּט ⟨שָׁנִי⟩
אֲשֶׁר הוֹלְבַּן
כִּבְוֹרִית וָשָׁלֶג

תָּר כָּאַיָּל
צֵאת מִן הַקֹּדֶשׁ
וְכַבִּירֵי עָם
יְלַוּוּהוּ לְנָוֵיהוּ

249. Song 6:9.

He made a feast
for his admirers and family.
Everyone rejoiced,
for he had come out safely.

תִּסְעוֹדָת יַעֲשֶׂה
לְאוֹהֲבָיו וּקְרוֹבָיו
וְהַכֹּל יָגִ‹ילוּ›
‹כִּי יָ›צָא בְשָׁלוֹם

5. Azkir Gevurot Elohah
"Let Me Recount the Wonders of God"

YOSE BEN YOSE

Yose ben Yose, who most likely lived in the fourth or fifth century C.E., is the first payetan known to us by name. However, nothing else is known about him except that he composed several important early piyyutim, including at least four Avodot. This composition, Yose ben Yose's masterpiece, is perhaps the most influential Avodah piyyut and was probably the best known of the ancient Avodah piyyutim. Although it may have been influenced by *Az be-ʾEn Kol*, it seems to have set the pattern for subsequent Avodah compositions.

Azkir Gevurot is distinguished by an elegant style, which describes its subjects with poetic precision, although without giving up the basic predisposition of piyyut toward elaboration. It also uses biblical history more selectively than *Az be-ʾEn Kol*, emphasizing cultic and priestly dimensions of Israel's past.

Ismar Elbogen discussed *Azkir Gevurot* in his pioneering studies of the Avodah.[1] Zvi Malachi included an edition of *Azkir Gevurot* in his 1974 dissertation; soon afterward Aaron Mirsky edited it in his collection of the piyyutim of Yose ben Yose.[2] T. Carmi included a partial prose translation in *The Penguin Book of Hebrew Verse*.[3] This translation is based on an improved version of Mirsky's edition based on Genizah manuscripts

---

1. Elbogen, *Studien*. Editions also appear in Davidson, Asaf, and Joel, eds., *Siddur Rav Saʿadiah Gaon*, 264–65; *Qoveṣ Maʿase Yede Geʾonim Qadmonim* (Berlin, 1856), 1–9; and *Anthologia Hebraica*, ed. H. Brody and M. Wiener (Leipzig 1922), 26–36.

2. Mirsky, *Yose ben Yose*, 122–72.

3. T. Carmi, ed., *The Penguin Book of Hebrew Verse* (New York: Penguin, 1981), 209–14.

[INTRODUCTORY PRAISE]

Let me recount the wonders
of the magnificent God,
Who is unique; there is no other,
self-sufficient and none second to Him.

There is none beyond Him in the universe,
none prior to Him in heaven;
none preceded Him,
and none can supplant Him.

When the Lord conceived,
when God invented,
He consulted but none could prevent Him,
He spoke and none constrained Him.

He speaks and fulfills,
decrees and enacts,
He is strong enough to support it,   **the world**
heroic enough to bear it.

5   He who is lauded
by the lips of his creatures,
from above and below,
let Him receive praise.

One God, unique on earth,
and holy in heaven,
among the great waters,
magnificent on high.

Exaltation from the depths,
praise from the lights,
speech[4] during the days,
melody during the nights.

Let fire announce His name;
let the trees of the forest sing for joy;

---

4. Heb. ʿomer (n.). According to Mirsky, the term here has connotations of song.

[השמים מספרים כבוד אל]

אַזְכִּיר גְּבוּרוֹת
אֱלוֹהַּ נֶאְדָּרִי
יָחִיד וְאֵין עוֹד
אֶפֶס וְאֵין שֵׁנִי

אַחֲרָיו אֵין בַּחֶלֶד
לְפָנָיו אֵין בַּשַּׁחַק
אֵין בִּלְתּוֹ קֶדֶם
זוּלָתוֹ בְּעָקֵב

אָדוֹן לַחֲשׁוֹב
אֱלֹהִים לַעֲשׂוֹת
נִמְלָךְ וְאֵין נֶעְדָּר
שָׂח וְאֵין מְאַחֵר

אוֹמֵר וְעוֹשֶׂה
יוֹעֵץ וּמֵקִים
אַמִּיץ לָשֵׂאת
וְגִבּוֹר לִסְבּוֹל

אֲשֶׁר לוֹ רְנָנוֹת
מִפִּי יְצוּרָיו
מִמַּעְלָה וּמִמַּטָּה
יִשָּׂא תְהִלָּה

אֵל אֶחָד בָּאָרֶץ
קָדוֹשׁ בַּשָּׁמַיִם
מִמַּיִם רַבִּים
אַדִּיר בַּמָּרוֹם

אֶדֶר מִתְּהוֹמוֹת
שֶׁבַח מִמְּאוֹרוֹת
אוֹמֶר מִיָּמִים
לֶמֶד מְלֵילוֹת

אֵשׁ תּוֹדִיעַ שְׁמוֹ
עֲצֵי יַעַר יְרַנְּנוּ

let each beast rehearse
the might of His awesome deeds.

[THE CREATION]

The Workman[5] was his amusement,	the Torah
the Law, his plaything;	
it was His occupation	
until **His treasure** arose.	Israel

At first, before a thousand generations,
it arose in his intention,
and from it came the plan
for all the works of the construction.[6]

On high He established	
the throne of His majesty;	
he spread His cloud,[7]	
and stretched out **the gauze** as a tent,	**heaven**

so that it shall not move,
nor will its pegs wander
until its end comes
and it is renewed with His word.

He strengthened, over the waters,
the pillars of the earth,
and he girded his loins
with chaos and storm.

They will not move,
nor will they slip
until the world wears out like a garment
and is exchanged as of old.[8]

15   Disorder and darkness
covered the face of the earth;

---

5. Heb. ʿoman, from Prov 8:30. See Gen Rabbah 1:1.
6. Heb. *tavnit*. There may be connotations of the building of the Temple.
7. Job 26:9.

בְּהֵמָה תְּלַמֵּד
עֱזוּז נוֹרְאוֹתָיו

[הבריאה]

התורה

אָמוֹן שַׁחֲקוֹ
דָּת שַׁעֲשׁוּעָיו
הִיא הֶגְיוֹנוֹ

ישראל

עַד עֲמוֹד **סְגֻלָּה**

אָז קֶדֶם לְאֶלֶף דּוֹר
עָלְתָה בְּמַחֲשֶׁבֶת
מִמֶּנָּה תְּכוּנַת
מַלְאֲכוֹת תַּבְנִית

בַּמָּרוֹם הֵכִין
כִּסֵּא הֲדָרוֹ
פִּרְשֵׂז עֲנָנוֹ

השמים

וְדוֹק נָטָה לְאֹהֶל

בַּל יִצְעָן
וּבַל יַסַּע יְתֵדוֹתָיו
עַד בּוֹא קִצּוֹ
וְיִתְחַדֵּשׁ בְּאוֹמֶר

בֵּרֵר עַל מַיִם
עַמּוּדֵי חָלֶד
שִׁיֵּס מָתְנֶיהָ
בְּתוֹהוּ וּבִסְעָרָה

בַּל תִּמּוֹט
וּבַל יָמָעֲדוּ מְכוֹנֶיהָ
עַד תִּבְלֶה כַבֶּגֶד
וְתוּמַר כְּמֵאָז

בֹּהוּ וַאֲפֵלָה   15
כִּסּוּ פְנֵי אֶרֶץ

---

8. Cf. the idea found in Gen Rabbah 3:7 and 9:2 that God created many worlds and destroyed them before creating this one.

then it shone with light
from the face of the King.

He cloaked the world with radiance for the day,
for humankind to go out to work,
and made darkness for **shadow**,   night
for animals to crawl out to the forest.

When the spirit hovered
between the heaven and the waters,
He placed a ceiling within
to bear half of **that which is measured**,   water

By them his marvel
in his handiwork can be known:
in the goodness of the fruit of rain,
the channel of all the waters.[9]

When he divided
between waters and waters,
He ignited **the Inferno**,[10]   Gehenna
the immeasurable Topheth,

with an unfanned fire,[11]
which can never be extinguished,
nor can a flood of many waters
affect it.

He banished to a pool
the mighty water,
and placed sand there
as a gate and bar.[12]

He made a fence for it
so that it would not cover the earth
until **the Faithful of his house**   Moses
cut it in half.

---

9. The idea here is that the rain is the conduit through which the upper waters reach the earth.
10. Heb. *ʿAluqah*, from Job 20:26. See the references in Mirsky, *Yose ben Yose*.

AZKIR GEVUROT ELOHAH 227

וַתָּבְהַק מָאוֹר
פְּנֵי מֶלֶךְ

בִּיהֵק נוֹגַהּ לַיּוֹם
לָצֵאת אָדָם לְפוֹעַל
וַיָּשֶׁת חֹשֶׁךְ **לָאִישׁוֹן**   לילה
לִרְמֹס חַיְתוֹ יַעַר

בְּרַחַף רוּחַ
בֵּין שְׁחָקִים לְמַיִם
שָׁת תִּקְרָה בַּתָּוֶךְ
שְׂאֵת חֲצִי **מְדוּדִים**   מים

בָּם יוֹדִיעַ
פִּלְאוֹ לְפָעֳלוֹ
בְּטוּב חֲשָׂרַת פְּרִי
פֶּלֶג מָלֵא מַיִם

בְּהַבְדִּילוֹ
בֵּין מַיִם לָמַיִם
הִסִּיק **עֲלוּקָה**   גיהנום
תּוֹפֶת לִבְלִי חֹק

בָּאֵשׁ לֹא נֻפַּח
לֹא נִכְבָּה נֶצַח
וְשֶׁטֶף מַיִם רַבִּים
לֹא יַגִּיעוּהוּ

גֵּרַשׁ לְמִקְוֶה
מַיִם אַדִּירִים
וְשָׂם לָהֶם חוֹל
בְּרִיחַ וּדְלָתַיִם

גָּדַר בַּעֲדָם
בְּלִי יְכַסּוּ אֶרֶץ
עַד נֶאֱמַן **בַּיִת**   משה
יַעֲשֶׂם גְּזָרִים

11. See Job 20:26.
12. See Deut 3:5.

He revealed the face of the earth
for humankind to work
and planted shrubs
and seed-producing grass.

He also planted in Eden
a luxuriant garden
as a canopy for the Glory
for **the foremost of all creatures.**[13]   the righteous

25   He finished obscuring
light sevenfold,
and arranged lamps
to rule the day and the night.

They did not transgress boundaries,   day and night
and they did not delay in their movement
until **the attendant in the tent**   Joshua
made them stand still in the valley.[14]

There arose from the water
the fugitives of the deep,[15]   the Leviathan
        and the sea serpent

protected by scales
and **sharp arrows.**   fins

He set some of them aside
for an eternal feast,
and prepared a prison in them
for **the deserting messenger.**   Jonah

The birds that fly upward
sprang from alluvial mud[16]
for those who will eat at the King's table
and the army of His hosts.

He proscribed as an abomination
impure fowl

---

13. The righteous will be enveloped by God's glory in Eden in the world to come. See Mirsky, *Yose ben Yose.* Here, as in several places in this section, the poet prefigures human history and eschatology in his account of creation.

	גִּילָה אֲדָמָה
	לַעֲבוֹדַת אֱנוֹשׁ
	וְהִדְשִׁיאָה שִׂיחַ
	וְעֵשֶׂב מַזְרִיעַ זָרַע
	גַּם נָטַע בְּעֵדֶן
	גַּן רַעֲנָנָה
	לַחֲפוֹת כְּבֻדּוֹת
הצדיקים	**אַדִּירֵי חֵפֶץ**
	גָּמַר לְהַעֲלִים 25
	אוֹר שִׁבְעָתַיִם
	וְעָרַךְ נֵרוֹת
	לִמְשׁוֹל בַּיּוֹם וּבַלַּיְלָה
	גְּבוּל לֹא יַשִּׂיגוּ
	וְלֶכֶת לֹא יְאַחֲרוּ
יהושע	עַד **מְשָׁרֵת אֹהֶל**
	יַדְמִימֵם בָּעֵמֶק
	גָּאוּ מִמַּיִם
הלויתן והתנינים	**בְּרִיחֵי תְהוֹמוֹת**
	אֲפִיקֵי מָגֵן
סנפירים	**שִׁנּוּנֵי חִצִּים**
	גָּנַז מֵהֶם
	לְמִשְׁתֶּה נְצָחִים
	וְהֵכִין בָּם כֶּלֶא
יונה	**לְצִיר הַבּוֹרֵחַ**
	גְּבִיהֵי עוֹף
	צָצוּ מֵרְקַק מַיִם
	לֶאֱכֹל שֻׁלְחַן מֶלֶךְ
	וְחֵיל צְבָאוֹתָיו
	גָּזַר לְתוֹעֵבָת
	עוֹף לֹא טָהוֹר

14. See Josh 10:12.

15. See Isa 27:1. Note that here a form of spontaneous generation is assumed, by which creatures spring forth from some substance, such as water or mud.

16. See Jastrow, *Dictionary*, s.v. *rqq*.

until **the Tishebite** came   Elijah the prophet
and the ravens fed him.[17]

There grew out of the earth
horned animals for slaughter,
edible beasts,
both cattle and those that crawl.

He pastured the Behemoth
with the produce of a thousand mountains,
for on the day when it is slaughtered,
He[18] will put His sword to it.

The Creator exulted
and rejoiced in His deeds
when He saw
that his work was good:

grasses for rest,
and food of choice;
the table was set,
but there was no one to relish it.

35   He said to Himself,
"Who will approach
for the butchered animals
and blended wine?

If he abides by My word,
he will be like God;[19]
if he defies My word,
I will send him back to matter."

He investigated and understood
and knew them to be worthless,
for he will not know enough
to pass the night in glory.[20]

---

17. Cf. the pattern in *Az be-ʾEn Kol* in which each thing is created so that (ʿad lo) it can serve a purpose in subsequent history.

18. That is, God himself.

אליהו הנביא

עַד בּוֹא **תִּשְׁבִּי**
וְעוֹרְבִים יְכַלְכְּלוּהוּ

דָּגוּ מֵחֶלֶד
מַקְרִינִים לְזֶבַח
חַיַּית מַאֲכָל
עִם טְמֵאָה וָרֶמֶשׂ

דִּשֵּׁן בְּהֵמוֹת
בְּבוּל הַרְרֵי אֶלֶף
כִּי בְיוֹם זִבְחוֹ
יַגֵּשׁ חַרְבּוֹ

דָּץ יוֹצֵר
וְשָׂמַח בְּמַעֲשָׂיו
בְּהַבִּיטוֹ
כִּי טוֹב פָּעֳלוֹ

דִּשְׁאֵי מְנוּחוֹת
וְאָכְלֵי מְגָדִים
וְשֻׁלְחָן עָרוּךְ
וְאֵין מִי יְדוּשָׁן

דִּבֶּר בְּלִבּוֹ 35
"מִי יָסוּר הֵנָּה
לְטָבַח הַטָּבוּחַ
וְיַיִן הַמָּסוּךְ

דְּבָרַי אִם יַעַשׂ
יְהִי כֵּאלֹהִים
אִם יָמִיר אוֹמֶר
לַחֲמֹרוֹ אֲשִׁיבֶנּוּ"

דָּרַשׁ וְהֵבִין
וְיָדַע מְתֵי שָׁוְא
כִּי לֹא יָבִין
לָלִין בִּיקָר

---

19. Because he was created in God's image.
20. See Ps 49:13.

[THE FIRST HUMANS]

He likened[21] him in His image,
engraved him in His shape,
so that on heaven and earth
he would be held in awe.

The **Distinguished One**[22] made   God
a beautiful bed in Eden;
of spun gold and precious stones
he fashioned its canopy.

He ornamented him with true knowledge[23]
and favored him with spirit
so that from the beginning
he could foresee the consequences.[24]

He let him rule
as a righteous ruler
so that he could provide names
for God and His works.

He warned him
about the tree of knowledge
lest he be struck
by the appealing food.

He put him to sleep
in a pleasant slumber
and took a bone from him
and prepared a young woman.

He adorned her as a bride,
with adornments of jewels,
and attached them together
to be one flesh.[25]

---

21. Heb. *dimmahu*.
22. From Song 5:10.
23. Heb. *qisheto*, implying both decoration and truth.

[אבות עולם]

אלוהים

דִּמָּהוּ בְצֶלֶם
חֲקָקוֹ בְתַבְנִית
הֱיוֹת בְּדוֹק וָחֶלֶד
פַּחַד מוֹרָאוֹ

דָּגוּל בְּתוֹךְ עֵדֶן
יִיפָּה יְצוּעוֹ
בְּפָז אֶבֶן יְקָרָה
חָק מְסוּכָּתוֹ

דַּעַת קִישְּׁטוֹ
וְרוּחַ חֲנָנוֹ
לְהַשְׂכִּיל מִקֶּדֶם
קֵץ אוֹתִיּוֹת

הִמְשִׁילוֹ
כְּצַדִּיק וּמוֹשֵׁל
לְכַלֵּיל שֵׁמוֹת
לָאֵל וּמִפְעָלָיו

הִזְהִירוֹ
עַל עֵץ הַדַּעַת
פֶּן יֻנָּקֵשׁ
בְּמַאֲכַל תַּאֲוָה

הִרְדִּימוֹ
בְּנוֹעַם שֵׁינָה
הֵרִים מֶנּוּ עֶצֶם
וְכוֹנֵן עַלְמָה

הֶעְדָּהּ כְּכַלָּה
עֲדִי קְשׁוּרִים
הִדְבִּיקָם הֱיוֹת
שְׁאֵר אֶחָד

---

24. Heb. *qeṣ otiot*.
25. On the Hebrew term used here, cf. Jastrow, *Dictionary*, s.v. *šʾr*

45   **He who crawls in the dust**   the snake
      duped the foolish woman
      into defying the command
      and returning to the dust.

      She caused man to die,
      by her appetite for idleness,
      and she caused many to fall
      and killed multitudes.[26]

      The snake was punished by means of his food
      and by means of his feet[27] for eternity,
      and he was made messenger
      for **those who break through the wall**.[28]   transgressors

      They felt naked and were covered
      by the leaf of **that which withers**,[29]   fig tree
      instead of being clothed in a cloud,
      enveloped in fog.

      Their stature was altered,
      and their fearsomeness was denied,[30]
      to be ruled by all
      and not to rule all.

      They were removed from Eden
      and were expelled from the garden,
      and the cleft of a rock was prepared
      as a home for them.

      The Creator placed the sense of lust
      into His creature
      and made a place in his helpmeet
      for him to lie down for his desire

      And she was in heat and conceived
      and went into labor and gave birth

---

26. Cf. Prov 7:26.
27. His feet were taken away from him.
28. Transgressors will be punished with snakebite. See Eccl 10:8.

	45	הַשִּׂיא פּוֹתָה
הנחש		**זֹחֵל עָפָר**
		לְהָנִיא אוֹמֶר
		וְלָשׁוּב לֶעָפָר

הֱמִיתָהּ אִישׁ
בְּתַאֲוַת עֵצֶל
הִפִּילָה רַבִּים
וְהָרְגָה עֲצוּמִים

הֻכָּה בְּטַרְפּוֹ
וּבִפְעָמָיו לָנֶצַח
הוּא יְשַׁלַּח צִיר
משיגי גבול		לְפוֹרְצֵי גָדֵר

הֶעֱרִמוּ וְכִסּוּ
תאנה		בַּעֲלֶה **נֹבֶלֶת**

תְּמוּר לְבוּשׁ עָנָן
חֲתוּלַת עֲרָפֶל

הוּמַר תָּאֳרָם
וְהוּסַר פַּחְדָּם
לְהֵרָדוֹת מִכֹּל
וְלֹא לִרְדּוֹת בַּכֹּל

הוּרְמוּ מֵעֵדֶן
וְגֹרְשׁוּ מִגַּן
וְהוּכַן נְקִיק סֶלַע
בֵּית מָלוֹן לָמוֹ

וְיוֹצֵר הֶחֱשִׁ
תַּאֲוַת יְצִירוֹ
וְהִרְגִּיל עֶזְרוֹ
לְרַבַּע תְּשׁוּקָתָהּ

וַיְחַיְּמָה וְהִזְרִיעָהּ
וְחִבְּלָהּ וְיִלָּדָהּ

---

29. See Isa 34:4.
30. God made them fearful of the animals and not the other way around.

	a first time to a **plower** **of furrows of earth.**	Cain
55	She gave birth a second time and sent forth **a youngster, bearer of a staff,** **a shepherd of flocks.**	Abel

And as a gift offering
they offered before the King
one from the fruit of the earth
and the other from first of the flock.

Then the Holy One looked
at the heart and not the appearance[31]
and paid heed to the service
of the fragrant offering of the younger.

He raised
the dejected brother on high
when he accepted the offering
of a fragrant sacrifice,

and made the elder dejected,
and he was aggrieved,
for He rejected his offering,
his choice food.

Then his anger raged,
and his fury stormed,[32]
and he cut off the earth
a brother and his kin.[33]

And blood that was spilled
let forth a scream,
and the first bloodletter
was punished with wandering.

---

31. Lit., "the eyes."
32. See Amos 1:11.

וּבִיכֵּירָהּ מְשַׁדֵּד
תַּלְמֵי אֲדָמָה

קין

וְהוֹסִיפָה שֵׁנִית
וְהִבְרִיכָה וְשִׁילֵּחָה
עָוִיל תּוֹמֵךְ שֵׁבֶט
רוֹעֶה עֲדָרִים

הבל

וּבִתְשׁוּרַת שַׁי
קִידְּמוּ פְּנֵי מֶלֶךְ
זֶה בִּפְרִי אֶרֶץ
וְזֶה בִּפְטָרֵי צֹאן

וְהִבִּיט קָדוֹשׁ
לַלֵּב וְלֹא לָעֵינַיִם
וְשָׁעָה עֶרֶךְ
נִיחוֹחַ צָעִיר

וְשִׂיגֵּב אָח
קוֹדֵר לַמָּרוֹם
בִּרְצוֹתוֹ שַׁי
רֵיחַ קָרְבָּנוֹ

וְהִקְדִּיר פְּנֵי רַב
וְגַם חָרָה לוֹ
כִּי מָאַס בְּשַׁי
יֶתֶר מַאֲכָלוֹ

וְטָרַף אַף
וְשָׁמַר עֶבְרָה
וְחִיבֵּל מֵאֶרֶץ
אָח וּמִשְׁפְּחוֹתָיו

וְהִצְרִיחַ זְעָקָה
דָּם הַשָּׁפוּךְ
וְנֶעֱנַשׁ בְּנָע וָנָד
רֹאשׁ לְשׁוֹפְכֵי דָם

55

---

33. His potential descendants, who were, as it were, eliminated with him.

And he confessed to the crime,
and He gave him a sign
lest his blood
be spilled by someone.

65 **This One** bound up the wound   God
of **his earliest creation**,[34]   Adam
for he had begun to drink the **cup
mixed**[35] **for generations**.   death

He remembered to give
a seed to **the sower**   Seth; Adam
to provide a surrogate
for **the forsaken fruit**.   Abel

His seed sprouted
poison weed,
and its plant grew perversely,[36]
yielding wild fruit.[37]

The crooked generation
plotted and began[38]
to substitute the name of an idol
for the name of the one God.

He called against them
the rage of the pent-up waters;
they broke through their boundaries,
and they tore up the land.

They annihilated all remembrance of humankind[39]
from the earth
when He washed away
mounds of dust of the earth.

The tendrils that were
in the trees of the forest

---

34. Adam was mourning for Abel at the time.
35. Ps 75:9.
36. Heb. *sigseg*; cf. Isa 17:11.

	וְנִתְוַדָּה עַל פֶּשַׁע
	וְנִתַּן לוֹ אוֹת
	פֶּן יִשָּׁפֵךְ
	דָּמוֹ בָאָדָם
הָאֵל	זֶה חָבַשׁ עֶצֶב 65
אָדָם	יְצִיר קַדְמוֹנִי
	כִּי הֵחֵל שְׁתוֹת כּוֹס
מָוֶת	מָסַךְ לְדוֹרוֹת
	זָכַר לָתֵת
שֵׁת; אָדָם	זֶרַע לַזוֹרֵעַ
	לְהַחֲלִיף לוֹ
הֶבֶל	פְּרִי הָאֻמְלָל
	זַרְעוֹ הִשְׁרִישׁ
	שׁוֹרֶשׁ פּוֹרֶה רֹאשׁ
	וְשִׂגְשֵׂג נִטְעוֹ
	עֲשׂוֹת פְּרִי בְאוּשִׁים
	זָמְמוּ וְהֵחֵלּוּ
	דּוֹר עֲקַלְקַלּוֹת
	לְהָמִיר בְּשֵׁם אֱלִיל
	שֵׁם אֵל אֶחָד
	זַעַף מַיִם עֲצוּרִים
	עֲלֵיהֶם קָרָא
	פָּרְצוּ גְבוּלָם
	וַיַּהַפְכוּ אָרֶץ
	זֵכֶר תִּקְוַת אֱנוֹשׁ
	הֶאֱבִיד מֵאֶרֶץ
	וְשָׁטַף יְסוֹדֵי
	סְפִיחֵי עֲפַר אָרֶץ
	זַלְזַלִּים אֲשֶׁר
	בַּעֲצֵי יַעַר

37. See Isa 5:2.
38. Heb. *ḥekhelu*, carrying connotations of blasphemy (*ḥillul*).
39. Heb. *Enosh*, alluding to the patriarch Enosh.

did not bear fruit
until the tenth generation.

A pure and innocent man   Noah
found among them,
and the fragrance of his deeds
was like perfume in his generation.[40]

Presumptuously they rebelled
during the seven days of sunshine.[41]
In the goodness and abundance
they said to God, "Leave us alone!"[42]

They were punished by the upper waters
and were crushed by the lower waters,
but **the righteous one** appealed to him with **a gift**[43]   Noah;
                                                                                                             sacrifice

for the waters of Noah not to flood.[44]

75   The face of the earth was renewed
and returned to its former state
from the few people
who went out from **prison**.   the ark

The fifth generation   the generation of Peleg
then took counsel and planned
to go up and put up
a nest on high.

The Living One did not withhold
from them their scheme—
He who scoffs at scoffers
fulfilled their purpose.

He divided the speech
of the tongue of the dissenters,
and they were broken up into factions
and fought each other to the death.

---

40. Cf. Gen 6:9.
41. Before the flood, God gave humanity a week of clear weather in order to repent.
42. Cf. Job 21:14.

	עַד דּוֹר עֲשִׂירִי
	לֹא עָשׂוּ פֶרִי
נוח	**זַךְ וְתָמִים**
	בְּקִרְבָּם נִמְצָא
	רֵיחַ מִפְעָלָיו
	כְּרֵקַח בְּדוֹרוֹתָיו
	זָדוּ וּמָרְדוּ
	בְּשִׁבְעַת יְמֵי נֹגַהּ
	בְּטוּב וּמֶרֶב כֹּל
	אָמְרוּ לָאֵל סוּר
	זָעֲמוּ בְּמֵי מַעְלָה
	וְדוֹכְאוּ בְּמֵי מַטָּה
נוח; קרבן	**וְרִיצָּהוּ צַדִּיק בְּשֵׂי**
	מֵעֲבוֹר מֵי נֹחַ

75

	חִוְּדְשׁוּ פְנֵי חֶלֶד
	וְשָׁבוּ לְקַדְמָתָן
	מִמְתֵי מִסְפָּר
התיבה	**יוֹצְאֵי מִמַּסְגֵּר**
	חָשְׁבוּ וְנוֹעֲצוּ
דור פלג	**אָז דּוֹר חֲמִישִׁי**
	לָרוּם וְלָשׂוּם
	קֵן בַּמָּרוֹם
	חַי לֹא בִיצֵּר
	מֵהֶם מְזִמָּה
	מֵלִיץ לַלֵּצִים
	חֶפְצָם הִשְׁלִים
	חִילֵּק שְׂפַת לָשׁוֹן
	בַּעֲלֵי מַחֲלוֹקוֹת
	וְכִתְּתוּ זֶה בָזֶה
	וְנִלְחֲמוּ לְמַשְׁחִית

43. Gen 8:20.
44. Cf. Isa 64:9.

[THE PATRIARCHS]

They vanished after the storm,
passed, and they were gone;
then **a righteous man** arose   Abraham
who was an everlasting foundation.

He reasoned, understanding
the secret of creation,[45]
which is controlled
by Him who governs and rules.

When he saw the course
of **that which glides and shines,**   the sun
eager as a hero when it emerges
and weak when it sets,

the windows of the sky,
in the east and the west,
through which the moon
leaps every day,

the arrows of lightning,
the rush of the stars
dashing to and fro—
and not one fails to appear—

the unenlightened became wise   Abram
and inferred by himself,[46]
saying, "There is a Lord of these—
Him I will follow."

85   Before he began,
God cleared the way for him,
"Go forth from death,
to the way of life."

---

45. Lit., "works."

[אֲבוֹת הָאוּמָּה]

אברהם

חָלְפוּ כַּעֲבוֹר
סוּפָה וְאֵינָם
וְהוּקַם **צַדִּיק**
יְסוֹד עוֹלָם

חִשֵּׁב לְהָבִין
סוֹד מִפְעָלוֹת
הַמִּתְנַהֲגִים
בְּשׁוֹטֵר וּמוֹשֵׁל

השמש

חֲזוֹתוֹ מְרוּצַת
שׁוֹאֵף וְזוֹרֵחַ
שָׁשׂ כְּגִבּוֹר בְּצֵאתוֹ
וְחַלָּשׁ בְּבוֹאוֹ

חַלּוֹנֵי שַׁחַק
אֲשֶׁר בְּקֵדְמָה וָיָמָּה
אֲשֶׁר בָּם תְּנַתֵּר
לִבְנֵה יוֹם יוֹם

חִצֵּי בְרָקִים
וְדוֹהַר כּוֹכָבִים
רָצִים וְשָׁבִים
וְאִישׁ לֹא נֶעְדָּר

אברם

חָכַם **סוּג לֵב**
וְשָׂכַל מֵאֵלָיו
וְשָׂח אָדוֹן לָאֵלֶּה
אַחֲרָיו אָרוּצָה

טֶרֶם הִקְדִּים
אֵל בֵּרֵר לוֹ דֶרֶךְ
לֹא לוֹ מִמָּוֶת
לְדֶרֶךְ הַחַיִּים

85

---

46. Abraham was not taught to understand monotheism but reasoned it on his own.

He who was pure in his deeds	Abraham
spoke heroically,[47]	
"O God of justice,	
judge with mercy!"	

He swept away the monarchs[48]
without shield or sword;
He lifted him up from fire,   God
aided him in war.

His generation was ignorant
and did not recognize **the Rock**.   God
So he informed them at the tamarisk[49]
of the name of the eternal God.

He placed in his flesh
a stamped impression of the covenant,
which **that which gapes** will see   Gehenna
and snap its mouth shut.[50]

He caused leaves to sprout
in old age,
when **the source of the withered bed**   Sarah's womb
was opened.

The One who tested him[51] placed the burden   God
of the ordeal on his shoulder;
indeed, he overpowered his urge,
giving his lamb to the slaughter.

He gave **a basket of first fruits**   Isaac
as an offering;
the father had no pity,
and the son did not hesitate.

When **the slaughterer of the lamb**   Abraham
grasped the sword,

---

47. That is, Abraham spoke to God regarding Sodom and Gomorrah; see Gen 18:25–32.
48. The four kings of Gen 14:9.
49. Gen 21:33. According to the midrash, it was a kind of inn, in which Abraham would extend hospitality and teach the guests about the eternal God.

אברהם	טָהוֹר בְּמַעֲשָׂיו
	דִּבֶּר גְּבוּרוֹת
	נָא אֱלֹהֵי מִשְׁפָּט
	שְׁפוֹט נָא בְּרַחֲמִים
	טָרַף רוֹזְנִים
	בְּלֹא מָגֵן וָחֶרֶב
האל	שִׂיגְּבוֹ מֵאֵשׁ
	עֲזָרוֹ בְמִלְחֶמֶת
	טָפַשׁ דּוֹרוֹ
האל	וְצוּר לֹא הִכִּירוּ
	וְהוֹדִיעָם בְּאֵשֶׁל
	שֵׁם אֵל עוֹלָם
	טַבַּעַת חוֹתָם בְּרִית
	שָׂם בִּשְׁאֵרוֹ
גיהנום	בָּהּ תִּפֶן פּוֹעֶרֶת
	וְאָז תִּקְפֹּץ פִּיהָ
	טַרְפֵּי צֶמַח
	זְקוּנִים הֵצִיץ
	בְּהִפָּתַח מָקוֹר
רחמה של שרה	לַעֲרוּגַת חוֹרֶב
האל	טוֹרַח בּוֹחַן מְנַסֵּיהוּ
	עָמַס עַל שְׁכֶם
	וְגַם מָשַׁל בְּיֵצֶר
	תֵּת שֵׂיוֹ לִזְבַח
יצחק	טָנָא בִּכּוּרִים
	מִנְחָה הוֹבִיל
	אָב לֹא חָמַל
	וּבֵן לֹא אֵחַר
אברהם	טוֹבֵחַ בְּעַד שֶׂה
	בְּעֵת תָּפַשׂ חֶרֶב

50. When Gehenna sees a Jew's circumcision, it will shut its gaping mouth so as to keep him out.
51. God tested Abraham at the binding of Isaac.

the angels of peace
let out a bitter cry.

The Good and Merciful One said:
"Do not harm the boy!
Your deed is accepted
as a sacrificer and sacrifice."

96 **The mild man** was settled					Jacob
in the **gates of testimony**:					Torah
before it was given,⁵²
he studied its words.⁵³

God has always
been glorified through him,
and in his name forever
He will be enthroned in praise.⁵⁴

The One who knows him stood
over him when he sojourned,
saying, "I am your guardian,
your shade at your right hand."⁵⁵

The holy ones ascended and descended				angels
on his behalf,
to get to know his image,
which was engraved on high.⁵⁶

100 **The Artisan** made him a little					God
less than God
when he caused (the goats) to mate by rods,⁵⁷
like clay in the hands of an artisan.

The fear of a vision
frightened **the Aramaean.**						Laban
"Do not touch the son,
supported since leaving the womb."

---

52. Lit., "before it was spoken."
53. That is, before the Torah was given at Sinai, he learned its content.
54. Alluding to the idea that Jacob's name and image are engraved on God's throne. On this idea, see Ginzberg, *Legends*, 5:290–91.

מַלְאֲכֵי שָׁלוֹם
מַר זָעֲקוּ בְכִי

טוֹב וְרַחוּם שָׂח
"אַל תַּשְׁחֵת נַעַר
נִרְצָה פָּעָלְכֶם
כְּזוֹבֵחַ וְנִזְבָּח"

יעקב	**יוֹסַד אִישׁ תָּם**	96
הַתּוֹרָה	בְּפִתְחֵי **תְעוּדָה**	
	טֶרֶם תֹּאמַר	
	שִׁינֵּן אֲמָרֶיהָ	

יָהּ מֵעוֹלָם
בּוֹ נִתְפָּאֵר
וּבִשְׁמוֹ לְעוֹלָם
יוֹשֵׁב תְּהִלּוֹת

יוֹדְעוֹ נִצָּב
עָלָיו בַּמָּלוֹן
וְשָׂח אֲנִי שׁוֹמְרֶךָ
צֵל עַל יְמִינֶךָ

המלאכים	יוֹרְדִים וְעוֹלִים
	קְדוֹשִׁים לְמַעֲנֵהוּ
	לְהַכִּיר תָּאֳרוֹ
	חָקוּק בַּמְּרוֹמִים

האל	**יוֹצֵר** חַסְרוֹ	100
	מְעַט מֵאֱלֹהִים	
	לְיַחֵם בַּמַּקְלוֹת	
	כְּחוֹמֶר בְּיַד יוֹצֵר	

לבן	יִרְאַת חָזוֹן
	אֲרַמִּי בְּעֶתַתּוּ
	"אַל תִּגַּע בְּבֵן
	עָמוּס מִנִּי בָטֶן"

---

55. Ps 121:5.
56. See note 54 above. The angels recognized his image from the throne and saw him on earth.
57. Gen 30:39.

When **the flying fiery flame**   the angel
struggled with him,
when he could not prevail over him,
he begged, crying out.

He saved him miraculously
from **the one who is girded with a sword**,   Esau
who resented and bore
eternal enmity.

He inherited the desires
of his parents' blessings.
twelve tribes
like the officers of the firmament.

[LEVI AND HIS CHILDREN]

The third was selected
to see the face of the King,
to sing and to serve
and to enter His chambers.

Like a tree planted
on the water,
his scepter sprouted
three holy vines: Moses, Aaron, and Miriam

those bent over by the load,[58]   the children of Merari
for the Tent and its planks;
those drivers of the pegs,
spreaders of the curtains;   the children of Gerson

an extended shoulder,   the children of Kehat
like a trained heifer,
for the yoke of the holy service
of the Lord of all.

Like a splendid vine
of beautiful branches and fruit,

---

58. The children of Merari built the framework of the Tabernacle. Num 3:36.

יִדּוֹד אֵשׁ לוֹהֵט	הַמַּלְאָךְ
בְּהֵאָבְקוֹ לוֹ	
כִּי לֹא יָכוֹל	
נִתְחַנַּן בִּבְכִי	
יֶשַׁע הִפְלִיא לוֹ	
מֵחֲגוֹר חֶרֶב	עֵשָׂיו
שׁוֹטֵם וְשׁוֹמֵר	
אֵיבַת עוֹלָם	
יָרַשׁ תַּאֲוֹת	
בִּרְכוֹת הוֹרָיו	
שְׁנֵים עָשָׂר שֶׁבֶט	
כְּשׁוֹטְרֵי רָקִיעַ	

[לוי ובניו]

יוּחַד שְׁלִישִׁי	
לִרְאוֹת פְּנֵי מֶלֶךְ	
לְשׁוֹרֵר לְשָׁרֵת	
לָבוֹא חֲדָרָיו	
כְּעֵץ שָׁתוּל	
עַל פַּלְגֵי מַיִם	
הִפְרִיחַ מַטֵּהוּ	
שְׁלֹשֶׁת בַּדֵּי קֹדֶשׁ	משה, אהרון ומרים
כְּפוּפֵי סֵבֶל	בני מררי
לְאֹהֶל וּקְרָשָׁיו	
תּוֹקְעֵי יָתֵד	
פּוֹרְשֵׂי יְרִיעוֹת	בני גרשון
כָּתֵף נְטוּיָה	בני קהת
כָּעֲגָלָה מְלֻמָּדֶת	
לְעוֹל עֲבוֹדַת קֹדֶשׁ	
אֲדוֹן כָּל הָאָרֶץ	
כְּגֶפֶן אַדֶּרֶת	
יְפַת פְּרִי וְעָנָף	

He caused Amram to sprout forth
from the root of Levi.

110 For it sent forth
three precious offspring:
a priest, a shepherd,   Aaron and Moses
and **a woman prophetess.**   Miriam

When **the time of love**[59] drew near,   the Exodus
his flower arose   Moses
to break the yoke-bands of **Zoan,**   Egypt
to break through the gate of **the hollow.**[60]   water

Hidden in a cloud
and sanctified for a week,
he stood inside
when the Word was given.

The power of **mighty ones**[61]   angels
was subdued before him;
for fear of him,
not a single one prevailed.

He nourished the holy flock
with flesh in the wilderness
from the bread of heaven
until they came to the land.[62]

The drumming maiden   Miriam
dug a well for the people;
she **perished and was gathered,**   died
and there was no water.[63]

The beloved were favored   Israel
with the accompaniment of the clouds of glory
by virtue of **the officiator,**[64]   Aaron
in peace and in ease.

---

59. Based on Ezek 16:8.
60. The term is from Isa 40:12. The meaning here is that Moses split the sea.
61. The angels opposed to the giving of the Torah to Moses.

הִצְמִיחַ עַמְרָם
מְשׁוֹרֶשׁ לֵוִי

110 כִּי שָׁלַח שְׁלוֹשֶׁת
שָׂרִיגֵי חֶמֶד
מְכַהֵן וְרוֹעֶה — אהרון ומשה
וְאִשָּׁה נְבִיאָה — מרים

כְּגֶשֶׁת עֵת דּוֹדִים — זמן הגאולה
פִּרְחוֹ הוּקַם — משה
לִשְׁבּוֹר מוֹסְרוֹת צֹעַן — מצרים
וְלִפְרוֹץ גֶּדֶר שׁוּעָל — המים

כּוּסָה בֶעָנָן
וְנִתְקַדַּשׁ שָׁבוּעַ
נִצָּב בַּתָּוֶךְ
בְּעֵת מַתָּן אוֹמֵר

כּוֹחַ אַדִּירִים — מלאכים
לְפָנָיו הוּכְנַע
מִמּוֹרָאוֹ
לֹא עָמַד אִישׁ

כִּלְכֵּל צֹאן קֹדֶשׁ
שְׁאֵר בִּישִׁימוֹן
וּמִלְחֶם שְׁחָקִים
עַד בּוֹאָם לָאָרֶץ

כָּרְתָה בְּאֵר לָעָם
עַלְמָה מְתוֹפֶפֶת — מרים
גָּוְעָה וְנֶאֶסְפָה
לֹא הָיָה מַיִם

לִוּוּיֵי עַנְנֵי הוֹד
יְדִידִים נְחָנֻנּוּ — ישראל
עַל יְדֵי מְכַהֵן — אהרון
בְּשָׁלוֹם וּמִישׁוֹר

---

62. The land of Israel.
63. Because of Miriam the people had water.
64. The clouds of glory accompanied Israel for Aaron's sake.

A covenant of salt
was engraved for him and his descendants
so that the covenant of salt of the fragrant offering
would never cease.

For the zealous wrath of **the hero**　　　　　　　　Pineḥas
God paid recompense
and renewed his office
for generations forever.

No foreigner shall ever acquire
the inheritance of their glory;
no other man shall inherit
their given portion.

120　The company of notables[65]
was taken down to the valley of the shadow;
and they settled **the king of power**[66]　　　　　　Uzziah
in isolated quarters.

They may not be jealous
of the lot of their brothers' portion;
God is called
their designated allotment.

Sacrificial bread
was reserved for them
when they came near to God,
in the time of the repulsive calf.[67]

The lawgiver taught them　　　　　　　　　　　Moses
the order of the Avodah
because he was in charge of it[68]
when they were at the gate[69]

to wash and anoint,
to cleanse their hands and feet,

---

65. See Num 16:2.
66. Uzziah's name literally means "the power of God"; he presumed to offer incense on the altar himself. See 2 Chr 26:16–21.

לוֹ וּלְזַרְעוֹ בְּרִית
אֱמֶת נֶחְקָקָה
בְּלִי תִּשְׁבּוֹת מֶלַח
בְּרִית הַנִּיחוֹחַ

פנחס

לְקִנְאַת חֲמַת **גֶּבֶר**
גְּמוּל גָּמַל אֵל
וְחִידֵּשׁ חֻקּוֹ
לְדוֹרוֹת עוֹלָם

לְזָר לֹא יָאֲתָה
נַחֲלַת כְּבוֹדָם
לֹא יִירַשׁ אֱנוֹשׁ
מַתַּת חֶלְקָם

לְצַלְמָוֶת הוּרְדוּ   120
עֲדַת אַנְשֵׁי שֵׁם

עוזיה

וְהוֹשִׁיבוּ **עֹז מֶלֶךְ**
בְּבֵית הַחָפְשִׁית

לֹא יְקַנְּאוּ בְחֶבֶל
אֲחֻזַּת אַחִים
כִּי אֱלֹהִים נִקְרָא
מְנָת גּוֹרָלָם

לֶחֶם הָאִשִּׁים
לָהֶם הוּכַן
בְּהִתְקָרְבָם לָאֵל
בְּעֵת רְחוּק עֲגָל

משה

לִימְּדָם **מְחוֹקֵק**
סִדְרֵי עֲבוֹדוֹת
כִּי בְּשִׁבְתָּם פֶּתַח
עֲלֵיהֶם הִפְקָד

לִרְחוֹץ וְלָסוּךְ
לְקַדֵּשׁ יָד וָרֶגֶל

---

67. The term *riḥuk* carries connotations of distance and abomination, in opposition to the verb *qrb*, "came near," in the same stanza.

68. The instructions concerning the Avodah.

69. The gate of the Tabernacle during the ceremony of ordination; see Lev 8:35.

to wear linens,
and to put on the girdle,

to ordain them
for seven days,
and to make it a law
for generations forever.

As it is written: Everything done today, the Lord has commanded to be done to make expiation for you (Lev 8:34).

[THE AVODAH]

Impeccable families
drew a lot
to magnify a chief
and to raise him in wealth.

From his bed where he lay,
they separated his wife,
lest he be impure for a week,
becoming tainted unintentionally.

The place where the chiefs gather　　　　the chamber
　　　　　　　　　　　　　　　　　　　　of Palhedrin

was his dwelling place;
would he not sleep there
all seven days?

He offered the minḥah,
placed the incense,
and arranged the lamps,
and was the first to offer the head and foot.[70]

Of the sale for the Sabbaths
and the portion of the priestly divisions,
his portion took precedence
over everyone else's.

---

70. Of the sacrificial animals.

לִלְבּוֹשׁ בַּדִּים
וְלַחֲגוֹר בְּמֵזַח

לְמַלֵּא יָדָם
יָמִים שִׁבְעָה
וַיְשִׂימֶהָ לְחוֹק
לְדוֹרוֹת עוֹלָם

ככת׳ כאשר עשה ביום הזה צוה יי לעשות לכפר עליכם

[העבודה]

מִשְׁפָּחוֹת בְּרוּרִים
גּוֹרָל יָטִילוּ
לְגַדֵּל סְגָן
וּלְעֲלוֹתוֹ בְּעוֹשֶׁר

מֵרֹבַע יְצוּעוֹ
שְׁאֵרוֹ יַבְדִּילוּ
פֶּן יִטְמָא שָׁבוּעַ
בְּשִׁגְגַת דָּוָה

מְקוֹם עֲצֶרֶת סְגָנִים   **לשכת פלהדרין**
בֵּית מוֹשָׁבוֹ
הֲלֹא שָׁם יָלִין
כָּל יְמֵי שִׁבְעָה

מַעֲלֶה מִנְחָה
וְנוֹתֵן סַמִּים
וְעוֹרֵךְ נֵרוֹת
וְרִאשׁוֹן בְּרֹאשׁ וָרֶגֶל

מִמַּכָּר שַׁבָּתוֹת
וְחֵלֶק מִשְׁמָרוֹת
חֶלְקוֹ בְּרֹאשׁ
כְּנֶגֶד כּוּלָם

Those who make wise the simple   the sages
stayed with him
to teach and train him
in the laws of the **tenth day**.   Yom Kippur

They brought him,
on the eve of the day of forgiveness,
his bull and his ram
and the sacrifices of his community.

"How pleasant," they said,
"is your service!
Be strong and of good courage,
for all these are your tasks."

135   They restricted food
from him toward evening
lest he fall asleep and there occur
a nocturnal pollution.

His instructors brought him to
the elders of his clan;
and in the incense-makers' house[71]
they adjured him by (God's) name.

He wept sadly
because he was accused of ignorance,[72]
and they cried
lest they accuse a righteous person.

They engaged him
with the strains of Midrash and scriptures
or occupied him
with the sacred writings.

They restored his soul
with talk of former kings
if he was a boor
and did not learn **Instruction**.[73]   Torah

---

71. The house of Avtinas, according to m. Sheqalim 5:1.

מַחְכִּימֵי פֶתִי	הַחכמים
יָעָמְתוּ לוֹ	
לְשַׁנְּנוֹ לַחֲנָכוֹ	
בְּחֻקֵּי עָשׂוֹר	יום כיפור
מַרְאִים לוֹ	
בְּעֶרֶב יוֹם סְלִיחָה	
פָּרוֹ וְאֵילוֹ	
וְזִבְחֵי קָהָל	
"מַה נָּאָה	
עֲבוֹדָתְךָ" יֹאמְרוּ	
"חֲזַק וֶאֱמָץ	
כִּי כָל אֵלֶּה פָּעֳלֶךָ"	
מַאֲכָל יַמְעִיטוּ	135
מֶנּוּ לְעֵת עֶרֶב	
פֶּן יֵרָדַם וְיִקָּר	
מִקְרֵה לָיְלָה	
מְחַנְּכָיו יְחַבְּרוּהוּ	
לְזִקְנֵי מַטֶּהוּ	
וּבְבֵית רוֹקְחֵי רֶקַח	
בַּשֵּׁם יַשְׁבִּיעוּהוּ	
נֶעְגַּם בִּבְכִי	
פֶּן יוּרְשַׁע כְּפֶתִי	
וְהֵמָּה יִבְכּוּ	
פֶּן צַדִּיק יַרְשִׁיעוּ	
נְעִימוֹת מִדְרָשׁ	
וּמִקְרָא יְשׂוֹחֵחַ	
אוֹ בְּכִתְבֵי קֹדֶשׁ	
הֵם יַעֲסִיקוּהוּ	
נַפְשׁוֹ יְשׁוֹבְבוּ	
בְּשִׂיחַ מַלְכֵי קֶדֶם	
אִם בַּעַר הוּא	
לֹא לָמַד לֶקַח	תורה

72. Heb. *peti*.
73. Heb. *Leqaḥ*; cf. Prov 4:2.

If he was inclined to doze,
they prevented him from sleeping
with a whistle of the middle finger,[74]
with the mouth, but not the harp.

In the tumultuous city[75]
they let forth a roar
to make him sated with sleeplessness
until the dawn.[76]

Those who guard the laws,
who plunder the commandments,[77]
got up before midnight
to remove the ashes.

They used to run hurriedly
on the ascent to the altar,
so they took care (to institute) a lottery
to put an end to disputes.[78]

They readied themselves vigilantly for immersion[79]
and tied the wreath[80]
and cast lots first
for taking the ashes.

145   They cast a second time,
for the case of the lamb
and for the ashes of the inner
altar and the lamps.

They cast the lots anew,
a third time, for the spices;
a fourth, for the combination[81]
to arrange (the offering of) the limbs.

---

74. See Zvi Malachi, "Makkin Lefanav be-ʾEṣbaʿ Seradah: Neʿima ba-Peh ve-Lo ba-Kinor," *Sidra* 2 (1986): 67–75.

75. Isa 22:2.

76. Job 7:4.

נָטָה לָנוּם
שְׁנָתוֹ יַפְרִידוּ
בְּנוֹעַם צְרָדָה
בְּפֶה וְלֹא בְכִינּוֹר

נוֹתְנִים שָׁאוֹן
עִיר הוֹמִיָּה
לְהַשְׁבִּיעוֹ נְדוּדִים
עֲדֵי נֶשֶׁף

נוֹצְרֵי חוּקִים
בּוֹזְזֵי מִצְווֹת
כַּחֲצוֹת לַיְלָה יַקְדִּימוּ
לְהָרִים דֶּשֶׁן

נֶהְדְּפוּ רָצִים
בְּמַעֲלוֹת מִזְבֵּחַ
וְשָׁקְדוּ בְפַיִס
לְהַשְׁבִּית מְדָנִים

נוֹעֲדוּ וְטָבְלוּ
וְעִינְּדוּ עֲטָרָה
וְהֵפִיסוּ תְחִלָּה
עַל תְּרוּמַת דֶּשֶׁן

נִצְבְּעוּ שֵׁנִית   145
עַל מַעֲשֵׂה כֶבֶשׁ
וְעַל דִּישּׁוּן מִזְבֵּחַ
פְּנִימִי וְנֵרוֹת

נִתְחַדְּשׁוּ
שְׁלִישִׁי לְסַמִּים
רְבִיעִי לְתַעֲרוֹבֶת
לְעֶרֶךְ הַנְּתָחִים

---

77. Alluding perhaps to the statement in m. Yoma 2:2 that specific duties are meted out to individual priests because of the intense competition for them in the past.
78. Prov 18:18.
79. Heb. *no'adu*. See Mirsky's note to this line (*Yose ben Yose*, 153).
80. The headdress. Other MSS read: they formed a circle.
81. Of old and new priests.

The overseeing chief officer
of the holy labor
sent to the east
faithful emissaries.

He said to them: "See
whether the dawn has arrived,
if the eastern light has spread
over the earth."

They told him
that the radiance had flashed,
and he ran to the purifying bath
for those who come to the court.

They spread a fine linen divider
between him and the people
to do him honor
not to see his nakedness.

Quickly he took off
the covering against his skin;
then he went down and bathed
and came up and dried himself.

The dressing attendant
wrapped him in linen
and added to his greatness
with ornamental garments of gold.

He rejoiced in his splendid attire,
but he was not too proud;
he wore them for God's honor
and not for his own.

He would inquire
about making war in them;
his eyes cast to his **Teacher**   **God**
like a student to his master.

155 A secret was revealed to him
in the judgment of the Urim:

שַׂר פָּקִיד נָגִיד
מְלֶאכֶת הַקֹּדֶשׁ
יִשְׁלַח לְקֶדֶם
צִירֵי אֱמוּנָה

שָׂח לָמוֹ "הַבִּיטוּ
אִם עָלָה הַשַּׁחַר
אִם הֵפִיץ אוֹר
קָדִים עֲלֵי אָרֶץ"

סֻפַּר לוֹ
כִּי בָרַק נוֹגַהּ
וְרָץ לְמִקְוֵה טוֹהַר
לְבָאֵי עֲזָרָה

סָכוּ מְחִיצַת שֵׁשׁ
בֵּינוֹ לְבֵין עַם
לִנְהוֹג בּוֹ בְגוֹדֶל
בְּלִי חֲזוֹת מַעֲרֵהוּ

שִׂמְלַת עוֹרוֹ
יְמַהֵר וְיִפְשׁוֹט
וְיֵרֵד וְיִטְבּוֹל
וְיַעַל וְיִסְתַּפֵּג

סְגַן הַמַּלְבִּישׁ
יַעֲטֵיהוּ בַדִּים
וְיוֹסִיף לְגַדְּלוֹ
בַּעֲדִי בִגְדֵי פָז

שָׂשׂ בְּמַעֲטֵי הוֹד
וְלֵב לֹא יַגְבִּיהַּ
לָבַשְׁם לִכְבוֹד אֵל
וְלֹא לְמַעֲנֵהוּ

סֵדֶר מִלְחָמוֹת
בָּהֶם יִשְׁאַל
עֵינָיו לְמוֹרֵהוּ
כְּתַלְמִיד לָרַב

סוֹד יְגַלֶּה לוֹ
בְּמִשְׁפַּט אוּרִים

האל

155

if he will succeed or fail,
whether to the sword or salvation.

Extol God,
children of a great nation!
He is near at all times
to proclaim redemption.

He rejoiced like an angel,
in the woven linen breeches,
like a vigilant horseman,[82]
a messenger faithful to those who send him.

With them he covered over
carnal nakedness,
for they were commanded
for covering indecency.

His strong body
filled his tunic,
doubled and woven[83]
as far as the sleeves.[84]

The sin of the house of Jacob
was atoned by this—
those who sold **the righteous one**   Joseph
over a sleeved tunic.[85]

The crown on his head
was like regal glory;
wrapped in a turban of fine linen
for glory and beauty.

He banished from the holy women[86]
the burden of uncovering the head,[87]

---

82. According to b. Niddah 13b, they resembled riding breeches.

83. Heb. *kefulah meshubeṣet*; according to some sources, such as y. Yoma 3:6 (40c) and Sifra Ṣav 2:1 (ed. Weiss, fol. 29d), it was a double garment. On the other hand, according to b. Yoma 71b, the term *shesh*, translated here as "fine linen," means that it was made of sixfold thread. On the possible interpretations of this line, see Mirsky, *Yose ben Yose*, 155.

84. Mirsky points out that, based on the meaning of *pas* as palm, Gen Rabbah 84:8 interprets *pasim* as sleeves: the tunic reached his palms (i.e., was long-sleeved).

אִם עָלֹה אִם חָדֹל
אִם לְחֶרֶב אִם לְיֵשַׁע

סוֹלוּ לֵאלֹהִים
בְּנֵי גּוֹי גָּדוֹל
קָרוֹב בְּכָל עֵת
לְבַשֵּׂר יְשׁוּעוֹת

עָלַץ כְּמַלְאָךְ
בִּשְׁיבּוּץ מִכְנְסֵי בַד
כְּפָרָשׁ מוּכָן
צִיר אֱמֶת לְשׁוֹלְחָיו

עֶרְוַת זִמָּה
בָּהֶם יְכַסֶּה
כִּי כֵן מִצְוָתָם
לְכַסּוֹת עֶרְוָה

עַלְמוּת קוֹמָה
יְמַלֵּא בְּכֻתֹּנֶת
כְּפוּלָה מְשׁוּבֶּצֶת
עַד פַּסֵּי יָד

עֲוֹן בֵּית יַעֲקֹב
יְכֻפַּר בְּזֹאת
מוֹכְרֵי צַדִּיק
עַל כְּתֹנֶת פַּסִּים

יוסף

עֲטֶרֶת רֹאשׁוֹ
כְּהוֹד הַמְּלוּכָה
צָנוּף צְפִירַת שֵׁשׁ
לְכָבוֹד וּלְתִפְאָרֶת

עֵסֶק פְּרִיעַת רֹאשׁ
יָסִיר מִקְדוֹשׁוֹת

---

85. Cf. also the motif of the emperor's exploitation of the sins of Jacob's sons against Israel in the Ten Martyrs complex.
86. Cf. Num 5:18.
87. The priest's headdress atoned for the adulterous woman (*sotah*) of Num 5, whose hair is to be unbound during her trial.

and he would justify the holy nation
with the diadem of his frontlets.

(God) will cleave to the jaw,
like a belt at the loins,
of those who stray after images
(of men) with girded loins.[88]

He girded himself with a belt,
a woven sash
made of unmixed linen,
unlike every other day of the year.

165 Wrapped in a blue robe
as bright as the firmament,
his rounded arms
filled the sleeves.[89]

The circular opening
for his head was like a coat of mail,
plaited all around
so that it could not be torn.[90]

At the edge of its hem
were colored pomegranates
and golden bells
between them.

When they struck each other,
the voice of one with the other,
they atoned for the voice
of one who strikes his neighbor in secret.[91]

The weave of the ephod
was a work of decoration,
fine twined linen,
bright blue and purple.

---

88. See Ezek 23:14–15.
89. Here following Carmi's translation.

וְיַצְדִּיק קְדוֹשִׁים
בְּנֵזֶר טוֹטָפוֹת

עוֹד יְדַבַּק בְּלֶחִי
כְּאֵזוֹר מָתְנַיִם
תּוֹעֵי בְצַלְמֵי
חֲגוֹרֵי מָתְנָיִם

עוֹז אַבְנֵט יִתְאַזַּר
בְּמַזַח אָרוּג בַּד
וְלֹא כִלְאַיִם
כָּכָל יְמֵי שָׁנָה

עֲטוּיֵי מְעִיל תְּכֵלֶת   165
כְּזוֹהַר הָרָקִיעַ
מְמַלֵּא בֵית יָד
גְּלִילֵי זְרוֹעוֹתָיו

עָגוֹל שְׂפַת פִּיו
רֹאשׁוֹ כְּתַחְרָא
מֵסַב קֶלַע
בְּלִי לְהִקָּרֵעַ

עַל שְׂפַת שׁוּלָיו
רִמּוֹנֵי צְבָעִים
וּפַעֲמוֹנֵי פָז
סָבִיב בְּתוֹךְ

עֵת יַשִּׁיקוּ
קוֹל זֶה בָּזֶה
יְכַפֵּר בְּעַד קוֹל
מַכֵּה רֵעַ בַּסָּתֶר

פְּעוּלַת חוֹשֵׁב
אֲרִיגַת הָאֵפוֹד
מָשְׁזָר שֵׁשׁ וְשָׁנִי
תְּכֵלֶת וְאַרְגָּמָן

---

90. Exod 28:32.
91. Verbally, through slander.

A golden cord
was spun into each thread,
and he was dressed in it
from heart to navel.

The corners of its shoulders
were like the brilliance of the luminaries;
they radiated light
from precious stones.[92]

He engraved them with a *shamir*[93]
as a remembrance of the tribes,
their names and letters
divided among them.

An ornamented band
extended from it;
it was embroidered like it;
he tied it on afterward.[94]

It banished sin against the commandment, (spoken)
at the beginning of **the Holy Utterances,**   the Decalogue
against sheathed images
of gods of gold.

175   In the breast of the ephod
was an opening of a span by a span
where it was bound to the breastpiece
by golden rings.[95]

The number of rows of stones
equaled the number of standards;[96]
their names were engraved on them,
and they were set into the breastpiece.

---

92. Heb. *Avne Shoham;* cf. Joshua Trachtenberg, *Jewish Magic and Superstition: A Study in Folk Religion* (New York: Atheneum, 1982), 137, who translates "onyx"; cf. Mirsky's note to this line, citing Saul Lieberman, *Tosefta Kifshutah,* vol. 8 (New York: Jewish Theological Seminary of America, 1973), 735–37. NJV: "Lazuli."

פְּתִיל זָהָב
נִטְוָוה בְּכָל חוּט
וְנִתְלַבֵּשׁ בּוֹ
מֵלֵב וְעַד טַבּוּר

פִּנּוֹת כְּתֵפָיו
כְּזוֹהַר הַמְּאוֹרוֹת
מַבְהִיקוֹת אוֹר
מֵאַבְנֵי הַשֹּׁהַם

פִּתְּחָם בְּשָׁמִיר
זִכְרוֹן שְׁבָטִים
הַמִּתְחַלְּקִים
בְּשֵׁמוֹת וְאוֹתוֹת

פֵּרַשׁ מִמֶּנּוּ
חֵשֶׁב הָאֵפוֹד
אָרוּג כְּמַעֲשֵׂהוּ
וַיַּעֲנְדוֹ לְאַחֲרָיו

פּוֹרֵק עָוֹן צַו
רֹאשׁ **דִּיבְּרוֹת קֹדֶשׁ**
אֲפֻדַּת מַסֵּכַת
אֱלֹהֵי זָהָב

עשרת הדיברות

פְּנֵי לֵב הָאֵפֹד   175
קָרוּעַ זֶרֶת עַל זֶרֶת
מְקוֹם יְרוֹפַס חֹשֶׁן
בְּטַבְּעוֹת זָהָב

פָּקַד טוּרֵי אֶבֶן
כְּמִסְפַּר דְּגָלִים
שָׁמָם חָקוּק בָּם
וַיְמַלְאוּ חֹשֶׁן

---

93. A hard stone or legendary worm. See Ginzberg, *Legends*, 5:53, and Michael Sokoloff, *A Dictionary of Jewish Palestinian Aramaic* (Ramat Gan: Bar Ilan University Press, 1990), s.v. shamir.
94. That is, after donning the ephod.
95. See Josephus Ant. 3.7.5
96. The divisions of the twelve tribes, three tribes per banner.

268   AVODAH

Framed in gold
in their setting,
their appearance was like
the appearance of eyes.

The gap of the rings[97]
between the ephod and the breastpiece
was covered by links
of golden cords.

The sin of perverters of justice
was wiped out by the breastpiece of justice;
may the God of justice
declare us righteous in justice.

Golden bells were placed around,
between the ephod and the breastpiece,[98]
attached to the holy diadem
on his two shoulders.

The gold frontlet was surrounded
with diadems of jewels;[99]
he[100] fastened and attached it
to the sacred diadem.

He placed the royal headdress on his forehead[101]
and the frontlet upon it;
there was a strip of hair
between it and the headdress.

The Rock of Eternity,
the powerful name,
was engraved on the diadem
like an inscription on a signet.

The filth of impurity
of transgressions of (sacrificial) blood and libations

---

97. Lit., "scales," after 1 Kgs 22:34; that is, the distance between the rings at the corners of the breastpiece and those of the shoulder straps of the ephod. The cords connect the two.

98. According to no extant tradition are bells on the upper part of the vestments; tradition has them only at the hem of the robe. Mirsky suggests that this stanza is corrupt and contains remnants

פָּז מוּסַבּוֹת
בִּמְלוּאוֹתָם
מַרְאֵה דְמוּתָם
כְּפִתְחֵי עֵינַיִם

פֶּרֶץ דְּבָקִים
בֵּין אֵפוֹד לַחֹשֶׁן
יְכַסֶּה בְשַׁרְשְׁרוֹת
עֲבוֹתוֹת זָהָב

פֶּשַׁע הוֹפְכֵי מִשְׁפָּט
יִמַּח בְּחֹשֶׁן מִשְׁפָּט
וְיַצְדִּיקֵנוּ בְמִשְׁפָּט
אֱלֹהֵי הַמִּשְׁפָּט

פַּעֲמוֹנֵי פָז מָקָף
בֵּין אֵפוֹד לַחוֹשֶׁן
חוּבַּר לְנֵזֶר הַקֹּדֶשׁ
עַל שְׁתֵּי כְתֵפָיו

צִיץ פָּז מָקָף
צִיצֵי פְנִינִים
דִּבֵּק וְחִבֵּר
לְנֵזֶר הַקְּדוֹשָׁה

צָנִיף הוֹד שָׂם בְּמֵצַח
וְעָלֶיהָ הַצִּיץ
וְשִׁיטַת שֵׂעָר
בֵּינוֹ לְמִצְנֶפֶת

צוּר עוֹלָמִים
שֵׁם הַנַּעֲרָץ
חָקוּק עַל צִיץ
בְּמִכְתַּב חוֹתָם

צוֹאַת טֻמְאַת
עֲוֹן דָּם וָנֶסֶךְ

---

of previous lines (cf. line 167).

99. Heb. *peninim,* usually "coral" or "pearls."

100. That is, the attendant; see above.

101. Heb. Ṣenif; this seems to be a kind of twisted rope of cloth worn around the diadem.

was absolved by the frontlet
like a pure, aromatic offering.

185 A fading flower,[102]
a worm not a man,
was found worthy of serving
Him who lives forever.

He saw the face of the King
and entered the holy chamber,
dressed in linens
and not in fine gold.

He commanded the death penalty
on those who come into the court
(without) washing their hands
and feet when they enter.

So **the emissary**, before   the priest
he approached to serve,
hastened to wash
his hands and his feet.

His assistants brought
the daily morning sacrifice.
He made the incision and collected
its blood and dashed it.

He stepped forth to offer the incense
and repair the lamps,
to sacrifice the head and **pieces**,   of the carcass
cakes and libation.

He hurried out
to the chamber of Parvah,
and they spread a partition of fine linen
between him and the people.

He washed and undressed
and bathed and dried himself

---

102. Heb. ṣiṣ, also used to signify "frontlet"; cf. Isa 28:1.

יְרַצֶּה הַצִּיץ
כְּנִיחוֹחַ טָהוֹר

185 צִיץ נוֹבֵל
תּוֹלַעַת וְלֹא אִישׁ
נֶחְשָׁב לְשָׁרֵת
לְחֵי הָעוֹלָמִים

צוֹפֶה פְּנֵי מֶלֶךְ
וּבָא בַּחֲדַר קֹדֶשׁ
לָבוּשׁ בַּדִּים
וְלֹא בְכֶתֶם אוֹפִיר

צַו עוֹנֶשׁ מִיתָה
לְבָאֵי עֲזָרָה
לְקַדֵּשׁ יָדַיִם וְרַגְלַיִם
בְּבוֹאָם לְשָׁרֵת

הכוהן

צִיר לָכֵן
בְּטֶרֶם גִּשְׁתּוֹ לְשָׁרֵת
יְמַהֵר יְקַדֵּשׁ
יָדָיו וְרַגְלָיו

צְעִירָיו יַגִּישׁוּ
אֶת תְּמִיד הַשַּׁחַר
קָרְצוֹ וְקִיבֵּל
דָּמוֹ וְזָרַק

צָעַד לְהַקְטִיר קְטוֹרֶת
לְהֵיטִיב נֵרוֹת
לְהַקְרִיב רֹאשׁ וְנֵתַח
חֲבִתִּים וָנֶסֶךְ

קִידֵּם בְּצֵאתוֹ
לְבֵית פַּרְוָה בַּקֹּדֶשׁ
וְסָכוּ מְחִיצַת שֵׁשׁ
בֵּינוֹ לְבֵין עָם

קִידֵּשׁ וּפָשַׁט
וְטָבַל וְסִיפֵּג

and put on linen clothes
and washed again.

He approached
the bull of his sin offering,
standing
between the portico and the altar.

He arose to place his hand
on its head firmly,[103]
to confess on behalf
of himself and his household.

Thus he would say: "O Lord, I have sinned, I have done wrong, I have transgressed before You, I and my household. O Lord, forgive the sins and iniquities and transgressions that I have committed against you, I and my household, as it is written in the Torah of Moses, Your servant: 'For on this day atonement shall be made for you to cleanse you of all your sins; before the Lord—'" (Lev. 16:30). And when the priests and the people standing in the court and serving in the Sanctuary heard the glorious explicit name coming forth from the mouth of the high priest in holiness and purity, they would kneel, prostrate themselves, and fall to their faces and say: "Blessed is the name of His Majesty's glory for ever and ever." He would also intend to finish the name while facing those saying the blessing and say to them, "You shall be pure."

Eastward, toward the Gate of Entrance,[104]
north of the altar,
the assistant priests
accompanied him respectfully.[105]

205   Was it not there
where the goats were placed,

---

103. Heb. *be-sevel*.
104. Heb. *Sha'ar ha-'Iton*, from Ezek 40:15, identified with the Middle Gate (y. Erubin 5:1 [22c]),

וְעָטָה כְּלֵי בַד
וְשָׁב וְנִתְקַדָּשׁ

קָרַב אֵצֶל
פַּר חַטָּאתוֹ
וְהוּא עוֹמֵד
בֵּין אוּלָם וְלַמִּזְבֵּחַ

קָם תֵּת יָדוֹ
עַל רֹאשׁוֹ בְּסֵבֶל
לְהִתְוַדּוֹת בְּעַד
עַצְמוֹ וְנָנֶיהוּ

וכך היה אומ' >"אָנָּא הַשֵּׁם. חָטָאתִי, עָוִיתִי, פָּשַׁעְתִּי לְפָנֶיךָ אֲנִי וּבֵיתִי: אָנָּא בַשֵּׁם, כַּפֶּר נָא לַחֲטָאִים וְלַעֲוֹנוֹת וְלַפְּשָׁעִים. שֶׁחָטָאתִי וְשֶׁעָוִיתִי וְשֶׁפָּשַׁעְתִּי לְפָנֶיךָ אֲנִי וּבֵיתִי. כַּכָּתוּב בְּתוֹרַת מֹשֶׁה עַבְדֶּךָ מִפִּי כְבוֹדֶךָ. כִּי בַיּוֹם הַזֶּה יְכַפֵּר עֲלֵיכֶם לְטַהֵר אֶתְכֶם מִכֹּל חַטֹּאתֵיכֶם לִפְנֵי יְהוָה: וְהַכֹּהֲנִים וְהָעָם הָעוֹמְדִים בָּעֲזָרָה כְּשֶׁהָיוּ שׁוֹמְעִים אֶת הַשֵּׁם הַנִּכְבָּד וְהַנּוֹרָא מְפֹרָשׁ יוֹצֵא מִפִּי כֹהֵן גָּדוֹל בִּקְדֻשָּׁה וּבְטָהֳרָה הָיוּ כּוֹרְעִים וּמִשְׁתַּחֲוִים וְנוֹפְלִים עַל פְּנֵיהֶם וְאוֹמְרִים: בָּרוּךְ שֵׁם כְּבוֹד מַלְכוּתוֹ לְעוֹלָם וָעֶד: וְאַף הוּא הָיָה מִתְכַּוֵּן כְּנֶגֶד הַמְבָרְכִים לִגְמֹר אֶת הַשֵּׁם, וְאוֹמֵר לָהֶם תִּטְהָרוּ"<

קֵדְמָה לְשַׁעַר אִיתוֹן
לִצְפוֹן מִזְבֵּחַ
יְלַוּוּהוּ בְכָבוֹד
כֹּהֲנֵי מִשְׁנֶה

205   קִימַת שְׂעִירִים
הֲלֹא שָׁם הָיְתָה

---

known also as the Nikanor Gate (m. Middot 1:4); see m. Yoma 3:9 and Mirsky's comment to this line, *Yose ben Yose*, 164.

105. Cf. Carmi: "with pomp."

as well as the container
where the golden lots were kept?

He gathered them in his hand[106]
and shook them and raised them,
one for Him who lives forever,
and the one for death in Ṣoq.[107]   Azazel

If in his right hand
he took the lot[108] engraved "for the Lord,"[109]
the assistant said to him,
"Raise your right hand!"

If (the lot for) of the severity of the generation's deeds
came up in his left hand,
the chief of the priest's division[110] said,
"Raise your left hand!"

He hastened to place them
on the two goats
and shouted in a loud voice,
"This one is a sin offering for the Lord!"

He tied a thread
to the head of the one who was to be dispatched;
he turned him over to the wilderness,
and the other to the place of slaughter.

Next he got up
and approached his bull[111]
and placed his two hands
on him and confessed.

And thus he would say: "O Lord, I have sinned, I have done wrong, I have transgressed before You, I and my household and the children of Aaron, Your holy people. O, by the Lord, forgive the sins and iniquities and transgressions that I have committed against you, I and my household and the children

---

106. Heb. *qoveṣam ʿal yad*, from Prov 13:11—there interpreted to mean "little by little"; here, perhaps, that he takes them one by one.

וּכְלִי בֵית הַנַחַת
גּוֹרָלוֹת זָהָב

קוֹבְצָם עַל יָד
וְטוֹרֵף וּמַעֲלֶה
זֶה לְחֵי עוֹלָם
וְזֶה לְמִיתַת צוֹק

עזאזל

קַחְתּוֹ בְיָמִין
פּוּר חָקוּק "לַשֵּׁם"
סְגָן יַשְׁמִיעַ לוֹ
"הַגְבֵּיהַּ יְמִינֶךָ"

קְשִׁי מַעֲלְלֵי דוֹר
בִּשְׂמֹאל אִם יַעַל
רֹאשׁ בֵּית אָב יָשִׂיחַ
הַגְבֵּיהַּ שְׂמֹאלֶךָ

קָפַץ וּנְתָנָם
עַל שְׁנֵי הַשְּׂעִירִים
וְהִצְרִיחַ בְּקוֹל רָם
"זֶה לְשֵׁם חַטָּאת"

קָשַׁר שָׁנִי
בְּרֹאשׁ הַמִּשְׁתַּלֵּחַ
הֲפָכוֹ לַמִּדְבָּר
וְזֶה לְבֵית שְׁחִיטָה

קָם וּבָא לוֹ
אֵצֶל פָּרוֹ שְׁנִיָּה
וְסָמַךְ שְׁתֵּי יָדָיו
עָלָיו וְהִתְוַדָּה

וְכָךְ הָיָה אוֹמֵר. "אָנָּא הַשֵּׁם. חָטָאתִי, עָוִיתִי, פָּשַׁעְתִּי לְפָנֶיךָ אֲנִי וּבֵיתִי וּבְנֵי אַהֲרֹן עַם קְדוֹשֶׁךָ. אָנָּא בַשֵּׁם. כַּפֶּר נָא לַחֲטָאִים וְלַעֲוֹנוֹת וְלַפְּשָׁעִים. שֶׁחָטָאתִי וְשֶׁעָוִיתִי וְשֶׁפָּשַׁעְתִּי לְפָנֶיךָ אֲנִי וּבֵיתִי וּבְנֵי אַהֲרֹן עַם קְדוֹשֶׁךָ. כַּכָּתוּב בְּתוֹרַת מֹשֶׁה עַבְדֶּךָ מִפִּי

---

107. The name Ṣoq refers to the precipice from which the goat was cast in m. Yoma 6:4 and 6:6.
108. Heb. *pur*, after Esther 9:24.
109. Heb. *la-shem*.
110. Heb. *rosh bet av*: the head of the family of priests on duty for that day.
111. That is, the bull for the priest's personal sin offering.

of Aaron, Your holy people, as it is written in the Torah of Moses, Your servant: 'For on this day atonement shall be made for you to cleanse you of all your sins; before the Lord—'" (Lev. 16:30). And when the priests and the people standing in the court and serving in the Sanctuary heard the explicit name coming forth from the mouth of the high priest in holiness and purity, they would kneel, prostrate themselves, and fall to their faces and say: "Blessed is the name of His Majesty's glory for ever and ever." He would also intend to finish the name while facing those saying the blessing and say to them, "You shall be pure."

221 He killed it[112] as required
and collected the blood in a vessel,
and another stirred it
at the steps of the portico.

He strode up the ramp
and ascended to the altar,
in his hands a fire-pan
made of red gold.

He filled it with glowing coals
from the western side.[113]
He went down and placed it
at the paved landing.[114]

His colleagues brought out
the ladle for him
and **the utensil for heaping
the finest of incense.**   the fire-pan

225 He put a handful of incense
into the ladle;
he held it in his left hand
and the fire-pan in his right.

---

112. Heb. *reṣaḥo*.
113. Of the altar; cf. Sifra Aḥare Mot 3:6 (ed. Weiss, fol. 81a), cited by Mirsky.

כְּבוֹדֶךָ. כִּי בַיּוֹם הַזֶּה יְכַפֵּר עֲלֵיכֶם לְטַהֵר אֶתְכֶם מִכֹּל חַטֹּאתֵיכֶם לִפְנֵי יְהֹוָה:
וְהַכֹּהֲנִים וְהָעָם הָעוֹמְדִים בָּעֲזָרָה כְּשֶׁהָיוּ שׁוֹמְעִים אֶת הַשֵּׁם הַנִּכְבָּד וְהַנּוֹרָא מְפֹרָשׁ
יוֹצֵא מִפִּי כֹהֵן גָּדוֹל בִּקְדֻשָּׁה וּבְטָהֳרָה הָיוּ כּוֹרְעִים וּמִשְׁתַּחֲוִים וְנוֹפְלִים עַל פְּנֵיהֶם
וְאוֹמְרִים: בָּרוּךְ שֵׁם כְּבוֹד מַלְכוּתוֹ לְעוֹלָם וָעֶד": וְאַף הוּא הָיָה מִתְכַּוֵּן כְּנֶגֶד
הַמְבָרְכִים לִגְמֹר אֶת הַשֵּׁם, וְאוֹמֵר לָהֶם "תִּטְהָרוּ":

	רְצָחוֹ כַּדָּת 221
	וְקִבֵּל דָּם בִּכְלִי
	וְאַחַר יְמָרְסֶנּוּ
	בְּמַעֲלוֹת אוּלָם
	רָמַס כֶּבֶשׁ
	וְעָלָה לְמִזְבֵּחַ
	וּבְיָדוֹ מַחְתַּת
	פָּז הָאָדוֹם
	רְשָׁפִים מְלֵאָה
	מִפְּנֵי מַעֲרָב
	יָרַד וְשָׂמָהּ
	בְּרוֹבֶד הַמִּרְצֶפֶת
	רֵיעָיו יוֹצִיאוּ לוֹ
	אֶת הַכַּף
	וּכְלֵי בֵּית צְבִירַת
המחתה	דַּקַּת הַדַּק
	רוֹקֵחַ מָלֵא חָפְנָיו 225
	נָתַן לְתוֹךְ כַּף
	נְטָלָהּ בִּשְׂמֹאל
	וּמַחְתָּה בְּיָמִין

114. In m. Yoma 4:3, the "fourth landing" between the steps leading up from the court to the sanctuary.

He joined the load
of the right hand to the left[115]
and went left to the sanctuary,
to the outer curtain.

He walked between the (curtains)
from south to north,
and when he arrived there he returned
to the middle of the house.

The ends of the rods[116]
stood out like breasts;
they pushed against the curtain,
for there was nowhere to pass.

He displayed his great strength
and pushed aside the curtain
and entered without stepping
between the two rods.

The first clump of earth,
the foundation stone,
the place where the ark was established,
was where he put the fire-pan.[117]

He poured the incense into it,
and the smoke rose straight up;
he turned his face to the side
and went out on his way.[118]

He pled on behalf of the people
briefly in the sanctuary
that the senior may not wield
power over the junior.[119]

The (priest) who was stirring the blood
returned it to him,

---

115. That is, he used the left hand along with his right to hold the fire-pan, which had a longer handle on Yom Kippur, according to m. Yoma 4:4.

116. The poles that project from the ark; see b. Yoma 54a and y. Yoma 42b, Jastrow, *Dictionary*, s.v. *bad*.

רִכֵּב כּוֹבָד
יָמִין עַל שְׂמֹאל
וְהַשְּׂמֹאל בַּהֵיכָל
בְּעֵקֶב הַפָּרוֹכֶת

רִגֵּל בְּקִרְבָּם
מִנֶּגֶב לְצָפוֹן
וּבְהַגִּיעוֹ שָׁב
עַד חֲצִי הַבַּיִת

רָאשֵׁי הַבַּדִּים
כְּמַרְאֵה שָׁדַיִם
לְחוּצִים בַּפָּרוֹכֶת
וְאֵין דֶּרֶךְ לַעֲבוֹר

רַב כֹּחַ יוֹדִיעַ
וְיִדְחֶה בַּפָּרוֹכֶת
וְיָבֹא בְּלֹא פֶסַע
בֵּין שְׁנֵי הַבַּדִּים

רֹאשׁ עַפְרוֹת תֵּבֵל
אֶבֶן הַשְּׁתִיָּה
מְקוֹם מְכוֹן אָרוֹן
שָׁם שָׂם מַחְתָּה

שָׁפַךְ בָּהּ קְטֹרֶת
וְתִימֶּר עָשָׁן
וְהִצְדִּיד פָּנָיו
וְיָצָא כְדַרְכּוֹ

שִׁוּוּעַ בְּעַד עַם
בְּקוֹצֶר בַּהֵיכָל
אֲשֶׁר לֹא יָשׁוֹר
רַב עַל צָעִיר

שׁוֹבֵב לוֹ דָּם
הַמְמָרֵס בּוֹ

---

117. According to m. Yoma 5:2, when the ark was removed, the foundation stone (*even shetiyah*) was exposed.
118. That is, the way he came in.
119. According to y. Yoma 5:3 (42c) and Lev Rabbah 20:4, the high priest prayed that no one in Israel assume high authority over the other.

and he approached and stood
where he was waiting.

He stretched out his most skilled finger[120]
and dipped it and swung it,[121]
once up
and seven times down.

235 And this is how he would count: "One, one and one, one and two, one and three, one and four, one and five, one and six, one and seven." He went out and set it down on the golden stand in the sanctuary.

He returned and placed it on the stand
and slaughtered the goat of the people
and collected the blood and entered
and swung (his finger with the blood) as required.

He placed it on its stand
and took the blood of the bull,
and so he sprinkled the Tent[122]
outside, opposite the ark.

And this is how he would count: "One, one and one, one and two, one and three, one and four, one and five, one and six, one and seven." He went out and set it down on the second stand in the sanctuary.

He returned and mixed it
with the blood of the goat
and dealt with it
according to the law for the blood of the bull.

He completed
the sprinkling of the inside;
he combined them[123] and went out
and expiated the incense altar.

---

120. The index finger of the right hand; see Sifra Aḥare Mot 3:12 (ed. Weiss, fol. 81a).
121. In a whipping motion.

וּבָא וְנִתְיַצֵּב
בִּמְקוֹם עָמְדוֹ

שָׁלַח אֶצְבַּע מְיֻמֶּנֶת
וְטָבַל וְהִצְלִיף
אַחַת לְמַעְלָה
וְשֶׁבַע לְמַטָּה

235 וְכָךְ הָיָה מוֹנֶה: "אַחַת. אַחַת וְאַחַת. אַחַת וּשְׁתַּיִם. אַחַת וְשָׁלֹשׁ. אַחַת וְאַרְבַּע. אַחַת וְחָמֵשׁ. אַחַת וָשֵׁשׁ. אַחַת וָשֶׁבַע": יָצָא מִקָּדְשֵׁי הַקֳּדָשִׁים וְהִנִּיחוֹ עַל כַּן הַזָּהָב שֶׁהָיָה בַּהֵיכָל:

שָׁב וְשָׂמוֹ בַּכַּן
וְשָׁחַט שְׂעִיר עַם
וְקִבֵּל דָּם וּבָא
וְהִצְלִיף כְּדַרְכּוֹ

שִׁנָּהוּ בְּכַנּוֹ
וְנָטַל דַּם פָּר
וְכֵן יַזֶּה בָּאֹהֶל
מוּל אָרוֹן חוּצָה

וְכָךְ הָיָה מוֹנֶה: "אַחַת. אַחַת וְאַחַת. אַחַת וּשְׁתַּיִם. אַחַת וְשָׁלֹשׁ. אַחַת וְאַרְבַּע. אַחַת וְחָמֵשׁ. אַחַת וָשֵׁשׁ. אַחַת וָשֶׁבַע": יָצָא וְהִנִּיחוֹ עַל כַּן הַזָּהָב הַשֵּׁנִי שֶׁהָיָה בַּהֵיכָל:

שָׁב וַיְמִירֶנּוּ
בְּדַם הַשָּׂעִיר
וַיִּפְעַל בּוֹ
כְּמִשְׁפַּט דַּם הַפָּר

שָׁלְמוּ כַדָּת
הַזִּיּוֹת פְּנִימָה
בְּלָלָם וְיָצָא
לְחַטֵּא מִזְבַּח הַקְּטוֹרֶת

---

122. Cf. Lev 16:16.
123. The two types of blood.

He had to begin
from the northeast direction,
and where he ended,
there he sprinkled seven times.

Afterward, he came to the scapegoat and placed his two hands on it and confessed[124] on our behalf. And thus he would say: "O Lord, they have sinned, they have done wrong, they have transgressed before You, Your people, the house of Israel. O, by the Lord, forgive the sins and iniquities and transgressions that they have committed against you, Your people, the house of Israel, as it is written in the Torah of Moses, Your servant: 'For on this day atonement shall be made for you to cleanse you of all your sins; before the Lord—'" (Lev. 16:30). And when the priests and the people standing in the court and serving in the Sanctuary heard the explicit name coming forth from the mouth of the high priest in holiness, they would kneel, prostrate themselves, and fall to their faces and say: "Blessed is the name of His Majesty's glory for ever and ever."

255 He appointed a man
who was designated to send it
and went up and burned
the fat of the bull and the goat.

He seized it by its yoke
outside the camp of the city.
They burned them entirely:
skin, flesh, and excrement.

They walked the goat
to the edge of the wilderness;
they took (the priest) to recite
from the Laws of the **Tenth Day**.[125]   Yom Kippur

First he washed
his hands and his feet

---

124. The second half of this sentence is not in the Mishnah.

שֶׁיַּתְחִיל מִקֶּרֶן
צָפוֹנָה מִזְרָחָה
וּבִמְקוֹם יִגְמוֹר
שָׁם יַזֶּה שֶׁבַע

צָעַד וּבָא לוֹ אֵצֶל הַשָּׂעִיר הַמִּשְׁתַּלֵּחַ לַעֲזָאזֵל לְהִתְוַדּוֹת עָלָיו אַשְׁמַת קְהָלוֹ, וְסָמַךְ שְׁתֵּי יָדָיו עָלָיו וְהִתְוַדָּה: וְכַךְ הָיָה אוֹמֵר. "אָנָּא הַשֵּׁם. חָטְאוּ. עָווּ. פָּשְׁעוּ לְפָנֶיךָ עַמְּךָ בֵּית יִשְׂרָאֵל: אָנָּא בַשֵּׁם. כַּפֶּר נָא לַחֲטָאִים וְלַעֲוֹנוֹת וְלַפְּשָׁעִים. שֶׁחָטְאוּ וְשֶׁעָווּ וְשֶׁפָּשְׁעוּ לְפָנֶיךָ עַמְּךָ בֵּית יִשְׂרָאֵל. כַּכָּתוּב בְּתוֹרַת מֹשֶׁה עַבְדֶּךָ מִפִּי כְבוֹדֶךָ. כִּי בַיּוֹם הַזֶּה יְכַפֵּר עֲלֵיכֶם לְטַהֵר אֶתְכֶם מִכֹּל חַטֹּאתֵיכֶם לִפְנֵי יְהוָה: וְהַכֹּהֲנִים וְהָעָם הָעוֹמְדִים בָּעֲזָרָה כְּשֶׁהָיוּ שׁוֹמְעִים אֶת הַשֵּׁם הַנִּכְבָּד וְהַנּוֹרָא מְפֹרָשׁ יוֹצֵא מִפִּי כֹהֵן גָּדוֹל בִּקְדֻשָּׁה וּבְטָהֳרָה הָיוּ כּוֹרְעִים וּמִשְׁתַּחֲוִים וְנוֹפְלִים עַל פְּנֵיהֶם וְאוֹמְרִים: בָּרוּךְ שֵׁם כְּבוֹד מַלְכוּתוֹ לְעוֹלָם וָעֶד:

יוֹם הַכִּפּוּרִים

255 תִּיכֵּן אִישׁ
מוֹעֵד לְשַׁלְּחוֹ
וְעָלָה וְהִקְטִיר
חֶלְבֵי פָר וְשָׂעִיר

תְּקָפָם בְּמוֹטוֹת
חוּץ לְמַחֲנֵה עִיר
שְׂרָפוּם כָּלִיל
עוֹר וּבָשָׂר וָפֶרֶשׁ

תָּאַר שָׂעִיר
לְרֹאשׁ הַמִּדְבָּר
מְשַׁכּוּהוּ לְשַׁנֵּן
בְּחֻקֵּי עָשׂוֹר

תְּחִלָּה יְקַדֵּשׁ
יָדָיו וְרַגְלָיו

125. Here the meaning is the Torah as a whole; see m. Yoma 7:1.

and took off the linen clothes
and wrapped himself in his rich clothes.[126]

He finished his reading,
undressed and immersed,
and put on the eight [vestments],
and washed again.

He burned his offering
of lambs and rams completely;[127]
he washed his hands
and his feet and undressed.

His steps led on
to the place of immersion;
he immersed and dried himself
and put on his linen garments.

He did what he had learned,
as was the custom,[128] and washed
and took the ladle and fire-pan
from inside.

He completed (the main)[129] service
in linen garments;
he washed and undressed
and laid them down forever.[130]

He immersed immediately
and put on his gold garments
and again washed
his hands and his feet.

265 He performed the Tamid
of the evening as required
and offered the incense
between the pieces and the libation.

---

126. A festive garment of his own; see m. Yoma 7:1.
127. Heb. *hikhlil*; so Mirsky. Alternatively, he offered them together.
128. Heb. *ke-dovro*.

וְיִפְשׁוֹט כְּלֵי בַד
וְיַעַט כְּלֵי עָשְׁרוֹ

תַּם הֲגִיוֹנוֹ
פָּשַׁט וְטָבַל
וְעָטָה שְׁמוֹנָה
וְשָׁב וְנִתְקַדָּשׁ

תְּשׁוּרַת כְּבָשִׂים
וְאֵלִים הַכְּלִיל
קִידֵּשׁ יָדָיו
וְרַגְלָיו וּפָשַׁט

תִּירְגֵּל פְּעָמָיו
לְבֵית הַטְּבִילָה
טָבַל וְסִיפֵּג
וְעָטָה כְּלֵי בַד

תַּלְמוּדוֹ יַעַשׂ
כְּדָבְרוֹ וְקִידֵּשׁ
וְיוֹצִיא מִפְּנִימָה
כַּף וּמַחְתַּת פָּז

תּוֹכֶן עֲבוֹדוֹת
כְּלֵי בַד הִשְׁלִים
קִידֵּשׁ וּפָשַׁט
וְהִנִּיחָם נֶצַח

תָּכַף טְבִילָה
וְלָבַשׁ כְּלֵי פָז
וְשָׁב וְקִידֵּשׁ
יָדָיו וְרַגְלָיו

תָּמִיד הָעַרְבַּיִם 265
יַעֲשֶׂה כַסֵּדֶר
וְהִקְטִיר קְטוֹרֶת
בֵּין נְתָחִים לָנֶסֶךְ

---

129. Heb. *tokhen 'avodot*.

130. According to Sifra (Aḥare Mot 6:7 [ed. Weiss, fol. 82b]), the garments are buried (*te'unim genizah*), never to be used again.

The deeds having being completed,   the sacrifices
he lit the lamps
and spread his hands
and washed and undressed.

The assistants ran
with the clothes for his body
and dressed him in reverence;
then he went out joyously.

His form radiated
like the sun rising in all its power.
To those who sent him[131]
he sent justice and healing.

It was the hope of the congregation
that **the vigilant man**[132] would emerge   the priest
bearing good news of redemption
and announcing forgiveness.

He gave praise
to God, facing the people,
and immersed five times
and washed ten times.

First he told them,
"Go, drink with a good heart!
God has pardoned sin
and passed over transgression."

"Give us a sign,"
they said to his ears,
"that we may know whether
He has forgiven sin."

He showed (them) the messenger who sent the goat,
and he announced redemption:

---

131. That is, Israel, whose emissary he is.

קרבנות היום

תַּכְלִית מַעֲשִׂים
נֵרוֹת הִבְעִיר
פֵּירַשׂ כַּפַּיִם
וְקִדַּשׁ וּפָשַׁט

תִּלְבּוֹשֶׁת שְׁאֵרוֹ
חֲנִיכָיו יָרִיצוּ
יַלְבִּשָׁם בְּכָבוֹד
וְיֵצֵא בְמָשׂוֹשׂ

תָּאֳרוֹ הֻקְרַן
כְּצֵאת הַשֶּׁמֶשׁ בִּגְבוּרָתוֹ
מְשַׁלֵּחַ לְשׁוּלְחָיו
צְדָקָה וּמַרְפֵּא

הכוהן

תִּקְוַת קָהָל
לָצֵאת **אִישׁ מָהִיר**
מְבַשֵּׂר יְשׁוּעוֹת
וּמוֹדִיעַ סְלִיחוֹת

תְּהִלָּה נָתַן לַשֵּׁם
אֶל פְּנֵי עַם
בְּחָמֵשׁ טְבִילוֹת
וְעֶשֶׂר קְדוּשׁוֹת

תְּחִלָּה הִשְׁמִיעָם
"לְכוּ שְׁתוּ בְּלֵב טוֹב
אֵל נוֹשֵׂא עָוֹן
וְעוֹבֵר עַל פֶּשַׁע"

"תֶּן לָנוּ מוֹפֵת"
בְּאָזְנָיו יֹאמְרוּ
"וְנֵדַע בַּמֶּה
יְכוּפַּר עָוֹן"

תִּתּוֹ צִיר שָׂעִיר
וְהוּא מְבַשֵּׂר יְשׁוּעוֹת

132. Heb. *ish mahir*.

the scarlet thread
had turned white as snow.[133]

They gave thanks,
for he had told good news
about the messenger of the faithful
who was sent to the wilderness.

275　Perfect and upright,
they accompanied him home,
and they rejoiced
when he came out unharmed.

Happy is the people
who have it so;
happy is the people
whose God is the Lord.[134]

---

133. Cf. Isa 1:18.

הִלְבִּין כַּשֶּׁלֶג
אוֹדֶם הַשָּׁנִי

תּוֹדָה נָתְנוּ
כִּי טוֹב הִשְׁמִיעָם
עַל צִיר אֱמוּנִים
הַמְשׁוּלָח לַמִּדְבָּר

תְּמִימִים יְשָׁרִים
לְנַוְוהוּ יְלַוּוּהוּ
וְשִׂמְחָה יַעֲשׂוּ
בְּצֵאתוֹ בְּלֹא פֶגַע

אַשְׁרֵי הָעָם
שֶׁכָּכָה לּוֹ
אַשְׁרֵי הָעָם
שֶׁיי אֱלֹהָיו

---

134. Ps 144:15.

6. Atah Konanta ʿOlam be-Rov Ḥesed
"You Established the World in Great Mercy"

YOSE BEN YOSE

This composition is a fully formed Avodah and provides another example of Yose ben Yose's handiwork. It is close in language and structure to *Azkir Gevurot,* and like it, this piyyut helped set the structure and themes of subsequent Avodah piyyutim. However, it varies in content and some of its emphases within the set themes. For example, this poem emphasizes not only that God created animals, including the Leviathan, for food but also that God embedded anatomical signs in kosher animals so they could be recognized as such. Although *Atah Konanta ʿOlam be-Rov Ḥesed* may not attain the elegance of *Azkir Gevurot,* it does contain some interesting details from Midrash and cultic lore.

Atah Konanta ʿOlam be-Rov Ḥesed was included in Saadia Gaon's liturgical handbook and entered the medieval French and Provençal liturgies. The following translation is based on an improved version of Mirsky's edition.[1]

---

1. Mirsky, *Yose ben Yose,* 172–99. See also Samuel David Luzzatto, *Maḥazor Kol ha-Shanah kefi Minhag Italiyani* (Livorno, 1855).

You established the world
in great mercy,
and (the world) shall be governed with it   mercy
till the end of days.

It will not shatter   **the world**
because of the sin of (Your) creatures,
and will not collapse
from the weight of transgression and sin.[2]

While the earth was still
desert and wasteland,[3]
You amused Yourself with the glow of the Law,
and it frolicked at Your feet.

You made up Your mind to make it
a cure for all humanity,
ere You made it
You assured its vitality.

You braced the skies
as a place for Your dwelling,
and extended the rafters
as a throne for Your glory;

You are hidden in (the skies),[4]
and no eye can see You,[5]
and from there Your eyes
survey every deed.

You contrived to cover
the abyss with land[6]
as a footstool for You
and a dwelling for Your creatures.

With chaos and storm
You suspended its foundations,

---

2. By rights, the world should be destroyed because of its sinfulness. But, out of mercy, God will not do so.

3. Heb. *ṣalmavet*.

4. Cf. Ps 91:1.

אַתָּה כּוֹנַנְתָּ עוֹלָם
בְּרֹב חֶסֶד
וּבוֹ יִתְנַהֵג
עַד קֵץ הַיָּמִין

חֶסֶד

אֲשֶׁר לֹא יִמּוֹט
מְעוֹן יְצוּרִים
וְלֹא יִמְעַד
מִכֹּבֶד פֶּשַׁע וַחֲטָאִים

הָעוֹלָם

אֲדָמָה בְּעוֹדָהּ
צִיָּה וְצַלְמָוֶת
בְּאוֹר דָּת שֶׁעֲשַׁעְתָּ
וְרַגְלָהּ שֹׂחֲקָה

אָמַרְתָּ לְתִתָּהּ
מַרְפֵּא לְכָל אֱנוֹשׁ
טֶרֶם תִּפְעָלֶנּוּ
חַיָּיו הֲכִינוֹתָ

בֵּרַרְתָּ שְׁחָקִים
לִמְכוֹן שִׁבְתֶּךָ
וְרִוַּחְתָּ עֲלִיּוֹת
לְכֵס הֲדָרֶיךָ

בָּם תִּסָּתֵר
בְּלִי תְשׁוּרְךָ עַיִן
וּמִשָּׁם עֵינֶיךָ
מְשׁוֹטְטוֹת בְּכָל פֹּעַל

בָּנִיתָ לִקְרוֹת
אֶרֶץ עַל בְּלִי מָה
לַהֲדוֹם רַגְלֶיךָ
וּמוֹשָׁב יְצוּרֶיךָ

בְּתֹהוּ וּבִסְעָרָה
יְסוֹדֶיהָ תָּלִיתָ

---

5. Lit., "without an eye being laid on You."
6. Heb. *banta liqrot 'ereṣ'al blimah*.

and when You oversee it,
its pillars quake.

You expelled darkness
and called light;
by name You called them,
and with measure You engraved them.[7]

10   You placed a border for them
and a division between them,
so that their lot cannot be diminished
and their order cannot be changed.

You defined the firmament
and stored away half of the waters,
and clouds sift out
(rain) from their produce.

You also kindled a fire pit[8]
for those who hate You;
and You will save those who love You
from fire and water.

You commanded to uncover
the appearance of the radiance of the land;
You suppressed **the other waters**   the lower waters
and gathered them together in a pool.

The pasture of the earth
sprang up with Your word,
the herbage of grass sprouting
and the Garden of Eden for those who trust You.

The lamps of the firmament   stars
were ignited with Your breath
so that the seasons and times
may be ascertained with them;

---

7. That is, the measure of light and darkness (and hence day and night) were also created with the creation of light.

וְעֵת תַּשְׁגִּיחַ בָּהּ
עַמּוּדֶיהָ יִתְפַּלָּצוּן

גֵּרַשְׁתָּ אוֹפֶל
וַתִּקְרָא אוֹר
בְּשֵׁם קְרָאתָם
וּבְמִדָּה חֲקַקְתָּם

10 גְּבוּל לָהֶם שַׂמְתָּ
וּפוּר בֵּינוֹתָם
לְבַל יִגְרְעוּ חֹק
וּבַל יְשַׁנּוּ סֵדֶר

גָּדַרְתָּ רָקִיעַ
וְכָמַסְתָּ חֲצִי מַיִם
וּמִפֵּירוֹתָם
עָבִים יַחְשֹׁרוּ

גַּם מְדוּרַת אֵשׁ
לְשׂוֹנְאֶיךָ הִסַּקְתָּ
וּמֵאֵשׁ וּמִמַּיִם
אוֹהֲבֶיךָ תַצִּיל

דְּמוּת זִיו אֲדָמָה
יָעַצְתָּ לְגַלּוֹת
הַמִּים הַתַּחְתּוֹנִים   דִּכִּיתָ שְׁאָר מַיִם
צְרַרְתָּם בִּמְקוֹמָהּ

דִּשְׁאֵי אֶרֶץ
צָצוּ בְמַאֲמָרֶיךָ
דֶּשֶׁא עֵשֶׂב מַזְרִיעַ זֶרַע
וְגַן עֵדֶן לְחוֹסֶיהָ

דָּלְקוּ בְרוּחַ פִּיךָ
כּוֹכָבִים   נֵרוֹת רָקִיעַ
לְהַפְקֵד בָּם
תְּקוּפוֹת וְעִתִּים

---

8. See Isa 30:33, in which a fire pit is prepared for Assyria.

You showed for them
a way through windows,⁹
one for day and one for night
so that none may falter.

You brought forth from the waters
those that fly on the wing,
hosts of fish
and a phalanx of sea monsters.

You made, as a sign for **those who know You,**   Israel
those who are clad with scales,   pure fish
and a fleeing serpent¹⁰
for the meal in eternity.¹¹

Did You not make out of the earth
in great abundance
cattle and crawling creatures
and the beasts of the earth?

20 You set signs to be known
of edibility and purity,
and for the company of the righteous
You made the Behemoth fit to eat.

And when the world was built,
in wisdom,
and when the table was set,
and its bounty,

You resolved¹²
to invite a guest
and to feed him
Your choice food,

and to make him dominant
over the work of Your hands,
to be like God,
a judge and a ruler,

---

9. According to a midrash in Exod Rabbah 15:22, God created 365 windows for the sun and moon.
10. See Isa 27:1.

דֶּרֶךְ חַלּוֹנוֹת
לָהֶם הוֹרֵיתָ
זֶה בַּיּוֹם וְזֶה בַּלַּיְלָה
לְבַל יְאַחֲרוּ פָּעַם

הִשְׁרַצְתָּ מִמַּיִם
מְעוֹפְפֵי כָנָף
צִבְאוֹת דָּגִים
וְתֹקֶף תַּנִּינִים

ישראל

הִתְוֵיתָ לְיוֹדְעֶיךָ
עֲטוּיֵי קַשְׂקֶשֶׂת
וְנָחָשׁ בָּרִיחַ
לַאֲרוּחַת נֶצַח

דגים טהורים

הֲלֹא מֵאֲדָמָה
לָרוֹב הֶעֱדַפְתָּ
בְּהֵמָה וָרֶמֶשׂ
וְחַיְיתוֹ אָרֶץ

הוֹדַעְתָּ סִימָנֵי   20
מַאֲכָל לְטָהֳרָה
וְלַחֲבוּרַת צֶדֶק
בְּהֵמוֹת הִכְשַׁרְתָּ

וּבִהְבָנוֹת
עוֹלָם בְּחָכְמָה
וּבְהֶעֶרְךָ נַחַת
שֻׁלְחָן וָדֶשֶׁן

וַתִּשְׁקֹד
לְהַזְמִין אוֹרֵחַ
וּלְהַאֲכִילוֹ
טוּב מַאֲכָלָךְ

וּלְהַרְדּוֹתוֹ
בְּמַעֲשֵׂה יָדְךָ
הֱיוֹת כֵּאלֹהִים
שׁוֹטֵר וּמוֹשֵׁל

---

11. On this concept, see pages 31–33 in the Introduction above and the sources cited there.
12. Heb. *va-tishqod*.

and to prevail over angels,[13]
to rend the measured waters,[14]
to dim the lights,[15]
and to revive the sleepers.[16]

You erected a body,
sculpted from clay;
You wrought him in the recesses,[17]
in the image of Your vision.

You kindled the lamp
of his lifebreath within him,
for it will search
the dark places of his innermost parts.[18]

You endowed him with **an honored woman**　　　　　　　Eve
in the canopy of Eden;
with gold and precious stone,
You adorned his bed.[19]

You filled this man
with the spirit of understanding,
to crown with names[20]
all of Your creatures.

You, who live forever,
wished to present him with a test:
whether he could bear
a slight commandment:[21]

30   "Abstain from the tree of knowledge,
lest you be snared,[22]
but from the trees of produce
you may fill your belly."

---

13. Referring to Jacob; see Gen 32:29.
14. Cf. Isa 40:12.
15. See Josh 10:12–13.
16. Both Elijah and Elisha revived the dead.
17. See Ps 139:15–16.
18. See Prov 20:27.
19. This may be an allusion to Edenic intercourse; see the Introduction, above.

וְלָשׁוּר אֶל מַלְאָךְ
וְלִקְרוֹעַ מֵי שׁוּעָל
לְהַדְמִים מְאוֹרוֹת
וּלְהַחֲיוֹת דְּדוּמִים

זִכְרוֹן גּוּלְמוֹ
מֵחוֹמֶר קָרַצְתָּ
רִקַּמְתּוֹ בַסֵּתֶר
בְּצֶלֶם חֶזְיוֹנֶיךָ

זֹהַר נֵר נְשָׁמָה
בְּגֵווֹ עָרַכְתָּ
כִּי הִיא תְּחַפֵּשׂ
חֶשְׁכֵי חֲדָרָיו

חוה   זְבַדְתּוֹ **כְּבוּדָּה**
בְּתוֹךְ חֻפַּת עֵדֶן
בְּפָז וְאֶבֶן יְקָרָה
יְצוּעוֹ יִפִּיתָ

זֶה מִלֵּאתוֹ
רוּחַ תְּבוּנָה
לְכַלֵּל שֵׁמוֹת
לְכָל מִפְעָלֶיךָ

חַי עוֹלָמִים
לְבָחֳנוּ רָצִיתָ
בְּמִצְוָה קַלָּה
אִם יוּכַל קוּם

30   "חֲדַל מֵעֵץ הַדַּעַת
פֶּן תִּנָּקֵשׁ
וּמֵעֲצֵי תְנוּבָה
תְּמַלֵּא בִטְנֶךָ"

---

20. This seems to imply that Adam knew the animals' (preexisting) names and did not make them up for himself.

21. *Miṣvah qalah*; cf. m. Avot 4:2: "Run to fulfill a light commandment as much as a weighty one."

22. Here perhaps employing both meanings of the verb *nqš*, implying both being smitten and being tempted by the serpent. Cf. Deut 12:30.

You saw him alone,
and said, "I will make him a helpmeet;
if he perverts the way,[23]
she will be a stumbling block."

You caused him to fall into
a sweet slumber;
You set aside a rib,
and prepared flesh.

You breathed grace into her;
You adorned her with favor;
You brought them to the canopy
and graced them with blessings.

The crawling creature seduced her
into a deceptive error.
He led her like an ox to the slaughter
to violate the command.

She devoured and gave to devour
fruit she was warned not to taste;
they were disgracefully naked
and covered themselves with **that which withers.**[24]   fig leaves

The feet of **the one with (forked) tongue**   the snake
were taken away from him;
and his food was **altered**[25]   into dust
incurably, forever.[26]

He will be bitterly despised,
being crushed at the head;
and he will strike at the heel
of those who secretly use their tongues viciously.[27]

He was sentenced to death[28]
and wearying toil,

---

23. That is, Torah.
24. See Isa 34:4. The Hebrew, *novelet*, is a play on "disgracefully," *be-navlut*.
25. Mirsky cites Pirqe de-Rabbi Eliezer ch. 14: any food he ate would end up tasting like dust.
26. The snake, unlike all other creatures, will not have his punishment revoked in the world to come.

חֲזִיתוֹ לְבַד וְשַׂחְתָּ
"אֶעֱשֶׂה לּוֹ עֵזֶר
אִם יְסַלֵּף אוֹרַח
תְּהִי לוֹ לְמִכְשׁוֹל"

חֲטִיפַת שֵׁינָה
עָלָיו הִמְתַּקְתָּ
צֵלָע אָצַלְתָּ
וּבָשָׂר כּוֹנַנְתָּ

טִפַּחְתָּהּ בְּחֵן
יִפִּיתָהּ בְּחֶסֶד
הֲבֵאתָם בְּחוּפָּה
חֲנַנְתָּם בְּרָכוֹת

טָעוּת כָּזָב
רֶמֶשׂ הִשִּׂיאָהּ
מְשָׁכָהּ כְּשׁוֹר לַטֶּבַח
לְהָנִיא צִוּוּי

טַעַם פְּרִי הֻזְהֲרוּ
לָעֲטָה וְהִלְעִיטָהּ
הֹעֲרָמוּ בְּנַבְלוּת
וְכֻסּוּ **בִּנוֹבֶלֶת**   עלי התאנה

טוֹרְדוּ פַעֲמֵי
בַּעַל הַלָּשׁוֹן   הנחש
וְנֶהְפַּךְ מַאֲכָלוֹ   לעפר
לְבַל יֵרָפֵא נֶצַח

יוּשְׁתַּן בְּאֵיבָה
לְהָרֵץ בָּרֹאשׁ
וְהוּא יְשׁוּף עָקֵב
לְמַלְשְׁנִי בַּסֵּתֶר

יָצָא דִין לַמָּוֶת
וִיגִיעַת עָמָל

---

27. Referring perhaps to those Israelites who spoke against God and Moses in the wilderness in Num 21:4–9 and who were bitten by snakes. See Tanḥuma Ḥuqqat 12, in which it is said that the snake, who used evil speech (lit., "evil tongue"), is the instrument of punishment against those who used evil speech against God.

28. Lit., "A death sentence was issued."

and she to birth pangs
and **the arid land** to thorns.   the earth

His urge was inclined
to desire for his mate;
and she sent forth her youngsters,
the worker and the shepherd.   Cain and Abel

40   They honored, with an offering,
the Maker of all,   God
the elder with the earth's fruit,   Cain
and **the younger** with the fat of the flock.   Abel

When You regarded, Exalted One,
the humility of **the lowly**,[29]   Abel
You preferred his offering,
and rejected **the fragrance** of the brother.   Cain's incense

He suppressed his mercy,
and did not conquer his inclination;
he raised his hand against the Image
and originated bloodshed.

When You heard, You who requite,
the voice of blood crying out,
You punished him with ceaseless wandering
and vain and empty toil.

When he confessed,
You engraved a sign for him
so that his murderer
would be punished sevenfold.

The generation of Enosh began[30]
to anger You, O God,
displacing Your glory
and calling on the name of an idol.

---

29. Cf. Ps 138:6, there referring to David, who, like Abel, was a shepherd (Mirsky).

	וְהִיא לְקוֹשִׁי לֵידָה
הָאֲדָמָה	וְצִוָּה לְשָׁמִיר
	יִצְרוּ הַוְרְגַּל
	לְתַאֲוַת רִבְעוֹ
	וְשִׁלְחָה עֲוִילֶיהָ
קין והבל	**עוֹבֵד וְרוֹעֶה**
	יַקְרִיבוּ בְמִנְחָה 40
הָאֵל	**לְיוֹצֵר הַכֹּל**
קין	**רַב** בִּפְרִי אֶרֶץ
הבל	וְרַךְ בְּחֶלְבֵי צֹאן
	כְּהַבִּיטְךָ רָם
הבל	**דְּכָאוּת שָׁפָל**
	שָׁעִיתָ בְּמִנְחָתוֹ
מנחת קין	**וְקַצְתָּ בְּנִיחֹחַ אָח**
	כָּפָה רַחֲמָיו
	וְלֹא כָבַשׁ יֵצֶר
	שָׁלַח יָד בְּצֶלֶם
	הֵחֵל שְׁפוֹךְ דָּם
	כְּשָׁמְעֲךָ דּוֹרֵשׁ
	קוֹל זַעֲקַת דָּם
	עֲנַשְׁתּוֹ בְּנָע וָנָד
	וִיגִיעַת רִיק וָהֶבֶל
	כְּהִתְוַדּוֹתוֹ
	אוֹת לוֹ חַקּוֹתָ
	לְהָשִׁיב לְהוֹרְגוֹ
	נָקָם שִׁבְעָתַיִם
	לְהַכְעִיסְךָ אֵל
	הֵחֵל דּוֹר אֱנוֹשׁ
	לְהָמִיר כְּבוֹדְךָ
	וְלִקְרוֹא בְּשֵׁם אֱלִיל

---

30. Here, as in *Azkir Gevurot*, line 68, the verb *ḥl* carries connotations of sacrilege.

For the sea You set the sand
as a boundary not to be transgressed;[31]
but You called it to destroy them
because they called (the idols) by name.

Those filled with lawlessness
were attracted to corruption;
they became fat and sleek
and said to God, "Leave us alone!"

Therefore You raged against them
with the springs of the deep,
and upon them You poured
a channel full of water.

Among them You found
a righteous, innocent man;   Noah
You sheltered him in Your tabernacle[32]
until the rage had passed.

50   From him you made many
families of **all creation,**   humankind
and when You were comforted by him,[33]
You said, "I will no more curse."

The residents of **Shinar**   Babel
transgressed against Your name,
climbing up to the throne
to make a name for themselves.

You fulfilled their wish,
making of them a mockery;
You scattered them in every direction,
perverting their language.

A lamp was lit in the chaos—
the father of a multitude appeared;   Abraham
and by the flame of his fire
ran those who falter.

---

31. Cf. Jer 5:22.
32. Heb. *be-sukkah*; cf. Ps 27:5. NJV translates the term as "pavilion."

לַיָּם חוֹל שַׂמְתָּ
חֹק לֹא יַעֲבוֹר
קְרָאתוֹ לְאָבְדָם
תְּמוּר קָרְאוּ בְשֵׁם

לָמְדוּ הַעֲוֵה
מְלֵאֵי חָמָס
שָׁמְנוּ עָשְׁתוּ
וְאָמְרוּ לָאֵל "סוּר"

לָכֵן זְעַמְתָּם
בְּמַעְיְנוֹת תְּהוֹם
וּפֶלֶג מָלֵא מַיִם
עֲלֵיהֶם שָׁפַכְתָּ

מֵהֶם מָצָאתָ
צַדִּיק תָּמִים
צְפַנְתּוֹ בְּסוּכָּה
עַד יַעֲבוֹר זָעַם

נח

מִמֶּנּוּ הָעֲצַמְתָּ 50
מִשְׁפְּחוֹת כָּל יְצִיר
וּבְהִנָּחֶמְךָ בּוֹ
"לֹא אֲקַלֵּל" שָׁחֹתָ

האנושות

מָרוּ בְשִׁמְךָ
יוֹשְׁבֵי שִׁנְעָר
לָרוּם עַד כֵּס
לַעֲשׂוֹת לָמוֹ שֵׁם

בבל

מִלֵּאתָ חֶפְצָם
בַּהֲלִעִיגְךָ לָמוֹ
נְפַצְתָּם בְּכָל רוּחַ
בְּסַלֶּפְךָ לְשׁוֹנָם

נֵר עָרוּךְ בַּתֹּהוּ
אַב הֲמוֹן נוֹדַע
וּלְשָׁבִיב אִשּׁוֹ
רָצוּ נִכְשָׁלִים

אברהם

---

33. When Noah brought an offering.

He announced to those astray
the straight path:
"Rely on the living God—
what good can an idol do you?"

He separated from his homeland
and was attracted to follow you;
and You presented Yourself to him
in **fire and war**.[34]   Nimrod's furnace

He wallowed in the blood of the covenant,
and his offspring after him,
for **it** will save   the covenant of circumcision
those who are carried from **the pit.**   Israel; Gehenna

You made him joyful
with a **lovingly tended fruit**[35]   Isaac
when he said: "I am deprived
and my roots have dried up."

He bore, like a hero,
the burden of ordeals;
You bade him to slaughter
his only son, and he prevailed.

The father was glad to bind,
and the son to be bound,
for by it **the burdened**   Israel
will be justified in judgment.

60   You placed a ram as his atonement,
and he was considered meritorious.
On this day (may we) hear:
"I have found ransom."[36]

> As it is written in Your Torah: And Abraham named that site Adonai-yireh, whence the present saying, "On the mount of the Lord there is vision" (Gen 22:14).

---

34. According to a widespread legend, Nimrod had the young Abraham cast into a fiery furnace, which Abraham survived. See Gen Rabbah 38:13 and b. Pesaḥim 118a; cf. Ginzberg, *Legends*, 1:198–203 and notes.

נְתִיב מֵישָׁרִים
הוֹדִיעַ לַתּוֹעִים
"הִשָּׁעֵנוּ בְּאֵל חַי
וּמַה יּוֹעִיל פֶּסֶל"

נָטַשׁ מְגוּרָיו
וְנִמְשַׁךְ אַחֲרֶיךָ
וּנְמְצֵאתָ לוֹ
בָּאֵשׁ וּבַמִּלְחָמֶת   כבשן נמרוד

נִתְבּוֹסֵס בְּדַם בְּרִית
וְזַרְעוֹ אַחֲרָיו   ברית מילה
כִּי הִיא תַצִּיל
עֲמוּסָיו מְשַׁחַת   ישראל; גיהנום

שִׂמַּחְתּוֹ
בִּפְרִי שַׁעֲשׁוּעִים   יצחק
בְּאָמְרוֹ "אֻמְלַלְתִּי
וְיַבְשׁוּ שָׁרָשַׁי"

סָבַל כְּגִבּוֹר
כֹּבֶד נִסְיוֹנוֹת
וּבִיחִידוֹ לִטְבּוֹחַ
בְּחַנְתּוֹ וְעָמָד

שָׂשׂ אָב לַעֲקוֹד
וּבֵן לְהֵעָקֵד
כִּי בָהּ יִצְדְּקוּ
עֲמוּסָיו בְּתוֹכַחַת   ישראל

שַׂמְתָּ כָּפְרוֹ אַיִל
וְנֶחְשַׁב לוֹ צֶדֶק
בְּיוֹם זֶה נַקְשִׁיב
מָצָאתִי כֹפֶר

ככתוב בתורתך ויקרא אברהם שם המקום ההוא יי יראה אשר יאמר היום בהר יי יראה

---

35. Cf. Isa 5:7.
36. Job 33:24.

Before You taught
the law from Your right hand,
an innocent man observed it   Jacob
and guarded its gates.

When You cast sleep upon him
in a dream, he found You,
and you promised him
that You would be his stronghold.

You sheltered him[37]
from the sword of **the pursuer**,   Esau
and You caused the **prince**   the angel with whom
of a flaming fire to become weak before him.   Jacob wrestled

You wreathed him
with **a number of banners**,   twelve tribes
and like grains (of sand) in the sea,
You increased his community.

You tithed a **youngster**
from his tribes to serve You   Levi
in return for tithing his fortune
for You at the pillar.[38]

You caused the fruit of the righteous to flourish
from the tribe of Levi:
Amram and his sons
like a vine and its shoots.

You watched over Your flock
with a **faithful man**,   Moses
saving it from **Zoan**   Egypt
passing it through measured water.

You ornamented him for a sanctification of **days**[39]   six days
and with the covering of a cloud,

---

37. Heb. *sakota*, possibly connoting a tabernacle (*sukkah*).
38. The phrase refers to the pillar Jacob erected at Bethel in Gen 28:18.

	עַד לֹא הוֹרַתָּ
	דָּת מִיָּמִין
יעקב	נָצְרָהּ אִישׁ תָּם
	וְשָׁקַד דְּלָתֶיהָ
	עֵת הִרְדַּמְתּוֹ
	בַּמָּלוֹן מְצָאָהּ
	וַתַּבְטִיחֵהוּ
	הֱיוֹת לוֹ לְמִשְׂגָּב
	עָלָיו סַכּוֹתָ
עשיו	מֵחֶרֶב רוֹדֵף
המלאך שיעקוב נאבק עמו	וְשַׂר אֵשׁ לוֹהֵט
	לְפָנָיו הֶחֱלַשְׁתָּ
	עֲטַרְתּוֹ
שנים עשר שבטים	בְּמִסְפַּר דְּגָלִים
	וְכִמְעוֹת יַמִּים
	קְהָלָיו הִרְבֵּיתָ
לוי	פֶּרַח מִשְּׁבָטָיו
	לְשָׁרֶתְךָ עִשַּׂרְתָּ
	תְּמוּר עֲשָׂרוֹ לָהּ
	הוּנוֹ בְּמַצֶּבֶת
	פְּרִי צַדִּיק הַצְּמַחְתָּ
	מִגֶּזַע לֵוִי
	עַמְרָם וְנִינָיו
	כְּגֶפֶן וְשָׂרִיגֶיהָ
	פָּקַדְתָּ צֹאנְךָ
משה	בְּיַד נֶאֱמָן
מצרים	לְחַלְּצָהּ מְצוֹעָן
	וּלְהַעֲבִירָהּ בְּשׁוֹעָל
שישה ימים	פֵּאַרְתּוֹ בְּקִדּוּשׁ יוֹם
	וּבְסִכּוּךְ עָנָן

39. On this phrase, see Mirsky, *Yose ben Yose*, 187.

	until he took **a captive**,[40]	Torah
	taking **the lady of the house**[41] as a spoil.	Torah
70	You have wreathed **Your holy one**	Aaron

with a crown of priesthood,
and he will bequeath it
to his children after him,

sheltered and preserved
for generations forever,
and those who disgrace their honor[42]
will be swallowed up and afflicted.

The Rock sustained them
with an abundance of gifts,
and from the table of the King
You prepared their food.

You commanded them to dwell
at the gates of Your tent,
to ordain them
for seven days.[43]

As it is written: Everything done today, the Lord has commanded to be done to make expiation for you (Lev 8:34).

75	The **holy ones** separated	priests
	a man from his abode,	the high priest

sequestering him in the chamber,
as in the law of ordination.[44]

They washed him and cleansed him
with water of expiation[45]
in place of the sprinkling of blood
and the anointing oil.[46]

---

40. This figure is based on Ps 68:19, "you went up to the heights, having taken captives," which is taken to refer to Moses receiving the Torah from heaven; see b. Shabbat 89a.
  41. Cf. Ps 68:13.
  42. Referring especially to Korah and his allies in Num 16.
  43. Referring to priestly ordination, according to Lev 8:35.

התורה	עַד יִשְׁבֶּה שֶׁבִי
תורה	וְיִשְׁלוֹל נְוַת בָּיִת
	צִיץ עֲטֶרֶת כְּהֻנָּה 70
אהרן	לִקְדוֹשְׁךָ הָעֲטֵיתָ
	וַיַּנְחִילֶנָּה
	לְבָנָיו אַחֲרָיו
	צְפוּנָה שְׁמוּרָה
	לְדוֹרוֹת עוֹלָם
	וּבוֹזֵי כְבוֹדָם
	יְבוֹלָעוּ וְיִנּוֹגָעוּ
	צוּר הֶעֱנַקְתָּם
	רֹב מַתָּנוֹת
	וּמִשֻּׁלְחַן מֶלֶךְ
	מַאֲכָלָם הֲכִינוֹתָ
	צִוִּיתָם שֶׁבֶת
	פִּתְחֵי אֹהָלֶיךָ
	לְמַלֵּא יָדָם
	יָמִים שִׁבְעָה

ככתוב כאשר עשה ביום הזה צוה יי לעשות לכפר עליכם

הכוהנים	קְדוֹשִׁים יַבְדִּילוּ 75
הכוהן הגדול	אִישׁ מִנַּוֵהוּ
	לְעָצְרוֹ בְלִשְׁכָּה
	כְּחֹק מִלּוּאִים
	קִדְּשׁוּהוּ וְחִטְּאוּהוּ
	בְּמֵימֵי נִדָּה
	תְּמוּר חַטּוּי דָּם
	וְשֶׁמֶן הַמִּשְׁחָה

44. The law of sequestration of the priest (m. Yoma 1:1) is derived by analogy from the law of ordination in Lev 8:34.

45. Heb. *ḥit'uhu*. See Mirsky, *Yose ben Yose*, 188: During those seven days they sprinkled him with water from the ashes of sin offerings in order to purify him. See y. Yoma 1:1 (38c), b. Yoma 4a; cf. m. Parah 3:1.

46. Of the priestly initiation; cf. Lev 8:30.

Discerning captains
joined him in fellowship
as brothers dwelling together[47]
to teach him **the order.**　　　　　　　　　order of sacrifice

He woke early, tossed blood,
offered incense, and trimmed lamps,
the first (to offer) the head and hind leg,
and the first to take a portion.[48]

The sacrifices of his atonement
and the sacrifices of the community[49]
were led before him
to acquaint him with them.

80　They withheld from him
excess of sleep and food
on the eve of forgiveness
lest he be lulled into emission.

The heads of his tribe
joined him in fellowship
to adjure him by the name
in the chamber of incense.

Tears ran down his eyes
that he was considered a simpleton,
and they broke into weeping
because it was necessary.

If he was wise,
they spoke before him
delighting him with Midrash[50]
and discoursing on holy scriptures.

If he was a boor,
they would occupy him
by recounting tales
of ancient kings.

---

47. Ps 133:1.
48. A paraphrase of m. Yoma 1:2.

סדר הקרבנות

קְצִינֵי מְזֻמָּה
הֵם נֶעֱמְתוּ לוֹ
כְּשֶׁבֶת אַחִים יַחַד
לְהוֹרוֹתוֹ **סֵדֶר**

קוֹרֵץ וְזוֹרֵק
מַקְטִיר וּמֵטִיב
רִאשׁוֹן בְּרֹאשׁ וָרֶגֶל
וְרֹאשׁ לִיטּוֹל חֵלֶק

רְצוּי זְבָחָיו
וְזִבְחֵי עֵדָה
לְפָנָיו יוֹבִילוּ
הֱיוֹת רָגִיל בָּם

רֹב שֵׁינָה וְאוֹכֶל   80
מִמֶּנּוּ יַמְעִיטוּ
עֶרֶב יוֹם סְלִיחָה
פֶּן יוֹרְגַּל לְקֶרִי

רָאשֵׁי שִׁבְטוֹ
הֵם נֶעֱמְתוּ לוֹ
לְהַשְׁבִּיעוֹ בְּשֵׁם
בַּעֲלִיַּת רַקָּחִים

רַד בִּדְמָעוֹת
כִּי נֶחְשַׁב לְפֶתִי
וְהֵם בְּכִי הִזִּילוּ
כִּי לְכָךְ הוּצְרְכוּ

שַׁעֲשׁוּעַ מִדְרָשׁ
וְהֶגֶא כִּתְבֵי קֹדֶשׁ
אִם יֶחְכַּם
לְפָנָיו יְשׂוֹחֵחוּ

שִׁנּוּן שִׂיחוֹת
מְלָכִים קַדְמוֹנִים
אִם יִהְיֶה בַּעַר
בָּם יַעֲסִיקוּהוּ

49. The animals of the priest's individual atonement, and those for the people of Israel.
50. According to Ps 119:92.

85 The young priests
Sang songs to him
By mouth and by pleasant laughter[51]
and by the sound of the middle finger.

The masses in [the city] full of people[52]   Jerusalem
raised a tumult:
For because of their voice
his sleep will disperse.

Those who offered the fat
assembled since midnight
to observe the commandment
of sacrifice at night.

A lottery was decreed
to be prepared for them
lest they push (someone) off
when they wanted to ascend the ramp.[53]

Those who stood in the court
cast lots at once
for performing the Tamid,
clearing the inner altar, and the lamps.

90 Those who desired blessings
from **the Guide**,   God
new priests, would cast
a lottery for the incense.

The prompt faithful
were sent to the east,
to see if the sun's light
had appeared for the slaughter.

His brothers accompanied him
to the outer place of immersion
where those who came to the court
were purified.

---

51. That is, not on musical instruments, according to y. Yoma 1:7. See Mirsky, *Yose ben Yose*, 190, and Malachi, "Makkin Lefanav."

	שִׁיר יְשׁוֹרְרוּ לוֹ 85
	פִּרְחֵי כְהוּנָּה
	בְּפֶה וּבְחֵיךְ עָרֵב
	וּבִנְעִימַת צְרָדָה
	שָׁאוֹן יַגְבִּירוּ
ירושלים	הֲמוֹן **רַבָּתִי עָם**
	כִּי מְקוֹלָם
	שְׁנָתוֹ תְפוֹרָר
	תּוֹרְמֵי דֶשֶׁן
	מֵחֲצוֹת נוֹעָדוּ
	לְקַיֵּם מִצְוַת חֹק
	עֲבוֹדַת לָיְלָה
	תַּקָּנַת פַּיִס
	לָהֶם הוּכָנָה
	פֶּן יֵהָדְפוּן
	בִּרִיצָתָם לַכֶּבֶשׁ
	תֵּכֶף לוֹ יָפִיסוּ
	עוֹמְדֵי עֲזָרָה
	לְמַעֲשֶׂה תָּמִיד
	וְדִשּׁוּן פְּנִימִי וְנֵרוֹת
	תְּאֵיבֵי בְרָכוֹת 90
האל	מִפִּי **מוֹרָה**
	לָשִׂים קְטֹרֶת
	חֲדָשִׁים יָפִיסוּ
	אֱמוּנֵי עִתִּים
	יִשְׁוֹלַח לַקָּדִים
	אִם בָּרָק נוֹגַהּ
	יָפֶן לִשְׁחִיטָה
	אֶחָיו יְלַוּוּהוּ
	לְבֵית טְבִילָה חוּצָה
	אֲשֶׁר שָׁם יְטוֹהֲרוּ
	בָּאֵי עֲזָרָה

---

52. According to Lam 1:1.
53. See m. Yoma 2:2.

They behaved toward him
with honor and dignity
and spread a screen
between him and the people.

His own clothes
he took off quickly,
and went down and immersed
and went up and dried himself.

95 With woven linen breeches
like those of horsemen
he first covered
the roundings of his thighs.[54]

In them he would cover
the licentious **sin of Shittim**[55]   sexual sin
and reveal to us
the merit of **the locked garden.**[56]   chastity

With a double linen tunic
he covered his flesh
from the palm of his hand
to the heel of his foot.

The One whose glory fills the earth,
looked upon them
and allayed the fear of
(Joseph's) sleeved tunic.[57]

The belt, the sash,
was different on the fast day,
for it was all linen,
not woven with mixed fabric.

100 He wrapped it and rolled it
in every direction

---

54. Cf. Song 7:2.
55. According to Num 25:1.
56. Cf. Song 4:12.

אָז יִנְהֲגוּ בוֹ
גְּדוּלָה וְכָבוֹד
וְיִפְרְשׂוּ מָסָךְ
בֵּינוֹ לְבֵין עָם

אֶת כְּסוּת עַצְמוֹ
יְמַהֵר וְיִפְשׁוֹט
וְיֵרֵד וְיִטְבּוֹל
וְיַעַל וְיִסְתַּפֵּג

בְּשִׁבּוּץ מִכְנְסֵי בַד   95
כְּעֵין פָּרָשִׁים
תְּחִלָּה יְכַסֶּה
חֲמוּקֵי יְרֵכָיו

גילוי עריות   בָּם יְכַסֶּה
פֶּשַׁע עֲרָוַת שִׂטִּים
וִיגַלֶּה לָנוּ
צניעות   זְכוּת גַּן נָעוּל

בְּכֶפֶל כְּתֹנֶת בַּד
יְכַסֶּה שְׁאֵרוֹ
מִפַּסֵּי יָד
עַד עִקְּבוֹת רֶגֶל

האל   בָּם יְפָן
מְלֹא הָאָרֶץ כְּבוֹדוֹ
וְיָסִיר דַּאֲגַת
כְּתֹנֶת הַפַּסִּים

גַּם מֵיזַח אַבְנֵט
יְשַׁנֶּה בְּיוֹם צוֹם
כִּי כֻלּוֹ בַד
בְּלִי אָרוּג כִּלְאַיִם

גּוֹלֵל וּמַקִּיף   100
וּמְשַׁלְשְׁלוֹ לְכָל עֵבֶר

---

57. The plain linen tunic atones for the sins of Joseph's brothers. The passage plays on the words *pase yad* (palms) and *ketonet passim* (sleeved tunic).

for the girded belts
of the figures of Chaldeans.⁵⁸

He was great and resplendent
in the [wreath] of kingship
when he raised his head
in the linen headdress.

Lo, with **that** he would cleanse   the headdress
the taint of **the loose-haired woman**⁵⁹   the suspected adulteress
and would take away the shame
of the harlot's hardheadedness.⁶⁰

His likeness was like **Tarshish**,   sea
like the look of the firmament
when he put on the blue robe,
woven like a honeycomb.

Its upper opening
was plaited like mail,
surrounding it
so that it could not tear.

105   Fastened to the hem
were colored pomegranates
and golden bells
encircling it.

When the **Prominent One**⁶¹ heard   God
the sound of his steps,
he atoned for the sound
of the slanderer's voice.

They wrapped him in an ephod,
(as thick as) felt,
woven of gold and crimson,
and fine linen blue and purple.

---

58. To atone for Israel's worship of Chaldean images (Ezek 23:14–15).
59. See the ritual of the suspected adulteress (*sotah*) in Num 5:11–29.

בְּעַד חֲגוֹרֵי אֵזוֹר
צַלְמֵי כַשְׂדִּים

גָּדוֹל וְנֶהְדָּר
בְּנֵזֶר הַמְּלוּכָה
בְּהַגְבִּיהוֹ רֹאשׁ
בְּמִצְנֶפֶת הַשֵּׁשׁ

במצנפת גַּם בָּהּ יָנָקֶה
הנואפת דּוֹפִי **פְּרִיעַת רֹאשׁ**
וְיַעֲבִיר כְּלִימּוֹת
אֵשֶׁת זְנוּת מֵצַח

ים דְּמוּתוֹ כְּ**תַרְשִׁישׁ**
כְּמַרְאֶה רָקִיעַ
בְּלָבְשׁוֹ מְעִיל תְּכֵלֶת
אָרוּג כְּכַוֶּרֶת

דַּלַּת שְׂפָתוֹ
גְּדִילָה כְתַחְרָא
מוּקֶּפֶת לוֹ
בְּלִי לְהִקָּרֵעַ

דָּבֵק לְשׁוּלָיו 105
רִמּוֹנֵי צְבָעִים
וּפַעֲמוֹנֵי פָז
עָגוֹל סָבִיב

אלוהים דָּגוּל בְּשָׁמְעוֹ
קוֹל פְּעָמָיו
מְכַפֵּר בְּעַד קוֹל
מוֹצִיא שֵׁם רַע

הֶעֱטוּהוּ בְאֵפוֹד
דּוֹמֶה כְּמִין לְבָד
אָרוּג פָּז וְשָׁנִי
וָשֵׁשׁ וּתְכֵלֶת וְאַרְגָּמָן

---

60. Lit., "forehead," a biblical figure for brazenness; see Jer 3:3.
61. Song 5:10.

On his shoulders were there not
two lapis lazuli,
and on them the names of the tribes,
like the number of banners?

As called by name,[62]
they were carved with letters,
engraved by the shamir,
which was formed at Creation.[63]

110 With them he justified
those who were ensnared by the ephod[64]
and exchanged God
for a bull eating grass.

And set at the heart
was the breastpiece, folded,
a span by a span square,
woven like the ephod.

And on it were rows of stones,
one for each tribe,
encircled with gold,
engraved by the shamir.

And it was bound with rings
so that it could not come loose;
it was covered like plates of armor
with braided chains.

And He who loves justice
called it "justice,"[65]   the "breastpiece of judgment"
to bring to justice
those who pervert justice.

115 He placed a wreath of gold
on a blue cap[66]

---

62. The names of the tribes are arranged on the stones as they were called by God to appear in the Temple; see Mirsky's note here, citing y. Sotah 7:4 (21d).

63. The creature known as the shamir, the only thing that could engrave the names of the tribes on the stones, was created during the six days of creation; see b. Sotah 48b.

הֲלֹא בִכְתֵפָיו
שְׁתֵּי אַבְנֵי שׁוֹהַם
וּבָם שְׁמוֹת שְׁבָטִים
כְּמִסְפַּר דְּגָלִים

הַגּוּיִים בַּשֵּׁמוֹת
חֲצוּיִים בָּאוֹתוֹת
בְּפִתּוּחַ שָׁמִיר
נוֹצַר מִבְּרֵאשִׁית

הִצְדִּיק בָּם   110
לְנוֹקְשֵׁי בָאֵפוֹד
וּמַחֲלִיפֵי אֵל
בְּשׁוֹר אוֹכֵל עֵשֶׂב

וְקָבוּעַ בְּלֵב חֹשֶׁן
כָּפוּל רָבוּעַ
זֶרֶת עַל זֶרֶת
אָרוּג כָּאֵפוֹד

וּבוֹ טוּרֵי אֶבֶן
אַחַת לְכָל שֵׁבֶט
מוּסַבּוֹת פָּז
חֲקוּקוֹת בְּשָׁמִיר

וַיְרַכְּסֵם בְּטַבָּעוֹת
כְּחֹק לֹא יִזַּח
וּבְשַׁרְשְׁרוֹת גַּבְלוּת
דְּבָקֵימוֹ יְכַסֶּה

וְאוֹהֵב מִשְׁפָּט
קְרָאוֹ **מִשְׁפָּט**   חושן המשפט
לְהַצְדִּיק בְּמִשְׁפָּט
מְעֻוְּתֵי מִשְׁפָּט

זֵר זָהָב שָׁם   115
עַל תְּכֵיפַת הָאֵפוֹד

---

64. Who worshiped the ephod idolatrously (Judg 8:27)
65. Exod 28:15.
66. Following Mirsky's suggested reading; on the cap, see b. Ḥullin 138a.

from ear to ear
opposite the headdress.

The remembrance of the esteemed Name
is engraved on the frontlet;
he placed it on his forehead;
it was attached to the diadem.

Intentional impurity of blood, flesh,
fat, the handful of incense, and libation
is atoned by the frontlet
so that they can arise[67] favorably.

The eight (garments) were designated
for **him who is greater than his brothers**[68]   the high priest
when he served
and when he inquired with the Urim.

120   He girded himself with them correctly
and put them on according to order;
then he washed
his hands and his feet.

His assistants brought him
the daily morning offering.
He slaughtered it
and collected its blood in the bowl.

He meted out a ***peras*** and offered it,   a measure of incense
and repaired the lamps,
and sacrificed the head and pieces,
cakes and libation.

He hurried to the Parvah chamber,
to the place of holy immersion,
and washed his hands
and feet and undressed.

He immersed and dried himself
and put on the linen vestments,

---

67. On the altar.

מֵאָז וְעַד אָז
מוּל פְּנֵי הַמִּצְנֶפֶת

זֵכֶר שֵׁם נַעֲרָץ
חָקוּק עַל צִיץ
נִתְּנוֹ עַל מֵצַח
מְחֻבָּר לַנֵּזֶר

זְדוֹן טֻמְאַת דָּם
וְקוֹמֶץ וּנְסָכִים
יְרַצּוּ בַצִּיץ
וְיַעֲלוּ לְרָצוֹן

זִמְּנוּ שְׁמוֹנָה
לְגָדוֹל מֵאֶחָיו
לְשָׁרֵת וְלִשְׁאוֹל
עֵצָה בָּאוּרִים

הכוהן הגדול

120 חֲגָרָם כַּדָּת
לְבָשָׁם כַּסֵּדֶר
וַיְקַדֵּשׁ
יָדָיו וְרַגְלָיו

חֲנִיכָיו יַגִּישׁוּ
אֶת תְּמִיד הַשַּׁחַר
קְרָצוֹ וְקִבֵּל
דָּמוֹ בְּמִזְרָק

מנת קטורת

חִלֵּק **פְּרָס** וְהִקְטִיר
וְנֵרוֹת הֵטִיב
הִקְרִיב רֹאשׁ וָנֵתַח
חֲבִיתִים וָנֶסֶךְ

חָשׁ לְגַב פַּרְוָה
לְבֵית טְבִילַת קֹדֶשׁ
וְקִדֵּשׁ יָדָיו וְרַגְלָיו
וּפָשַׁט

טָבַל וְסִפֵּג
וְעָטָה כְּלֵי בַד

68. Lev 21:10.

and again he washed
his hands and his feet.

Pure, he approached
the bull designated for him,
which stood between
the portico and the altar.

His secrets were revealed
before the Creator of all;
he could not conceal sin,
for thus he would receive mercy.

The Good One forgave him
when he confessed
and placed his hands
on the bull firmly.

And thus he would say: "O Lord, I have sinned, I have done wrong, I have transgressed before You, I and my household. O, by the Lord, forgive the sins and iniquities and transgressions that I have committed against you, I and my household, as it is written in the Torah of Moses, Your servant: 'For on this day atonement shall be made for you to cleanse you of all your sins; before the Lord—'" (Lev. 16:30). And when the priests and the people standing in the court and serving in the Sanctuary heard the glorious explicit name coming forth from the mouth of the high priest in holiness and purity, they would kneel, prostrate themselves, and fall to their faces and say: "Blessed is the name of His Majesty's glory for ever and ever." He would also intend to finish the name while facing those saying the blessing and say to them, "You shall be pure." And You, in your great beneficence, arouse Your mercy and pardon Your pious man [the high priest].

The prefect and the head of the father's house[69]
encircled him
and he entered the inner gate
at the east of the court.

---

69. The head of the one of the families of the priestly division in attendance at the Temple; cf. the Introduction, above, and *Shiʿvat Yamim*.

וַיְקַדֵּשׁ עוֹד
יָדָיו וְרַגְלָיו

טָהוֹר נִגַּשׁ
אֵצֶל פַּר מָמוֹנוֹ
הָעוֹמֵד
בֵּין הָאוּלָם וְלַמִּזְבֵּחַ

טְמוּנוֹתָיו יְגַלֶּה
לְיוֹצֵר הַכֹּל
וְלֹא יְכַסֶּה פֶּשַׁע
כִּי בְכֵן יְרוּחָם

טוֹב יִסָּלַח לוֹ
בְּהִתְוַדּוֹתוֹ
בְּסָמְכוֹ יָדָיו
עַל פָּרוֹ בְּכוֹבֶד

וכך היה אומר: אנא השם. חטאתי, עויתי ופשעתי לפניך אני וביתי אנא בשם כפר נא לחטאים ולעונות ולפשעים שחטאתי ושעויתי ושפשעתי לפניך אני וביתי ככתוב בתורת משה עבדך כי ביום הזה יכפר עליכם לטהר אתכם מכל חטאתיכם לפני יהוה והכהנים והעם העומדים בעזרה כשהיו שומעים את השם הנכבד והנורא מפרש יוצא מפי כהן גדול בקדושה ובטהרה היו כורעים ומשתחוים ונופלין על פניהם ואומרים: ברוך שם כבוד מלכותו לעולם ועד: ואף הוא היה מכוין לגמור את השם כנגד המברכים ואומר להם תטהרו ואתה בטובך הגדול תעורר רחמיך וסלח לאיש חסידך:

יַקִּיפוּהוּ סְגָן
וְרֹאשׁ בֵּית אָב
וּבָא לְשַׁעַר הַתִּיכוֹן
לְמִזְרַח עֲזָרָה

There they would find
two goats of the people
and the golden lots
placed in the urn.

He shook it
and raised up the lots:
One for the Esteemed One
and one for Azazel.

If the lot of the goat for the Lord
came up in his right hand,
the prefect would call in a loud voice
joyously, "Raise your right hand!"

If it came up
in his left hand,
the head of the father's house would say,
"Raise your left hand!"

140 When he placed them
on the two goats,
he called out in a loud voice,
"This is for the Ḥatta't."

He directed himself to
the second bull
to confess for sin,
transgression, and offense.

He pressed his hands
heavily between its horns
to confess again
for the transgression of his family and clan.

And thus he would say: "O Lord, I have sinned, I have done wrong, I have transgressed before You, I and my household and the children of Aaron, Your holy people. O, by the Lord, forgive the sins and iniquities and transgressions that I have committed against you, I and my household and the children of Aaron, Your holy people, as it is written in the Torah of Moses, Your servant:

יִמְצָא שָׁם
שְׁנֵי שְׂעִירֵי עַם
וְגוֹרָלוֹת זָהָב
נְתוּנִים בְּקַלְפֵּי

יִטְרוֹף בָּהּ
וְיַעַל גּוֹרָלוֹת
זֶה לְשֵׁם נַעֲרָץ
וְזֶה לַעֲזָאזֵל

יְמִינוֹ אִם תַּעַל
גּוֹרַל שָׂעִיר שֵׁם
סְגַן יַשְׁמִיעַ לוֹ בְּגִיל
הַגְבַּהּ יְמִינֶךָ

כְּהַעֲלוֹתוֹ בְּיַד
הַשְּׂמָאלִית
רֹאשׁ בֵּית אָב יָשִׂיחַ
הַגְבַּהּ שְׂמֹאלָךְ

140 כְּהִנָּתְנָם
עַל שְׁנֵי הַשְּׂעִירִים
קוֹרֵא בְּקוֹל רָם
זֶה לְשֵׁם חַטָּאת

כִּוֵּן וּבָא לוֹ
אֵצֶל פָּרוֹ שְׁנִיָּה
לְהִתְוַדּוֹת בְּעַד חֵטְא
עָוֹן וָפֶשַׁע

כָּבַשׁ יָדָיו
בֵּין קַרְנָיו בְּכוֹבֶד
לְהִתְוַדּוֹת עוֹד
בְּעַד עָוֹן בֵּיתוֹ וּמַטֵּהוּ

וכך היה אומר: אנא השם. חטאתי, עויתי ופשעתי לפניך אני וביתי אנא בשם כפר נא לחטאים ולעונות ולפשעים שחטאתי ושעויתי ושפשעתי לפניך אני וביתי ובני אהרון עם קדושיך ככתוב בתורת משה עבדך כי ביום הזה יכפר עליכם לטהר

'For on this day atonement shall be made for you to cleanse you of all your sins; before the Lord—'" (Lev. 16:30). And when the priests and the people standing in the court and serving in the Sanctuary heard the explicit name coming forth from the mouth of the high priest in holiness and purity, they would kneel, prostrate themselves, and fall to their faces and say: "Blessed is the name of His Majesty's glory for ever and ever." He would also intend to finish the name while facing those saying the blessing and say to them, "You shall be pure." And You, in Your great beneficence, arouse Your mercy and pardon Your ministering tribe [the priests].

[152] He turned to slaughter it
and collected its blood
and assigned it to be stirred
on the terrace of the court.

He went up and around
the altar of the flame,
in his hand the fire-pan
of beaten gold.

He put down the embers,
facing west,
and went down and put it
on the terrace of the court.

They brought before him
the golden ladle
and the dish that contained
the fine incense.

He took a handful
and put it in the ladle;
he placed it in his left hand,
with the fire-pan in his right.

He walked into the sanctuary
until he came to the curtain;
he stepped inside
until he reached the ark.

אתכם מכל חטאתיכם לפני יהוה והכהנים והעם העומדים בעזרה כשהיו שומעים את השם הנכבד והנורא מפרש יוצא מפי כהן גדול בקדושה ובטהרה היו כורעים ומשתחוים ונופלין על פניהם ואומרים: ברוך שם כבוד מלכותו לעולם ועד: ואף הוא היה מכוין לגמור את השם כנגד המברכים ואומר להם תטהרו ואתה בטובך הגדול תעורר רחמיך וסלח לאיש חסידך:

[152] לְשָׁחֲטוֹ נִפְנָה
וְקִבֵּל דָּמוֹ
וְצִוָּה לְמָרְסוֹ
בְּרוֹבֶד הָעֲזָרָה

לְמִזְבַּח מוֹקְדָה
עָלָה וְהִקִּיף
וּבְיָדוֹ מַחְתַּת
זָהָב שָׁחוּט

לוֹחֲשׁוֹת חָתָה
מִפְּנֵי מַעֲרָב
וְיָרַד וְשָׂמָהּ
בְּרוֹבֶד הָעֲזָרָה

לְפָנָיו יוֹבִילוּ
כַּף הַזָּהָב
וְהַמַּגֵּס אֲשֶׁר בָּהּ
קְטֹרֶת הַדַּקָּה

מִלֵּא חָפְנָיו
וְנָתַן לְתוֹךְ כַּף
נְטָלָהּ בִּשְׂמֹאל
וּמַחְתָּה בְּיָמִין

מְהַלֵּךְ בַּהֵיכָל
עַד בֹּא לַפָּרֹכֶת
צוֹעֵד בְּקִרְבָּהּ
עַד גֶּשֶׁת לָאָרוֹן

He put the fire-pan
between the two rods,
and if there was no ark,
on the Foundation Stone.⁷⁰

He poured the incense
on the burning coals;
a cloud covered over;⁷¹
he turned aside and went out.

160 He was careful to pray
briefly in the sanctuary
that the senior not
subjugate the junior.

He said to the stirrer,
"Bring the blood of the bull."
He took it and entered
and stood between the rods.

Facing the cover,
he sprinkled with his finger,
once up
and seven down, whipping.

He put **it** on the golden stand   **the bowl**
in the sanctuary,
and he slaughtered the people's goat
and collected its blood.

He turned around the way (he came)
and stood at his place
and whipped some of it
as he had done with the bull.

He put it on a second
stand in the sanctuary
and took the blood of the bull
and came to the cover.

---

70. See m. Yoma 5:2.

מַחְתָּה שָׁם
בֵּין שְׁנֵי בַדִּים
וְאִם אֵין אָרוֹן
בְּאֶבֶן שְׁתִיָּה

מְעָרָה קְטֹרֶת
עַל גַּחֲלֵי אֵשׁ
כִּסָּה עָנָן
צָעַד וְיָצָא

נִבְהַל לְשַׁוֵּעַ 160
בְּקוֹצֶר בַּהֵיכָל
לְבִלְתִּי רְדוֹת עַם קֹדֶשׁ
רַב בְּצָעִיר

נָם לַמְמָרֵס
הַגֵּשׁ דַּם פָּר
נָטְלוּ וְנִכְנַס
וְקָם לְבֵין הַבַּדִּים

נוֹכַח הַכַּפֹּרֶת
הִזָּה בְאֶצְבָּעוֹ
אַחַת לְמַעְלָה
וְשֶׁבַע לְמַטָּה כְּמַצְלִיף

נָתְנוּ עַל כַּן
זָהָב בַּהֵיכָל
וְשָׁחַט שְׂעִיר עַם
וְקִבֵּל דָּמוֹ

סוֹבֵב כְּדַרְכּוֹ
וְעָמַד בְּעָמְדוֹ
וְהִצְלִיף מִמֶּנּוּ
כְּמִשְׁפַּט דַּם פָּר

שָׂמוֹ עַל כַּן
שֵׁנִי בַּהֵיכָל
נָטַל דַּם פָּר
וּבָא לַפָּרֹכֶת

---

71. A cloud of smoke filled the room.

He counted as he sprinkled
opposite the ark outside,
once up
and seven times down.

He turned and exchanged it
for the blood of the goat
and did with it
as he had done at first.

He made it into a mixture[72]
as one expiation;
then he went out to the altar
of gold to expiate it.

On its horns he sprinkled
and put his finger
around **the four
quarters** and expiated it.   **the four horns of the altar**

170 On the eastern side
he finished his expiation
and from there sprinkled
seven times on its top.

When he had finished, he came
to the live goat
and placed his two hands on it
to confess for the people.

Thus he would say: "O Lord, they have sinned, they have done wrong, they have transgressed before You, Your people, the house of Israel. O, by the Lord, forgive the sins and iniquities and transgressions that they have committed against you, Your people, the house of Israel, as it is written in the Torah of Moses, Your servant: 'For on this day atonement shall be made for you to cleanse you of all your sins; you shall be clean before the Lord'" (Lev. 16:30). And when the priests and the people standing in the court and

---

72. The blood of the goat and the blood of the bull, thus using them together in one act of purification.

סָפַר וְהִזָּה
מוּל אֲרוֹן חוּצָה
אַחַת לְמַעְלָה
וְשֶׁבַע לְמַטָּה כְּמִסְפָּר

סָר וְהֶחֱלִיפוֹ
בְּדַם הַשָּׂעִיר
וַיִּפְעַל בּוֹ
כְּסֵדֶר הָרִאשׁוֹן

עֲשָׂאוֹ בְּתַעֲרוֹבֶת
חַטָּאת אֶחָד
וְיָצָא לַמִּזְבֵּחַ
הַזָּהָב לְחַטְּאוֹ

עַל קַרְנוֹתָיו הִזָּה
וְנָתַן בְּאֶצְבָּעוֹ
סָבִיב עַל **אַרְבַּעַת**
רִבְעָיו וְחִטְּאוֹ

ארבע קרנות המזבח

170 עַל צֵלַע מִזְרָח
גָּמַר חִטּוּיוֹ
וּמִשָּׁם הִזָּה
שֶׁבַע עַל טָהֳרוֹ

עֵת גָּמְרוֹ בָא
אֵצֶל שָׂעִיר חַי
וְסָמַךְ שְׁתֵּי יָדָיו עָלָיו
לְהִתְוַדּוֹת בְּעַד עַם

וכך היה אומר. אנא השם חטאו. עוו ופשעו לפניך עמך בית ישראל: אנא בשם. כפר נא לחטאים ולעונות ולפשעים שחטאו ושעוו ושפשעו לפניך עמך בית ישראל. ככתוב בתורת משה עבדך. כי ביום הזה יכפר עליכם לטהר אתכם מכל חטאתיכם לפני יי: והכהנים והעם העומדים בעזרה כשהיו שומעים את השם

serving in the Sanctuary heard the explicit name coming forth from the mouth of the high priest in holiness, they would kneel, prostrate themselves, and fall to their faces and say: "Blessed is the name of His Majesty's glory for ever and ever." And You, in Your great beneficence, arouse Your mercy and pardon the community of Jeshurun.

180 He commanded that it be sent forth
by a designated man,
burdened with the sins
of the nation and its offenses.

He set his face
to the bull and the goat,
cut them open, and took out
their fat and burned it.

The young priests
carried them on poles;
and burned their skin, flesh, and excrement
outside the city.

The goat headed out
for the edge of the desert;
they waved turban cloths
one to another to tell the news.[73]

He exulted on displaying
the riches of his majesty
and to take pleasure in
his **splendid garments**.[74]   the gold vestments

He stepped forth and washed
his hands and his feet
and took off the linen garments
and put on his clothing.

He announced the order
of the commandment to the congregation;

---

73. Messengers would signal with towels from one post to another when the goat had reached the wilderness; see m. Yoma 6:8.

הנכבד והנורא מפורש יוצא מפי כהן גדול היו כורעים ומשתחוים ונופלין על פניהם ואומרים: ברוך שם כבוד מלכותו לעולם ועד: ואף הוא היה מכוין לגמור את השם כנגד המברכים ואומר להם תטהרו. ואתה בטובך תעורר רחמיך וסלח לעדת ישורון:

פְּקָדוֹ לְשַׁלְּחוֹ 180
בְּיַד אִישׁ עִתִּי
עָמוּס עֲוֹנוֹת
אֹם וּפְשָׁעֶיהָ

פָּנָיו שָׂם
בְּפַר וְשָׂעִיר
קָרְעָם וְהוֹצִיא
חֶלְבָּם וְהִקְטִיר

פִּרְחֵי כְהֻנָּה
יְסַבְּלוּם בְּמוֹטוֹת
וְיִשְׂרְפוּ חוּץ לָעִיר
עוֹר וּבָשָׂר וָפֶרֶשׁ

פָּשַׁט שָׂעִיר
לְרֹאשׁ הַמִּדְבָּר
מְנִיפֵי צְנִיפוֹת
זֶה לָזֶה יְבַשְּׂרוּ

צָהַל לְהַרְאוֹת
עוֹשֶׁר תִּפְאַרְתּוֹ
וּלְהִתְנָאוֹת
בְּמַלְבּוּשׁ יְקָרוֹ **בגדי הזהב**

צָעַד וְקִדֵּשׁ
יָדָיו וְרַגְלָיו
וּפָשַׁט כְּלֵי בַד
וְעָטָה כְּסוּתוֹ

צִוּוּי סֵדֶר
יוֹדִיעַ לָעֵדָה

---

74. His own vestment; see m. Yoma 7:1.

he recounted by heart
the law of **the tenth day**.   Yom Kippur

He **fulfilled the need for blessing**;[75]   recited prayers
then he washed and undressed
and went down and immersed
and went up and dried himself.

He put on the holy
garments of gold
and again washed
his hands and his feet.

He hastened to sacrifice
the goat for the additional offering
and included his ram and the ram for the people
with the fat for the day.

190   He washed his hands
and feet and undressed
and went down and immersed
and went up and dried himself.

They brought before him
white garments;
he put them on and washed
his hands and his feet.

He ran like a sprinter[76]
to the place between the rods
and took out from there
the ladle and the gold fire-pan.

His hands and his feet
he washed as was his custom;
then he took off his linen garments
and laid them down forever.

He bathed and dried himself
and put on the gold garments,

---

75. See m. Yoma 7:1.

יוֹם הַכִּפּוּרִים

וַיּוֹרְגַּל בְּפֶה
חָק הֶעָשׂוֹר

צֹרֶךְ בְּרָכוֹת הִשְׁלִים
וְקִדֵּשׁ וּפָשַׁט
וְיָרַד וְטָבַל
וְעָלָה וְסִפֵּג

קְדוּשַׁת בִּגְדֵי
זָהָב לָבַשׁ
וַיְקַדֵּשׁ עוֹד
יָדָיו וְרַגְלָיו

קָדַם וְעָשָׂה
שְׂעִיר הַמּוּסָף
וְהִכְלִיל אֵילוֹ וְאֵיל עַם
עִם חֶלְבֵי יוֹם

קִדֵּשׁ יָדָיו וְרַגְלָיו   190
רָץ וּפָשַׁט
וְיָרַד וְטָבַל
וְעָלָה וְסִפֵּג

קֵרְבוּ לְפָנָיו
בִּגְדֵי לָבָן
לְבָשָׁם וְקִדֵּשׁ
יָדָיו וְרַגְלָיו

רָץ כְּאִישׁ מָהִיר
לְבֵין הַבַּדִּים
וְהוֹצִיא מִשָּׁם
כַּף וּמַחְתַּת פָּז

רַגְלָיו וְיָדָיו
קִדֵּשׁ כְּדִבְרוֹ
וּפָשַׁט כְּלֵי בַד
וְהִנִּיחָם נֶצַח

רָחַץ וְסִפֵּג
וְעָטָה כְּלֵי פָז

76. Lit., "swift man."

and again he washed
his hands and his feet.

He offered the desired
daily sacrifice in the evening
and offered the incense
between the pieces and the libation.

He waited until evening
to light the lamps,
for the requirement
is from evening to evening.[77]

He returned to lift up his hands
to bless the people;
then washed his hands
and his feet and undressed.

He covered his body
in his own clothes;
he was accompanied by officers
resplendently to his abode.

Safe as he departed,
no fault having occurred,
the congregation celebrated
in joy and high spirits.

200 The messenger who sent the goat
brought cause for giving praise[78]—
the news that **the wayward daughter's**[79]   Israel's
sins had been pardoned.

"Give us a sign,"
his couriers said,
"how we may know
that offense has been atoned."

---

77. The lamps are only to be lit each evening.
78. Following Mirsky's suggested reading.

וִיקַדֵּשׁ עוֹד
יָדָיו וְרַגְלָיו

רָצוּי תָּמִיד
הִגִּישׁ בָּעַרְבַּיִם
וְהִקְטִיר קְטֹרֶת
בֵּין נְתָחִים לָנָסֶךְ

שָׁמַּר לָעֶרֶב
דְּלִיקַת נֵרוֹת
כִּי מִצְוָתָם
מֵעֶרֶב וְעַד עֶרֶב

שָׁב שְׂאֵת כַּפַּיִם
לְבָרֵךְ אֶת הָעָם
וְקִדֵּשׁ יָדָיו וְרַגְלָיו
וּפָשַׁט

שְׁאָרוֹ יְכַסֶּה
בְּבִגְדֵי עַצְמוֹ
וְשָׂרִים יְלַוּוּהוּ
בְּהָדָר לְנָוֵיהוּ

שָׁלוֹם בְּצֵאתוֹ
בְּלִי הוּקְרָה פִיסוּל
תְּרַנֵּן עֵדָה
בְּשִׂמְחָה וּבְטוּב לֵבָב

תְּהִלָּה יְבַשֵּׂר   200
שְׁלִיחַ הַשָּׂעִיר
כִּי נִרְצוּ עֲוֹנוֹת
בַּת הַשּׁוֹבֵבָה

ישראל

תֵּן לָנוּ מוֹפֵת
שׁוֹלְחָיו יֹאמֵירוּ
בַּמֶּה נֵדַע
כִּי כֻפַּר פֶּשַׁע

79. Jer 31:21.

"The appearance of the crimson
thread has turned white,
and I led the goat,
and it was pushed and died."

They clothed themselves in beauty,
dressed themselves in splendor;
they found joy
and gained jubilation.

תּוֹאֶרֶת לְשׁוֹן
הַשָּׁנִי הִלְבִּינָה
וְשָׂעִיר הוֹלַכְתִּי
וְנִדְחָה וָמֵת

תִּפְאֶרֶת יַעֲטוּ
וְהָדָר יִלְבָּשׁוּ
שִׂמְחָה יִמְצָאוּ
וְשָׂשׂוֹן יַשִּׂיגוּ

7. Emet Mah Nehedar
"Truly, How Beautiful"

This poem, simple in structure but vivid in its use of imagery, has its origins in the apocryphal Book of Ben Sira, or Ecclesiasticus, which served as perhaps the most influential model for the Avodah genre.[1] In chapter 50, a seminal composition in which Ben Sira describes the service of Simeon, the son of Yoḥanan, the high priest in the Temple, he includes a twelve-line passage describing the beatific radiance that overcame the high priest as he emerged from the sanctuary.[2] Several poems dating from late antiquity and the Middle Ages expand on Ben Sira's rhapsody, using acrostic and extravagant images and figures. Particularly prominent is the poet's use of cosmic images, such as stars, to describe the high priest's face, and allusions to objects in the Temple and even aspects of the priestly vestments. In keeping with the late antique aesthetic, the author, in contrast to Ben Sira, tends to place his dazzling images into frameworks, such as the garden and the window.

This text, which is not attributed to a single author, is published in Goldschmidt's edition of the Maḥzor[3] and is recited in Ashkenazic communities.

---

1. See the Introduction, above. On this composition, see Yahalom, *Piyyut u-Meṣiʾut*, 15 16
2. The Hebrew text of chapter 50 is only found in manuscript B. For translation and analysis, see Patrick W. Skehan and Alexander A. Di Lella, *The Wisdom of Ben Sira: A New Translation with Notes* (New York: Anchor Bible Doubleday, 1987), 546–55, and Hayward, *Jewish Temple*, 38–84.
3. Goldschmidt, *Maḥazor*, 483–84.

Truly, how beautiful was the high priest when he emerged from the holy of holies safely, without harm!

Like a tent stretched out among the **dwellers on high**[4]   **angels**
    was the appearance of the Priest;
Like bolts of lightning going forth from the radiance of the Holy Creatures
    was the appearance of the Priest;
Like the size of the fringes on the four corners[5]
    was the appearance of the Priest;
Like the image of a rainbow inside a cloud[6]
    was the appearance of the Priest;
Like the majesty with which **the Rock** clothed His creatures **God**
    was the appearance of the Priest;
Like a rose planted in a delightful garden
    was the appearance of the Priest;
Like a wreath placed on the forehead of a king
    was the appearance of the Priest;
Like the grace on the face of a bridegroom
    was the appearance of the Priest;
Like the purity inherent in a pure diadem[7]
    was the appearance of the Priest;
Like **the one who dwells in shelter** assuaging the countenance of the King[8]   **Moses**
    was the appearance of the Priest;
Like the planet Venus in the eastern sky[9]
    was the appearance of the Priest;
Like one clad in the garments and helmet of triumph
    was the appearance of the Priest;
Like an angel standing at the beginning of the road
    was the appearance of the Priest;
Like a lamp shining through windows
    was the appearance of the Priest;

---

4. Heaven is stretched out over the angels like a tent.
5. According to Num 15:38, fringes (ṣiṣit) are to be worn on a four-cornered garment.
6. Cf. Ezek 1:28 and Ben Sira 50:7.
7. See Zech 3:5, where the prophet envisions a pure diadem being placed on the high priest's head.

אֱמֶת מַה נֶּהְדָּר הָיָה כֹּהֵן גָּדוֹל בְּצֵאתוֹ
מִבֵּית קָדְשֵׁי הַקֳּדָשִׁים בְּשָׁלוֹם בְּלִי פֶגַע

שמים; מלאכים	**כְּאֹהֶל הַנִּמְתָּח בְּדָרֵי מַעְלָה**
	מַרְאֵה כֹהֵן
	כִּבְרָקִים הַיּוֹצְאִים מִזִּיו הַחַיּוֹת

מַרְאֵה כֹהֵן
כְּגֹדֶל גְּדִילִים בְּאַרְבַּע קְצָווֹת
מַרְאֵה כֹהֵן
כִּדְמוּת הַקֶּשֶׁת בְּתוֹךְ הֶעָנָן
מַרְאֵה כֹהֵן

אלוהים	כְּהוֹד אֲשֶׁר הִלְבִּישׁ **צוּר** לִיצוּרִים

מַרְאֵה כֹהֵן
כְּוֶרֶד הַנָּתוּן בְּתוֹךְ גִּנַּת חֶמֶד
מַרְאֵה כֹהֵן
כְּזֵר הַנָּתוּן עַל מֵצַח מֶלֶךְ
מַרְאֵה כֹהֵן
כְּחֶסֶד הַנִּתָּן עַל פְּנֵי חָתָן
מַרְאֵה כֹהֵן
כְּטֹהַר הַנָּתוּן בְּצָנִיף טָהוֹר
מַרְאֵה כֹהֵן

משה	**כְּיוֹשֵׁב בְּסֵתֶר** לְחַלּוֹת פְּנֵי מֶלֶךְ

מַרְאֵה כֹהֵן
כְּכוֹכַב הַנֹּגַהּ בִּגְבוּל מִזְרָח
מַרְאֵה כֹהֵן
כִּלְבוּשׁ מְעִיל וּכְשִׁרְיָן צְדָקָה
מַרְאֵה כֹהֵן
כְּמַלְאָךְ הַנִּצָּב עַל רֹאשׁ דֶּרֶךְ
מַרְאֵה כֹהֵן
כְּנֵר הַמֵּצִיץ מִבֵּין הַחַלּוֹנוֹת
מַרְאֵה כֹהֵן

---

8. As Goldschmidt notes, the line refers to Moses pleading before God to spare Israel; cf. Deut 9:25–26.

9. Heb. *kokhav nogah*.

Like the army commanders at the head of the holy people
> was the appearance of the Priest;

Like the magnificence with which purity adorns **the purified**[10]
>> **the priest at his ordination**
> was the appearance of the Priest;

Like the golden bells on the hem of the robe[11]
> was the appearance of the Priest;

Like the form of the sanctuary and the Curtain of Testimony[12]
> was the appearance of the Priest;

Like a [chamber][13] enveloped in blue and purple
> was the appearance of the Priest;

Like the sight of the sunrise over the earth
> was the appearance of the Priest;

Like a lily of the garden among thorns
> was the appearance of the Priest;

Like the shape of Orion and Pleiades from Teman
> was the appearance of the Priest.

---

10. Cf. Lev 8.
11. Of the high priest.

כּוֹהֵן בִּימֵי הַמִּילּוּאִים

כְּשָׂרֵי צְבָאוֹת בְּרֹאשׁ עַם קֹדֶשׁ
מַרְאֵה כֹהֵן
כְּעֹז אֲשֶׁר הִלְבִּישׁ טָהוֹר **לַמִּטָּהֵר**

מַרְאֵה כֹהֵן
כְּפַעֲמוֹנֵי זָהָב בְּשׁוּלֵי הַמְּעִיל
מַרְאֵה כֹהֵן
כְּצוּרַת הַבַּיִת וּפָרֹכֶת הָעֵדוּת
מַרְאֵה כֹהֵן
כְּקִילָה מְכָסָּה תְּכֵלֶת וְאַרְגָּמָן
מַרְאֵה כֹהֵן
כְּרוֹאִי זְרִיחַת שֶׁמֶשׁ עַל הָאָרֶץ
מַרְאֵה כֹהֵן
כְּשׁוֹשַׁנַּת גַּן בֵּין הַחוֹחִים
מַרְאֵה כֹהֵן
כְּתַבְנִית כְּסִיל וְכִימָה מִתֵּימָן
מַרְאֵה כֹהֵן

---

12. Those in the Temple, which were very colorful.
13. Reading *ke-qilah* for *ke-qehilah*, with Goldschmidt.

8. En Lanu Kohen Gadol
"We Have No High Priest"

YOSE BEN YOSE

This poem, attributed to Yose ben Yose, is one of several laments of its kind and is meant to be recited in the confession of sins for Yom Kippur. The poem has a strict form and repeats verbs and motifs for the sake of the literary structure and the acrostic. Its literary and historical value lies in its constant wordplay, using clever puns and alliterations, and in its tone, which combines bitter lament with an almost ludic preoccupation with the details of the cult and their relationship to Israel's tragic fate. It is impossible to convey the full impact of the poem's wordplay in English translation. However, we have endeavored to give the reader a taste of its complexity and style by noting examples of the wordplay in our notes and by occasional free translations that convey similar puns in English. This translation is based on an improved version of Mirsky's edition based on manuscript evidence (*Yose ben Yose*, 210–17).

We have no high priest
to atone for us;
how shall we be expiated
on account of our misdeeds?

We have no Urim and Thummim
to inquire;[1]
how can we have light
while our desire[2] lies in darkness?

We have sinned ...

The service[3] has been abolished
from the place of service;
how can we serve the Righteous One
while in servitude to a foreigner?

The sacrificial fire and guilt offering[4]
have been withheld from us;
how can we make fires
while the fire of the altar is extinguished?

We have sinned ...

The rejoicing over the lots[5]
is absent from among us;
how can we go up in joy
while we are in exile?

---

1. Cf. the prayers to be recited before practicing divination, on which, see Michael D. Swartz, "Sacrificial Themes in Jewish Magic," in *Magic and Ritual in the Ancient World*, ed. Marvin Meyer and Paul Mirecki (Leiden: Brill, 2002), 311–12.

2. The Temple, that is, the place of our desire. The phrase is based on Ps 132:13. Cf. Eleazar ben Qallir's phrase *be-'ohel 'ivvui*, "the desired tent," in his *qerovah* for Sukkot *Az Hayetah*, in *Maḥazor*

אֵין לָנוּ כֹּהֵן גָּדוֹל
לְכַפֵּר בַּעֲדֵנוּ
וְאֵיךְ יִתְכַּפֵּר לָנוּ
עַל שִׁגְגוֹתֵינוּ

אֵין לָנוּ אוּרִים וְתֻמִּים
לִשְׁאוֹל בָּהֶם
וְאֵיךְ יֵאוֹר לָנוּ
וְאִוּוּיֵינוּ מְאוֹפָל

חטאנו צורנו סלח לנו יוצרנו

בָּטְלָה עֲבוֹדָה
מִבֵּית עֲבוֹדָה
וְאֵיךְ נַעֲבוֹד לָזָךְ
וְזָר מַעֲבִיד בָּנוּ

בָּטְלוּ מִמֶּנּוּ
אִשִּׁים וְאָשָׁם
וְאֵיךְ נַעַשׂ אִשִּׁים
וְאֵשׁ מִזְבֵּחַ כָּבָה

חטאנו צורנו סלח לנו יוצרנו

גִּיל גּוֹרָלוֹת
חָדַל מִמֶּנּוּ
וְאֵיךְ נַעַל בְּגִילָה
וְאָנוּ בְגוֹלָה

Sukkot, Shemin ʿAṣeret, ve-Simḥat Torah, ed. Daniel Goldschmidt (Jerusalem: Koren, 1981), 105, line 12; see Abraham Even-Shoshan, *Ha-Milon he-Ḥadash* (Jerusalem: Kiryat Sefer, 1989), s.v. ʾwwy.
   3. Heb. ʿAvodah.
   4. Heb. *asham*.
   5. That is, the lots cast for the goats.

Repairers of broken walls[6]   Israel's leaders
are broken down because of our sins;
how shall we repair what is broken,
when there is none to stand in the breach?[7]

We have sinned ...

We have been deprived of
juice and succulent fruit offerings;
how can we offer moist fruit
when our eyes are moist with tears?[8]

The blood sprinkled in slaughter
has passed from the house of slaughter;
how can we sprinkle blood
when our blood has been spilled?

We have sinned ...

Offerings of aromatic incense
have been taken away from us;
how can we offer aroma
when our aroma has gone foul?

10   Light has been extinguished
from **the place of our desire;**   Temple
how can we repair the lamps
when our light has gone out?

We have sinned ...

And the savor has ceased
at our Divine resting place;
how can we set forth offerings[9]
when there is no Divine place of rest?

---

6. See Isa 58:12.
7. Cf. Ezek 22:30.

מנהיגי העם	**גּוֹדְרֵי פְּרָצוֹת** נִפְרְצוּ בַּאֲשָׁמֵינוּ וְאֵיךְ נִגְדּוֹר פֶּרֶץ וְאֵין עוֹמֵד בַּפֶּרֶץ

חטאנו צורנו סלח לנו יוצרנו

דִּמְעָה וּמְלֵאָה
דָּלְלוּ מִמֶּנּוּ
וְאֵיךְ נִתְרוֹם דֶּמַע
וְדִמְעָה בְּעֵינֵינוּ

דַּם זְרִיקַת זֶבַח
פַּס מִבֵּית זֶבַח
וְאֵיךְ נִזְרוֹק דָּם
וְנִשְׁפַּךְ דָּמֵינוּ

חטאנו צורנו סלח לנו יוצרנו

הַקְטָרַת רֵיחַ סַמִּים
הוּסַר מִמֶּנּוּ
וְאֵיךְ נַקְטִיר רֵיחַ
וְהוּבְאַשׁ רֵיחֵנוּ

בית המקדש	הֲטָבַת נֵרוֹת הוֹדַעְכוּ מֵאִוּוּיֵנוּ וְאֵיךְ נֵטִיב נֵרוֹת וְכָבָה נֵירֵנוּ	10

חטאנו צורנו סלח לנו יוצרנו

וְנִיחוֹחַ חָדַל
מִמְּנוּחָתֵנוּ
וְאֵיךְ נָבִיא מִנְחָה
וְאֵין בֵּית מְנוּחָה

---

8. Playing on fruit offerings, *demaʿ*, and tears, *demaʿot*.
9. Heb. *Minḥah*, playing on the root *nwḥ*, "to rest."

And our first-fruit offerings
have ceased to be offered;
how can we ascend on the festival of first fruits
when there is no early fruit?

We have sinned ...

Whole-sacrifices[10]
have passed from **that which was wholly beautiful**;   the Temple
how shall we sacrifice
when the house of sacrifice is destroyed?

The abject (people)
has been ridiculed by foreigners;
how can we approach the inheritance
when our inheritance belongs to foreigners?

We have sinned ...

Fat offerings
are no longer given;
how can we offer fat
when there is no fat of the land?[11]

We are bereft of
goats for the sin offering;
how can we perform the sin offering
when our sins are overwhelming?

We have sinned ...

There is no more purifying immersion
in the chamber of Parvah;
how can we immerse in purity
when our immersions have ceased?

---

10. Heb. *zivḥe kalil*, see Ps 51:21.

וּבִיכּוּרִים
חָדְלוּ לְבַכֵּר
וְאֵיךְ נַעַל בְּבִיכּוּר
וְאֵין בִּיכּוּרָה

חטאנו צורנו סלח לנו יוצרנו

זִבְחֵי כָלִיל
פַּסּוּ מִמִּכְלַל יֹפִי
וְאֵיךְ נַעֲשׂ זֶבַח
וְחָרַב בֵּית זֶבַח

המקדש

זֹלֵלָה
זִלְזְלוּהָ זָרִים
וְאֵיךְ נָבוֹא לְנַחֲלָה
וְנַחֲלָתֵנוּ לְזָרִים

חטאנו צורנו סלח לנו יוצרנו

חֲלָבִים
פַּסּוּ מֵהַקְטִירָם
וְאֵיךְ נַקְטִיר חֵלֶב
וְאֵין חֵלֶב חִטָּה

חָדְלוּ מִמֶּנּוּ
שְׂעִירֵי חַטָּאת
וְאֵיךְ נַעֲשׂ חַטָּאת
וְגָבְרוּ חֲטָאֵינוּ

חטאנו צורנו סלח לנו יוצרנו

טְבִילַת טַהֲרָה
אֵין בַּפַּרְוָה
וְאֵיךְ נִטְבּוֹל בְּטוֹהַר
וּפָסְקוּ טְבִילוֹת

---

11. Lit., "when there is not one grain (ḥelev) of wheat."

The rows of stones
have disappeared from **that which was filled with stones;**[12]   the breastpiece
how shall we **remove the heart of stone**[13]   repent
when **they**[14] have thrown stones at us?   Israel's enemies

We have sinned …

The forest of Lebanon[15]   the Temple
has been reduced to a wreckage;[16]
how shall **the bride from Lebanon**[17]   Israel
sing love songs to her beloved?[18]

20   **Our beauty** has been laid waste   the Temple
and our light has dimmed;
how can **she whose eyes are beautiful**   Israel
beautify herself for **the Preeminent One?**[19]   God

We have sinned …

The atoning bull
has passed from **the palanquin;**[20]   the Temple
how can we sacrifice a bull
when there is no one who can atone?[21]

Our (sacrifices of) atonement
have departed from the **place of our desire;**   the Temple
how shall we present a gift
when **the root of Jesse** is no more?[22]   David

We have sinned …

---

12. Precious stones were embedded in the breastpiece.
13. See Ezek 11:19.
14. See Lam 3:53.
15. Since cedars of Lebanon were used to build the Temple, references to Lebanon are taken as references to the Temple.
16. Cf. Isa 10:6.
17. Song 4:8–9.

	טוּרֵי אָבֶן
חושן המשפט	פַּסּוּ מִמְּלוּאַת אָבֶן
נחזור בתשובה	וְאֵיךְ נָסִיר לֵב אָבֶן
	וְיָדוּ בָנוּ אֶבֶן

חטאנו צורנו סלח לנו יוצרנו

המקדש	יַעַר הַלְּבָנוֹן
	הוּשַׁת לְמִרְמָס
האל	וְאֵיךְ תְּלַבֵּב לְדוֹד
ישראל	כַּלַּת הַלְּבָנוֹן

המקדש	יָפְיֵנוּ הוּשַׁם	20
	וְאוֹרֵנוּ אֹפֶל	
האל	וְאֵיךְ תִּיפֶה לְדָגוּל	
ישראל	יְפַת עֵינַיִים	

חטאנו צורנו סלח לנו יוצרנו

	כֹּפֶר פָּר
המקדש	פַּס מֵאַפִּרְיוֹן
	אֵיךְ נַקְרִיב פָּר
	וְאֵין מִי יְכַפֵּר

	כַּפָּרוֹתֵינוּ
המקדש	פַּסּוּ מֵאַוְוֵינוּ
	וְאֵיךְ נַגִּישׁ שַׁי
	וְאֵין שׁוֹרֶשׁ יִשַׁי

חטאנו צורנו סלח לנו יוצרנו

18. Ibid.
19. See Song 5:10.
20. See Song 3:9.
21. The stanza plays on words containing the ordered consonants *p* and *r*: *par* (bull), *kpr* (atone), and *apirion* (palanquin).
22. From a variant reading (see Mirsky, *Yose ben Yose*, 213), playing on *shai*, "gift," and *Yishai*, Jesse. The alternative text reads: "when You have dissolved our bodies?"

We have not made incense
on the hill of Lebanon;
how can **her** sins be whitened   Israel's
who is as beautiful as the moon?[23]

The *log* of oil is gone
from **the fruitful hill**;[24]   the land of Israel
how can we pour oil
on **that which is mixed with oil**?[25]   the meal offering

We have sinned …

She who is perfumed with myrrh[26]   Israel
is bereft of flowing myrrh;
how, on **the mountain of myrrh**,   Zion
can **the Sachet of Myrrh**[27] reside?   God

The shovel for gathering coals
has been ruined;
how can we use the shovel
when we are in ruins?[28]

We have sinned …

The aroma of nard and saffron
has drifted away;[29]
how can we say, "My nard
has given forth its fragrance"?[30]

The libation of fermented drink
is no longer offered;[31]
how shall we offer libations
as (we) poured them of old?

We have sinned …

---

23. Playing on *lavan* (white) and *levanah* (moon).
24. Isa 5:2; Heb. *qeren ben shemen*, using the word *shemen*, which also means oil.
25. Lev 2:4.
26. Song 3:6.
27. Song 1:13.

	לְבוֹנָה לֹא עָשְׂנוּ
	בְּגִבְעַת הַלְּבָנוֹן
	וְאֵיךְ יְלוּבַּן חֵטְא
ישראל	**יָפָה כַלְּבָנָה**

	לוֹג שֶׁמֶן פַּס
ארץ ישראל	**מְקֶרֶן בֶּן שֶׁמֶן**
	וְאֵיךְ נְצוֹק שֶׁמֶן
קרבן מנחה	**עַל בְּלוּלָה בַשֶּׁמֶן**

חטאנו צורנו סלח לנו יוצרנו

	מָר דְּרוֹר אָפַס
ישראל	**מְמֻקְטֶרֶת מוֹר**
ציון	**וְאֵיךְ בְּהַר הַמּוֹר**
האל	**יָלִין צְרוֹר הַמּוֹר**

מַחְתָּה הוּחַתָּה
מְלֹחֲתוֹת גֶּחָלִים
וְאֵיךְ נַעַשׂ מַחְתָּה
וְאָנוּ בִמְחִיתָה

חטאנו צורנו סלח לנו יוצרנו

נֵרְדְּ וְכַרְכֹּם
נָדַד רֵיחוֹ
וְאֵיךְ נַעַן
נִרְדִּי נָתַן רֵיחוֹ

נִסְכֵּי שֵׁכָר
פַּסּוּ מֵהֲסֵךְ
וְאֵיךְ נְנַסֵּךְ
כְּנִיסַּכְתּוֹ מֵרֹאשׁ

חטאנו צורנו סלח לנו יוצרנו

---

28. The stanza plays on *maḥtah*, "incense shovel," and *meḥitah*, "destruction" or "ruin."
29. Heb. *nadad*, playing on the sound of *nerd*, "nard."
30. Song 1:12, applied to Israel offering incense before God.
31. See Num 28:7.

Choice flour has been diverted
from the arrangement of loaves;[32]
how can we prepare choice flour
when we have been captured in a siege?[33]

30   Spices have been taken away
from the handful;[34]
how shall we offer the spices
when we have been depleted by taxes?[35]

We have sinned ...

The burnt offering has been removed
from **the forest of burnt offerings**;[36]   the Temple
how can we perform the burnt offerings
when our burden is heavy?[37]

The arranged wood[38]
has vanished from the wood altar;
how can we be purified with wood[39]
when we have been **defeated on wood**?[40]   crucified

We have sinned ...

Bull and ram
are no longer burned;
how can we burn the bull
when our Temple has been burned?

The curtain has crumbled,
and the cover has been cut up;
how can we cry out in prayer
when we have been crushed?

We have sinned ...

---

32. The ḥalot of Lev 24:5–6.
33. Playing on *solet*, "choice flour," and *solelot*, "siege."
34. The handful of incense that the high priest offered on Yom Kippur.
35. Playing on *samim*, "incense," *husam*, "melted" or "depleted," and *missim*, "taxes."
36. Heb. *ya'ar ha-'olot*.

EN LANU KOHEN GADOL

סוֹלֶת סוֹלְפָה
מְסֻדָּר חַלּוֹת
וְאֵיךְ נַיֵּפֶּה סוֹלֶת
וְנִלְכַּדְנוּ מְסוֹלָלוֹת

סַמִּים הוּסַר 30
מִמִּלּוּא חָפְנַיִם
וְאֵיךְ נַעַשׂ סַמִּים
וְהוּמַסְנוּ בְמָסִים

חטאנו צורנו סלח לנו יוצרנו

עוֹלָה עָתְקָה
מִיַּעַר עוֹלוֹת — המקדש
וְאֵיךְ נַעַשׂ עוֹלוֹת
וְהוּכְבַּד עוֹלֵנוּ

עֲצֵי עֶרֶךְ
חָדְלוּ מִמִּזְבַּח עֵץ
וְאֵיךְ נִטְהַר בָּעֵץ
וְכָשַׁלְנוּ בָעֵץ — נצלבנו

חטאנו צורנו סלח לנו יוצרנו

פַּר וְשָׂעִיר
פַּסּוּ מִלְּהִשָּׂרֵף
וְאֵיךְ נִשְׂרוֹף פַּר
וּמִקְדָּשׁ נִשְׂרַף

פָּרוֹכֶת פוֹרְכָה
וְכַפּוֹרֶת כּוֹרָתָה
וְאֵיךְ נַפְצִיחַ פֶּלֶל
וְאָנוּ בְּפֶרֶךְ

חטאנו צורנו סלח לנו יוצרנו

---

37. Lit., "yoke," *'ol*, playing on *'olah*, "burnt offering."
38. The pile of wood on the altar in the Temple.
39. Which provides fire for purifying sacrifices.
40. Cf. Lam 5:13.

Zion is desert,
Jerusalem has gone to the beasts;
how can we set up
signposts for ourselves?[41]

The diadem of the frontlet has been stripped
from **the atoning forehead;**[42]   forehead of the high priest
how can we atone with the diadem
when we are dried up like a flower?[43]

We have sinned ...

The voice that spoke[44]
is absent from **the tent;**   the Temple
how can we pitch our tent
when our tent has been plundered?

The sacrificial victims[45] are absent
from the (storeroom) of the lamb sacrifices;
how shall we offer the victims
when **Shalem** has been victimized?[46]   Jerusalem

We have sinned ...

The myriads have been sent afar;   Israel
the boiled cakes have gone cold;[47]
how can we make boiled cakes,
when we ourselves boil in oil?[48]

40   The **wide place** has been narrowed;   Jerusalem
the **winding passage** has been shut;   Jerusalem
how can we open our mouths wide
when our enemies prosecute us?

We have sinned ...

---

41. So that we can find our way back to the destroyed Zion. The line plays on Ṣiyyon, "Zion," and siyyun, "signpost."
42. The frontlet, which was worn on the high priest's forehead, was said to have atoning power.
43. Cf. Isa 40:7; playing on the meaning of ṣiṣ as flower and priestly frontlet.
44. Cf. Num 7:89.

צִיּוֹן צִיָּיה
יְרוּשָׁלַיִם לְעִיִּים
וְאֵיךְ נַצִּיב לָנוּ
נַצִּיב צִיּוּנִים

ציץ נֵזֶר נוֹצַל
הכוהן הגדול מִמֵּצַח **מְרֻצֶּה**
וְאֵיךְ נֵרָצֶה בְּצִיץ
וְחַסְדֵּנוּ כְּצִיץ

חטאנו צורנו סלח לנו יוצרנו

קוֹל מְדַבֵּר
חָדַל מֵאֹהֶל
אוהל מועד וְאֵיךְ נִטָּה **אֹהֶל**
וְשֻׁדַּד אָהֳלֵינוּ

קָרְבָּן חָדַל
מִטָּלֶה קָרְבָּן
וְאֵיךְ נַקְרִיב קָרְבָּן
ירושלים וְשָׁלֵם בְּחָרְבָּן

חטאנו צורנו סלח לנו יוצרנו

ישראל **רְבָבָה** הָרְחָקָה
רְבוּכָה הֻקָּרָה
וְאֵיךְ נַעַשׂ מַרְבֶּכֶת
וְאָנוּ מְרֻבָּכִים

ירושלים **רַחֲבָה** הוּצְרָה 40
וְנָסְבָּה הוּסְגְּרָה
וְאֵיךְ נַרְחִיב פֶּה
וְאוֹיְבֵנוּ פְלִילִים

חטאנו צורנו סלח לנו יוצרנו

---

45. That is, the animals for sacrifice.
46. Lit., "in ruins" (*be-ḥurban*, playing on *qorban*, "sacrifice").
47. Heb. *rekhivim*, cakes boiled in water and cooked in oil; cf. Lev 6:14 and M. Men. 7:1. NJV: "soaked cakes."
48. Are sentenced by the Romans to boil in oil.

The whole ones[49] agonize;	Israel
the whole offerings have ceased;	
how can we pay tribute	
when we are bereft of peace?[50]	

The seven flawless sacrifices
have ceased from our land,
how can we praise God sevenfold
when we have been punished sevenfold?

We have sinned …

Prayer has come to an end
in the house of prayer;
how can we say prayers
when (God) has screened Himself off from prayer?[51]

The *Temidim* have ceased	
in **the forest of *Temidim*;**	the Temple
who shall we offer *Temidim*	
when the Tamid has been annulled?	

We have sinned …

---

49. Israel is called "whole" because it once lacked nothing.
50. Cf. Lam 3:17. The stanza plays on *shalem*, "whole," *shilem*, "pay," and *shalom*, "peace."

ישראל   **שְׁלָמִים** הָאָנְחוּ
                       שְׁלָמִים שָׁבָתוּ
                       וְאֵיךְ נְשַׁלֵּם שַׁי
                       וּמִשָּׁלוֹם זְנַחְנוּ

                       שִׁבְעָה תְמִימִים
                       תַּמּוּ מֵאַרְצֵנוּ
                       וְאֵיךְ נְהַלֵּל שֶׁבַע
                       וְיִסַּרְנוּ בְשֶׁבַע

חטאנו צורנו סלח לנו יוצרנו

                       תְּפִלָּה פָּסְקָה
                       מִבֵּית תְּפִלָּה
                       וְאֵיךְ נַעַן תְּפִלָּה
                       וְסָךְ בְּעַד תְּפִלָּה

המקדש   תְּמִידִים כָּלוּ
                       מִיַּעַר תְּמִידִים
                       וְאֵיךְ נַעַשׂ תְּמִידִים
                       וּבָטַל הַתָּמִיד

חטאנו צורנו סלח לנו יוצרנו

---

51. See Lam 3:44.

CONCLUSION

The Avodah: Poetry, History, and Ritual

IN THIS VOLUME, we have presented the most important examples from the early history of the Avodah genre. In doing so, we hope to have conveyed something of the range, variety, and literary and historical significance of this poetry and, indeed, of ancient piyyut in general. These examples demonstrate considerable continuity of form and theme; on the other hand, the individual poems differ in how they handle forms and themes.

CONTINUITY AND DIVERSITY

In many ways the Avodah is a very stable genre, preserving a basic form, structure, and set of themes since the first poetic preamble to the recitation of the Mishnah in *Atah Barata* and the elaborations of the Mishnah's procedure in *Atah Konanta ʿOlam Me-Rosh*. The genre retained its basic structure throughout the Middle Ages. All of our examples begin with praise of God and His planning of creation, continue with a narrative of the history of Israel, emphasizing God's selection of the Levites and Aaronites, and relate the procedure of the Yom Kippur sacrifice. In each of these examples, the historical preamble contains much of relevance to the theme of the Yom Kippur sacrifice. Some present biblical figures in terms of their fulfillment of their obligation to present offerings to God; some emphasize that the earth was created so that humanity could enjoy its fruits and observe the commandments; and most focus on Levi as the chosen clan. Moreover, all of the Avodah piyyutim engage in the valorization of the priesthood, presenting the high priest as a virtuous and skilled man and, in some cases, a splendid physical specimen.

At the same time, the poems exhibit a good deal of diversity in style, form, and theme. One variable is the degree of elaboration of historical details. For example, the anonymous piyyut *Atah Konanta ʿOlam Me-Rosh* is quite concise and concerned with giving the most important details of the historical sequence from creation to the Temple service. This concern with choosing the most relevant details extends to the selection of Aaron, who is mentioned, while Moses is omitted. In contrast, *Az be-ʾEn Kol* lavishes attention on each major stage of human and Israelite history, presenting a rich tapestry of myths and homiletics on the relevance of the Torah to creation, Adam and Eve, the patriarchy, and ensuing history. For its author, the Temple and sacrifice, while central to the program of the Avodah, do not eclipse the pageant of Israel's heroes in their complexity and grandeur.

Likewise, the poems differ in their use of metonymy and other poetic figures. These differences may be due to historical development. Over the centuries, piyyut became more elaborate and cryptic as it evolved from brief compositions embedded in Talmudic literature and the statutory liturgy[1] to the ornate classical style of Eleazar ben Qallir. Whereas *Atah Konanta ʿOlam Me-Rosh* uses terms for historical figures and objects that would have been understood by literate ancient Jews, *Az be-ʾEn Kol* and *Azkir Gevurot* use metonymy (*kinnui*) at every opportunity, to the point of referring to water as "that which is measured in His hollow," based on Isa 40:12. In addition, the midrashic interpretations are integral to *Az be-ʾEn Kol* and other later compositions but not to the earlier poems such as *Atah Konanta*. For example, *Az be-ʾEn Kol* alludes to the legend that Jacob was born circumcised. This is based on a midrash that interprets the biblical description of him as *ish tam* (Gen 25:27) to mean that Jacob was a perfect man. Likewise, an entire section of that piyyut is based on the myth found in Genesis Rabbah that the Torah was the blueprint for the world.

POETRY AND HISTORY

The Avodah stands in a long history of Hebrew literature that portrays the saga of Israel and its heroes as precedents for later holy men. The most prominent example of this motif is the long section in praise of the ancestors in Ben Sira chapters 44–50. There, as in the Avodah piyyutim, the patriarchs, lawgivers, and progenitors of the priesthood are praised for their loyalty to God and assiduousness in building the nation's fundamental institutions. There too the sacred history culminates

---

1. On the earliest stages of piyyut, see Aaron Mirsky, "Gidre ha-Piyyut shel ha-Payetanim ʾAlume ha-Shem," *Peraqim* 1 (1969): 109–14; idem, "Ha-Shirah bi-Tequfat ha-Talmud," *Yerushalaim: Shenaton le-Divre Sifrut ve-Hagut* 3-4 (1970): 161–70; idem, *Maḥṣavtan shel ṣurot ha-Piyyut* (Jerusalem: Schocken, 1968–69); and idem, *Reshit ha-Piyyut* (Jerusalem: Ha-Sokhnut ha-Yehudit, 1965). On the development of the forms of piyyut in general, see Fleischer, *Shirat ha-Qodesh*.

CONCLUSION: THE AVODAH: POETRY, HISTORY, AND RITUAL

in the high priest's offering of the sacrifice on behalf of the people and emerging radiant from the divine presence.

Likewise the Avodah is organized according to the succession of ancestors. However, in this case the individual ideal figures are chosen unambiguously in keeping with the themes of Yom Kippur, especially the Temple cult and the theme of reward and punishment. From the standpoint of the holiday's drama of repentance and expiation, the story of humankind is the story of its moral failures and their rectification. At the same time, in the Avodah piyyutim, human history culminates in the chosen priest and the moment when he enters the holy of holies once a year to offer the incense that purifies Israel of its sins. We can see how selection of ideal figures reveals the author's conception of sacred history in the earliest full Avodah piyyut, *Atah Konanta ʿOlam Me-Rosh*. While its narrative begins with the creation of the earth, humanity is presented as the crown of this creation, created from the choice portions of the earth:

> Also from [the earth]
> You formed Adam
> and You caused his descendants to thrive
> like the sands of the sea.

The chain of tradition continues according to a pattern in which a moral hero is chosen after the failure of a generation. Thus, after the wicked generation of the Nephilim,

> Then there arose among them
> a small remnant:
> this is Noah
> whom You called "righteous."

After the flood (which is not described in *Atah Konanta*), the succession continues with Abraham:

> From his descendants You produced
> a pure and upright man:
> Abraham, who loved You
> with all his heart.

The divine plan seems on the brink of collapse with the binding of Isaac—a sacrifice that is not a sacrifice—but is set right with the birth of Jacob:

> From him You produced
> a beloved from the womb:
> this is Jacob
> whom You called firstborn.

From here the saga proceeds to the selection of Levi and Aaron, the progenitors of the priesthood.

Similar narratives of succession, known as chains of tradition, appear elsewhere in Jewish literature of the same period. The best-known example is the opening of the tractate Avot, known as the "Sayings of the Fathers." This tractate of the Mishnah, which constitutes a kind of rabbinic manifesto, presents a history of Torah whereby it is handed down from Moses at Sinai to the prophets, elders, "men of the great assembly," through a succession of Second-Temple sages, to the rabbis of the Mishnah's day.[2] In the Avodah, however, the chain of tradition emphasizes the cult and priesthood. *Atah Konanta* again serves as an excellent example. Its narration of the saga of Israel from Jacob's sons to the establishment of the cult omits Moses and proceeds directly to Levi and Aaron:

> You distinguished a treasure
> from among his children:
> this is Levi,
> the third from the womb.

---

2. Elie Bickerman, "La chaîne de la tradition pharisienne," *Revue biblique* (1952): 44–54, repr. in *Essays in Greco-Roman and Related Talmudic Literature*, ed. Henry A. Fischel (New York: Ktav, 1977), 127–37; Anthony Saldarini, "The End of the Rabbinic Chain of Tradition," *Journal of Biblical Literature* 93 (1974): 97–106; Steven D. Fraade, *From Tradition to Commentary: Torah and Its Interpretation in the Midrash Sifre to Deuteronomy* (Albany: State University of New York Press, 1991), 69–70; Henry A. Fischel, "The Uses of Sorites (*Climax, Gradatio*) in the Tannaitic Period," *Hebrew Union College Annual* 44 (1973): 119–51; Moshe David Herr, "Ha-Reṣef she-be-Shalshelet Mesiratah shel ha-Torah: Le-Verur ha-Historiografiyah ha-Miqra'it be-Hagutam shel Ḥazal," *Zion* 44 (1979): 43–56. On variations of this motif in early Jewish magical and mystical literature, see Swartz, *Scholastic Magic*, 173–99.

> You looked favorably
> on those who came forth from his loins:
> this is Aaron,
> the first holy man.

Aaron, not Moses, is given pride of place in the chain of transmission. The rest of the piyyut concerns the service performed by "one of [Aaron's] clan," who stands "in his place." The creation of earth, human prehistory, and Israel's patrimony therefore culminate in the selection of Aaron and the latter-day priests. The effect of this progression is to place the Temple and its priesthood at the center of all existence.

THE AVODAH AND THE HISTORY OF JUDAISM

Yet the Avodah piyyutim arose at a time in history in which the Temple was destroyed and priests did not in fact hold a central place in Jewish society and religion. These piyyutim were recited in the synagogue, that place known in rabbinic literature as the "smaller sanctuary." This paradox seems to have inspired the synagogue poets of late antiquity to create an epic literature in which the lost rituals are reconstructed in finely crafted words. By his use of the imagery of the Temple and his poetic skill, the poet sought to evoke in the listener a vivid sense of the experience of the high priest as he prepared for his role, carried out the sacrifice, entered the holy of holies, and emerged luminous with the splendor of his encounter with the divine.

The Avodah therefore stands as testimony to several features of Jewish society in Palestine in late antiquity that deserve the attention of historians and students of Judaism. It is testimony to the persistence of the prestige of the priesthood, even when rabbinic sources such as the Mishnah reveal a deep ambivalence toward the priests as a class. It also testifies to the persistence of the notion of sacrifice as an activity with deep resonance for a community whose main form of worship was verbal prayer. It attests as well to Israel's consciousness of its history as theologically and ritually meaningful. Overall, the Avodah piyyutim serve as fine examples of the literary creativity of the Jewish community of Byzantine times.

BIBLIOGRAPHY

Anderson, Gary A. "Celibacy or Consummation in the Garden? Reflections on Early Jewish and Christian Interpretations of the Garden of Eden." *Harvard Theological Review* 82 (1989): 121–48.
Bickerman, Elie. "La chane de la tradition pharisienne," *Revue biblique* (1952): 44–54. Repr. in *Essays in Greco-Roman and Related Talmudic Literature,* edited by Henry A. Fischel, 127–37. New York: Ktav, 1977.
Branham, Joan R. *Sacred Space in Ancient and Early Medieval Architecture.* Cambridge: Cambridge University Press, forthcoming.
———. "Vicarious Sacrality: Temple Space in Ancient Synagogues." In *Ancient Synagogues: Historical Analysis and Archaeological Discovery,* edited by Dan Urman and Paul V. M. Flesher, 2:319–45. Leiden: Brill, 1995.
Bronznick, Nahum M. "Li-Meqoro u-le-Horaʾato shel ha-Munaḥ Qefiṣat ha-Derekh." *Lešonénu* 37 (1972–73): 15–20.
———. Review of *Az be-'En Kol,* by Yahalom. *Lešonénu* 62 (1999): 145–58.
Buber, Solomon, ed. *Midrash Ekhah Rabbah.* Vilna, 1899.
———. ed. *Midrash Tanḥuma ʿal Ḥamishah Ḥumshe Torah.* Vilna: Rom, 1913.
Carmi T., ed. *The Penguin Book of Hebrew Verse.* New York: Penguin, 1981.
Charlesworth James H., ed. *Pseudepigrapha of the Old Testament.* 2 vols. Garden City, N.Y.: Doubleday, 1983.
Danby, Herbert. *The Mishnah Translated from the Hebrew with Introduction and Brief Explanatory Notes.* London: Oxford University Press, 1933; repr., 1974.
Davidson, I., S. Assaf, and B. I. Joel. *Siddur Rav Saʿadiah Gaʾon.* Jerusalem: Reuben Mass, 1985.
Dr. Einhorn's Olat Tamid: Book of Prayers for Jewish Congregations. N.p., 1921.

Elbogen, Ismar. *Jewish Liturgy: A Comprehensive History.* Translated by Raymond P. Scheindlin. Philadelphia: Jewish Publication Society; New York: Jewish Theological Seminary of America, 1993.

———. *Studien zur Geschichte des jüdischen Gottesdienstes.* Berlin: Mayer & Müller, 1907.

Elior, Rachel. "From Earthly Temple to Heavenly Shrines: Prayer and Sacred Song in the Hekhalot Literature and Its Relation to Temple Traditions." *Jewish Studies Quarterly* 4 (1997): 217–67.

Epstein, J. N. *Mavoʾ le-Nusaḥ ha-Mishnah.* 2 vols. Jerusalem: Magnes; Tel Aviv: Devir, 1964.

———. *Mevoʾot le-Sifrut ha-Tannaʾim.* Jerusalem: Magnes; Tel Aviv: Devir, 1957.

Eshel, Esther, Hanan Eshel, Carol Newsom, Bilhah Nitzan, Eileen Schuller, and Ada Yardeni. *Qumran Cave 4.: Poetical and Liturgical Texts, Part* . Discoveries in the Judaean Desert 11. Oxford: Clarendon Press, 1998.

Eshel, Hanan. "Shever Ketovet shel K-D Mishmerot ha-Kohanim mi-Naṣrat?" *Tarbiz* 61 (1991): 159–61.

Even-Shoshan, Abraham. *Ha-Milon he-Ḥadash.* Jerusalem: Kiryat Sefer, 1989.

Fine, Steven. "Art and the Liturgical Context of the Sepphoris Synagogue Mosaic." In Eric M. Meyers, *Galilee Through the Centuries: Confluence of Cultures,* 227–37. Winona Lake, Ind.: Eisenbrauns, 1999.

———. *This Holy Place: On the Sanctity of the Synagogue During the Greco-Roman Period.* Notre Dame, Ind.: Notre Dame University Press, 1997.

Finkelstein, Louis, ed. *Sifre ʿal Sefer Devarim.* New York: Jewish Theological Seminary of America, 1969.

Fischel, Henry A. "The Uses of Sorites (*Climax, Gradatio*) in the Tannaitic Period." *Hebrew Union College Annual* 44 (1973): 119–51.

Fleischer, Ezra. *Shirat ha-Qodesh Ha-ʿIvrit Bi-Yeme ha-Benayim.* Jerusalem: Keter, 1975.

———. "ʿIyyunim be-Hashpaʿat ha-Yesodot ha-Maqhelatiyim ʿal ʿIṣuvam ve-Hitpatḥutam shel Suge ha-Piyyuṭ." *Yuval* 3 (1974): 18–48.

Fraade, Steven D. *From Tradition to Commentary: Torah and Its Interpretation in the Midrash Sifre to Deuteronomy.* Albany: State University of New York Press, 1991.
Genack, Yakov. "Miṣvat Sukkah ba-Halakhah shel Ḥazal: Ben Bayit le-Miqdash." *Daat* 42 (1999): 283–98.
Ginzberg, Louis. *The Legends of the Jews.* 7 vols. Philadelphia: Jewish Publication Society, 1909–38.
Glatzer, Nahum N. "Franz Rosenzweig: The Story of a Conversion." *Judaism* 1 (1952): 69–79.
Goitein, S. D. *A Mediterranean Society: The Jewish Communities of the Arab World as Portrayed in the Documents of the Cairo Geniza.* 5 vols. Berkeley and Los Angeles: University of California Press, 1967–89.
———. *Sidre Ḥinukh.* Jerusalem: Hebrew University Press, 1962.
Goldschmidt, Daniel. *Seder ha-Qinot le-Tishʿah be-Av.* Jerusalem: Mossad Harav Kook, 1968.
———. ed. *Maḥazor le-Yamim Noraʾim (Ashkenaz).* 2 vols. Jerusalem: Mosad Bialik, 1970.
———. ed. *Maḥazor Sukkot, Shemini ʿAṣeret, ve-Simḥat Torah.* Jerusalem: Koren, 1981.
Goldstein, Naftali. "Avodat ha-Qorbanot be-Hagut Ḥazal she-le-Aḥar Ḥurban Bet ha-Miqdash." *Daat* 8 (1982): 29–51.
Gruenwald, Ithamar. "Meqoman shel Masorot Kohaniot be-Yeṣiratah shel ha-Misṭiqah shel ha-Merkavah ve-shel Shiʿur Qomah." *Meḥqere Yerushalayim be-Maḥshevet Yisraʾel* 6 (1987): 65–120.
Haberman, A. M. "*Sefer Qerovah.*" *Yediʿot ha-Makhon le-Madaʿe ha-Yahadut* 3 (1927): 91–132.
Hayward, C. T. R. *The Jewish Temple: A Non-Biblical Sourcebook.* London: Routledge, 1996.
Heinemann, Joseph. "ʿAl Defus Piyyuti Qadum." *Bar Ilan* 4–5 (1977): 132–37.
———. *Prayer in the Talmud: Forms and Patterns.* Berlin: De Gruyter, 1977.
———. "Qedushah u-Malkhut bi-Qeriʾat Shemaʿ de-ʿAmidah." In *Shai le-Heman: Meḥqarim li-Khevod A.M. Haberman,* 107–17. Jerusalem: Reuben Mass, 1977. Repr. in Joseph Heinemann, *ʿIyyune Tefilah,* edited by Avigdor Shinan, 12–21. Jerusalem: Magnes, 1981.

Herr, Moshe David. "Ha-Reṣef she-be-Shalshelet Mesiratah shel ha-Torah: Le-Verur ha-Historiografiyah ha-Miqra'it be-Hagutam shel Ḥazal." *Zion* 44 (1979): 43–56.
Himmelfarb, Martha. *Ascent to Heaven in Jewish and Christian Apocalypses.* New York: Oxford University Press, 1993.
Hoffman, Lawrence A. *Beyond the Text: A Holistic Approach to Liturgy.* Bloomington: Indiana University Press, 1987.
———. *The Canonization of the Synagogue Service.* Notre Dame, Ind.: Notre Dame University Press, 1979.
Horovitz, H. S., ed. *Sifre De-Ve-Rav.* Jerusalem: Wahrman, 1966.
Idel, Moshe. "Tefisat ha-Torah be-Sifrut ha-Hekhalot ve-Gilguleha ba-Qabbalah." *Meḥqere Yerushalayim be-Maḥshevet Yisrael* 1 (1981–82): 23–84.
Jaffee, Martin S. "Writing and Rabbinic Oral Tradition: On Mishnaic Narrative, Lists, and Mnemonics." *Journal of Jewish Thought and Philosophy* 4 (1994): 123–46.
Kahle, Paul. *Masoreten des Westens.* Stuttgart: Kohlhammer, 1927.
Klein, Earl, ed. and trans. *Ḥazon Yeḥezkel: A Prayerbook for Yom Kippur According to the Oriental Sephardic Rite.* Los Angeles: Kahal Joseph Sephardic Congregation, 1994.
Knohl, Yisrael, and Shlomo Naeh. "Milu'im ve-Khippurim." *Tarbiz* 62 (1992): 17–44.
Kook, S. H. "Godel ha-Torah ve Yaḥasah le-Godel ha-ʿOlam." *Iyyunim u-Meḥqarim* (Jerusalem, 1967): 108–19.
Levine, Baruch A. *In the Presence of the Lord.* Leiden: Brill, 1974.
———. *The JPS Torah Commentary: Leviticus.* Philadelphia: Jewish Publication Society, 1989.
———. "The Presence of God in Biblical Religion." In *Religions in Antiquity: Essays in Memory of E. R. Goodenough,* edited by Jacob Neusner, 71–87. Leiden: Brill, 1968.
Lieberman, Saul. *Tosefta Kifshutah.* 10 vols. New York: Jewish Theological Seminary of America, 1955–88.
Lieberman, Saul. "Some Notes on Adjurations in Israel." In *Texts and Studies,* 21–28. New York: Ktav, 1974.
Luzatto, Samuel David. *Mavo' le-Maḥazor Bene Roma.* Edited by Daniel Goldschmidt. Tel Aviv: Devir, 1966.
Maḥzor ha-Miqdash. Jerusalem: Temple Institute, 1995–97.

Maier, Johann. *Vom Kultus zum Gnosis: Bundeslade, Gottesthrone und Märkābāh.* Salzburg: Otto Müller, 1964.
Malachi, Zvi. *Be-Noʿam Siaḥ: Peraqim mi-Toldot Sifrutenu.* Lod: Haberman Institute for Literary Research, 1983.

———. *Ha-"ʾAvodah" le-Yom ha-Kippurim—ʾOfiyah, Toledoteha ve-hitpatḥuta ba-Shirah ha-ʿIvrit.* 2 vols. Ph.D. diss., Hebrew University, 1974.

———. "Makkin Lefanav be-ʿEṣbaʿ Ṣeradah: Neʿima ba-Peh ve-Lo ba-Kinor." *Sidra* 2 (1986): 67–75.

Mandelbaum, Bernard, ed. *Pesikta de-Rav Kahana.* New York: Jewish Theological Seminary of America, 1962.

Midrash Tanḥuma ʿal Ḥamishah Ḥumshe Torah. Jerusalem: Levin-Epstein, 1964.

Miller, Stuart S. "The Rabbis and the Non-Existent Monolithic Synagogue." In *Jews, Christians, and Polytheists in the Ancient Synagogue: Cultural Interaction During the Greco-Roman Period,* edited by Steven Fine, 57–70. London: Routledge, 1999.

———. *Studies in the History and Traditions of Sepphoris.* Leiden: Brill, 1984.

Mirsky, Aaron. "Gidere ha-Piyyut shel ha-Payetanim ʿAlume ha-Shem." *Peraqim* 1 (1969): 109–14.

———. "Ha-Shirah bi-Tequfat ha-Talmud." *Yerushalaim: Shenaton le-Divre Sifrut ve-Hagut* 3–4 (1970): 161–70.

———. *Maḥṣavtan shel Ṣurot ha-Piyyut.* Jerusalem: Schocken, 1968–69.

———. *Piyyute Yose ben Yose.* 2nd ed. Jerusalem: Mosad Bialik, 1991.

———. *Reshit ha-Piyyut.* Jerusalem: Ha-Sokhnut ha-Yehudit, 1965.

Neusner, Jacob. *The Mishnah: A New Translation.* New Haven: Yale University Press, 1988.

Newsom, Carol. *Songs of the Sabbath Sacrifice: A Critical Edition.* Atlanta: Scholars Press, 1985).

Nitzan, Bilhah. *Qumran Prayer and Religious Poetry.* Leiden: Brill, 1994.

Petuchowski, Jakob J. "The Liturgy of the Synagogue: History, Structure, and Contents." In *Approaches to Ancient Judaism,* edited by William S. Green, 4:1–64. Chico, Calif.: Scholars Press, 1983.

———. *Prayerbook Reform in Europe: The Liturgy of European Liberal and Reform Judaism.* New York: World Union for Progressive Judaism, 1968.

Rabbinowitz, Zvi M. *Maḥazor Piyyute Rabbi Yannai la-Torah u-Moʿadim.* Jerusalem: Mosad Bialik, 1985.

Roberts, Michael. *The Jeweled Style: Poetry and Poetics in Late Antiquity.* Ithaca: Cornell University Press, 1989.

Roth, Cecil. "Ecclesiasticus in the Synagogue Service." *Journal of Biblical Literature* 71 (1952): 171–78.

Saldarini, Anthony. "The End of the Rabbinic Chain of Tradition." *Journal of Biblical Literature* 93 (1974): 97–106.

Schäfer, Peter. *Synopse zur Hekhalot-Literatur.* Tübingen: Mohr, 1981.

Schechter, Solomon, ed. *Avot de-Rabbi Natan.* London, Vienna, and New York, 1887.

Schirmann, Jefim. "The Battle Between Behemoth and Leviathan According to an Ancient Hebrew Piyyut." *Proceedings of the Israel Academy of Sciences and Humanities* 4 (1969–70): 327–69.

Schmeltzer, Menahem H. "How Was the High Priest Kept Awake on the Night of Yom ha-Kippurim?" In *Saul Lieberman (1898-1983), Talmudic Scholar,* edited by Meir Lubetski, 59–70. Lewiston, N.Y.: Edwin Mellen, 2002.

Schwartz, Seth. *Josephus and Judaean Politics.* Leiden: Brill, 1990.

Seder Rav Amram Gaon. Edited by Daniel Goldschmidt. Jerusalem: Mossad Harav Kook, 1971.

Segal, Moshe Zvi. *Sefer Ben Sira ha-Shalem.* Jerusalem: Mosad Bialik, 1976.

Skehan, Patrick W., and Alexander A. Di Lella. *The Wisdom of Ben Sira: A New Translation with Notes.* New York: Anchor Bible Doubleday, 1987.

Sky, Hyman I. *Redevelopment of the Office of Hazzan Through the Talmudic Period.* San Francisco: Mellen Research University Press, 1992.

Sokoloff, Michael. *A Dictionary of Jewish Palestinian Aramaic.* Ramat Gan: Bar Ilan University Press, 1990.

Sperber, Daniel. "Meḥqarim be-Milim ve-Girseʾotehen." *Teʿudah* 7 (1991): 149–53.

Stemberger, Günter. *Introduction to the Talmud and Midrash.* Translated and edited by Markus Bockmuehl. Edinburgh: T. & T. Clark, 1996.

Stone, Michael E. *A Commentary on the Fourth Book of Ezra.* Minneapolis: Augsburg Fortress, 1990.

Swartz, Michael D. *Mystical Prayer in Ancient Judaism: An Analysis of Maʿaseh Merkavah.* Tübingen: Mohr, 1992.

———. "Ritual About Myth About Ritual: Toward an Understanding of the *Avodah* in the Rabbinic Period." *Journal of Jewish Thought and Philosophy* 6 (1997): 135–55.

———. "Sacrificial Themes in Jewish Magic." In *Magic and Ritual in the Ancient World,* edited by Marvin Meyer and Paul Mirecki, 303–15. Leiden: Brill, 2002.

———. "Sage, Priest, and Poet: Typologies of Leadership in the Ancient Synagogue." In *Jews, Christians, and Polytheists in the Ancient Synagogue: Cultural Interaction During the Greco-Roman Period,* edited by Steven Fine, 101–17. London: Routledge, 1999.

———. *Scholastic Magic: Ritual and Revelation in Early Jewish Mysticism.* Princeton: Princeton University Press, 1996.

Theodor, Julius, and Albeck, Chanoch, eds. *Midrash Bereshit Rabbah.* 3 vols. 2nd ed. Jerusalem: Wahrman, 1965.

Trachtenberg, Joshua. *Jewish Magic and Superstition: A Study in Folk Religion.* New York: Atheneum, 1982.

The Union Prayer-Book for Jewish Worship. 2 vols. New York: Central Conference of American Rabbis, 1906.

Urbach, Ephraim. "Seride Tanḥuma-Yelamedenu." *Qoveṣ ʿal Yad,* n.s., 6 (1966): 1–54.

Weinfeld, Moshe. "ʿIqvot shel Qedushat ha-Yoṣer u-Fesuqe de-Zimra bi-Megilot Midbar Yehudah u-ve-Sefer Ben Sirah." *Tarbiz* 45 (1976): 15–26.

Weiss, J. H., ed. *Sifra de-Be Rav.* Vienna: Schlossberg, 1862.

Weiss, Zeʾev, and Ehud Netzer. *Promise and Redemption: A Synagogue Mosaic from Sepphoris.* Jerusalem: Israel Museum, 1996.

Yahalom, Joseph. *Az be-ʾEn Kol: Seder ha-ʿAvodah ha-Ereṣ-Yisreʾeli ha-Qadum le-Yom ha-Kippurim.* Jerusalem: Magnes, 1996.

———. *Maḥzor Ereṣ Yisrael: Qodeqs ha-Genizah.* Jerusalem: Magnes, 1987.

———. *Piyyut u-Meṣiʿut be-Shilhe ha-Zeman ha-ʿAtiq.* Tel Aviv: Hakibbutz Hameuchad, 1999.

———. "The Temple and the City in Liturgical Hebrew Poetry." In *The History of Jerusalem: The Early Muslim period, 638–1099,* edited by Joshua Prawer and Haggai Ben-Shammai, 270–94. Jerusalem: Yad Izhak Ben-Zvi; New York: New York University Press, 1996.

Yavetz, Ze'ev. "Ha-Piyyutim ha-Rishonim." In *Festschrift zum siebzigsten Geburtstage David Hoffman's,* edited by Simon Eppenstein, Meier Hildesheimer, and Joseph Wohlgemuth, 69–70 [Hebrew section]. Berlin: Lamm, 1914.

Yehudah Al-arizi. *Taḥkemoni.* Edited by Y. Toporowski. Jerusalem: Mossad Harav Kook, 1952.

Zeidman, A. "Matbeaʿ Seder ha-ʿAvodah Le-Yom ha-Kippurim." *Sinai* 13 (1944): 173–82, 255–62.

Zohar, Zvi. "U-Mi Metaher ʾEtkhem—ʾAvikhem ba-Shamayim: Tefilat Seder ha-ʿAvodah shel Yom ha-Kippurim: Tokhen, Tifqud u-Mashmaʿut." *Association for Jewish Studies Review* 14 (1989): 1–28 [Hebrew section].

Zulay, Menahem. *ʾEretz Yisrael u-Fiyuṭeha: Meḥqarim be-Fiyute ha-Genizah.* Jerusalem: Magnes, 1995.

GLOSSARY

Avodah: Literally "service," the sacrificial procedure in the Temple. In Jewish liturgy, the prayer service recited at Yom Kippur describing the sacrifice for the Day of Atonement as described in Leviticus 16.

Azazel: According to Rabbinic interpretation of Leviticus 16:8–10, the precipice in the wilderness from which the scapegoat was cast. Also identified as oq.

Ḥataʾat: The purification ceremony or "sin-offering" described in Leviticus 16.

Ḥazan: A synagogue official who in antiquity served as a prayer leader, composer of piyyut, or schoolteacher.

Kinnui: Metonymy; a poetic device used in piyyut whereby a word or phrase, often based on a biblical verse, stands for another.

Midrash: Rabbinic interpretation of the Bible.

Minḥah: A sacrificial offering (see Genesis 4:3–5), especially a grain offering (Leviticus 2:1–16).

Payetan: A composer and performer of piyyut.

Piyyut: Hebrew and Aramaic liturgical poetry, which began in the first centuries of the Common Era and flourished in Palestinian synagogues from the third to eighth centuries C.E.

Shamir: An extremely hard stone, or perhaps a living creature, which was used to hew stone in the Temple and engrave the names on the stones of the High Priest's breastpiece according to rabbinic legends.

Tamid: The daily sacrificial offering as described in Exodus 29:38–42 and Numbers 28:1–8.

SOURCE INDEX

Biblical and rabbinic sources are listed in Jewish canonical order. Other ancient and medieval sources are listed in alphabetical order.

Bible

Gen
- 1:1, 27, 34
- 1:2, 112
- 2, 132
- 3:15, 142
- 3:19, 145
- 3:24, 145
- 4:7, 146
- 4:8, 147
- 4:9, 148
- 4:11, 149
- 6:4, 150
- 6:9, 240
- 8:1, 150
- 8:20, 241
- 11:4, 159
- 12:1, 163
- 14:9, 244
- 15:5, 46, 118, 162
- 15:8, 162
- 15:13–16, 164
- 17:5, 165
- 17:21–23, 172
- 18:25–32, 244
- 19:4–5, 164
- 21:33, 244
- 22:14, 306
- 25:27, 71, 180, 183, 368
- 27:46, 152
- 28:22, 171
- 30:39, 247
- 49:3, 182
- 49:14, 182
- 49:19, 184
- 49:20, 184
- 49:26, 184

Exod
- 4:10–11, 12
- 15:2, 122
- 28:32, 265
- 28:41, 175
- 29:10–14, 6
- 29:39, 6
- 31:17, 130

Lev, p. 88
- 2:4, 358
- 6:13, 78
- 6:14, 363
- 8, 346
- 8:30, 311
- 8:34, 174, 254, 311
- 8:35, 253, 310
- 16, 13, 24, 41, 88
- 16:1–34, 16
- 16:3, 48, 58
- 16:7–9, 60
- 16:10, 60
- 16:12, 62
- 16:16, 281
- 16:18, 66
- 16:22, 60
- 16:30, 58, 62, 66, 82, 206, 215
- 19:18, 147
- 21:10, 34, 323
- 23:26–32, 16
- 24:5–6, 360

Num
- 3:36, 248
- 5, 263
- 5:11–29, 318
- 5:18, 263
- 15:38, 344
- 16, 310
- 16:2, 252
- 17, 178
- 18, 194
- 20:10, 173
- 21:4–9, 301
- 25:1, 316
- 28:7, 359
- 29:7, 88
- 29:7–11, 16

Deut
- 3:5, 227
- 9:25–26, 345
- 12:30, 299
- 18:2, 195
- 26, 6

Josh
33:12, 185
33:19, 183
33:23, 184

Josh
7, 172
10:12, 229
10:12–13, 298
19:47, 183

Judg
5:20–22, 118

2 Sam
17:8, 86

1 Kgs
17:2–6, 109
22:34, 268

2 Kgs
2:8, 114

Isa
1:18, 182, 207, 288
5:2, 239, 358
5:7, 307
5:14, 192
10:6, 356
11:15, 115
17:11, 238
18:18, 259
20:26, 226
20:26, 227
22:2, 258
27:1, 32, 33, 108, 229, 296
28:1, 270
30:33, 295
34:4, 235, 300
35:7, 98
37:1, 122
38:1–8, 118
40:3, 36, 178
40:7, 362
40:12, 116, 174, 250, 298
40:13, 102, 142
40:14, 102
40:26, 162, 185
40:6, 190
41:2, 28
44:13, 151
46:7, 161
54:12, 99
56:2, 132
58:12, 352
59:17, 36, 179
64:9, 241
75:9, 238

Jer
3:3, 319
5:22, 304
12:7, 208
17:9, 146
17:10, 146
31:21, 339

Ezek
1, 98
1:7, 99
1:28, 344
3:12, 99
9:2, 98
11:19, 356
13:11, 128
16:8, 250
22:30, 352
23:14–15, 264
28:13, 132
28:14, 136

Hos
11:4, 180
14:3, 5

Joel
2:10, 118
2:17, 204

Amos 1:11, 236

Hab
3:1, 156, 156
3:3, 205

Zech 3:5, 344

Mal
2:7, 37, 174
3:20, 119

Ps
8:2, 170
8:5, 131, 168
16:5, 195
18:13–16, 108
19:6, 200
19:8, 110
19:13, 209
27:5, 304
49:13, 231
49:21, 144
50:2, 12, 201
51:21, 354
62:0, 136
68:5, 151
68:13, 310
68:14, 181
68:19, 310
91:1, 8, 126, 292

SOURCE INDEX

Prov

103:15, 150
104:2, 105
104:7, 107
104:19, 120
104:24, 128
104:31, 128
114:3, 114
119:92, 313
121:5, 247
129:3, 130
132:13, 350
133:1, 312
136:6, 162
138:6, 302
139:15, 133
139:15–16, 298
140:12, 138
144:15, 92, 289
145:17, 142
147:4, 120

1:9, 72
3:16, 104
4:2, 258
7:26, 234
8:22, 27
8:28, 110
8:30, 174, 224
10:12, 160
13:11, 274
16:29, 138
19:13, 141
24:31, 160
28:10, 138

Job

7:4, 258
9:13, 99
9:26, 99
10:3, 70
11:9, 26, 104
10:10, 109
11:20, 152
21:14, 240
24:15, 148
28:9, 167
33:6, 109
33:24, 307
34:10, 166
34:11, 166
35:10, 200
38:10, 107
38:16, 107
40:29, 123

41:17, 125

Song

1:12, 359
1:13, 358
3:6, 358
3:9, 357
4:3, 178
4:8–9, 356
4:12, 316
5:3, 176
5:10, 198, 232, 319, 357
6:9, 217
7:2, 36, 177, 316
7:6, 178

Lam

1:1, 315
2:13, 188
3:17, 364
3:44, 365
3:53, 356
5:13, 361

Eccl

7:26, 139
10:8, 234
36:26, 140

Dan

7:9–10, 97
7:10, 98
7:19, 187
8:22, 181
10:6, 99

Neh 9:6, 128
2 Chr 26:16–21, 252

Apocrypha, Pseudepigrapha, and Hellenistic Jewish Literature

2 Baruch
    29:4, 33
    56:6, 28
Apocalypse of Abraham 7, 27
Ben Sira (Ecclesiasticus), p. 17
    44–50, 368
    50:7, 344
1 Enoch 60:24, 33
4 Ezra 6:49, 33
Josephus
    Antiquities 3.7–5, 267
    Jubilees 3:2–5a, 6 , 28; 50:8, 29
Philo
    On the Virtues 62, 27
    On Drunkenness, 27

Dead Sea Scrolls

Serekh ha-Berakhot
    25:5, 37
1Q28b 4/25–26, 37

Mishnah

Bikkurim 3:5, 6
Pesaḥim, p. 16
Sheqalim 5:1, 256
Yoma, pp. 16, 24–25, 41
    1:1, 18
    1:2, 312
    1:5, 25
    1:6, 199
    2:2, 18, 259, 315
    3:1, 201
    3:3, 18
    3:9, 273
    4:3, 277
    5:1, 75
    5:2, 279, 330
    6:4, 275
    6:7, 88
    6:8, 275, 334
    7:1, 16, 216, 283, 335, 336
    7:4, 216
Sota 10:3–5, 153
Avot 4:2, 299
Menaḥot 7:1, 363
Tamid, p. 16
    3:3–4, 57
    7:3, 57
Middot 1:4, 273
Negaʿim, p. 156
Parah, p. 16
    3:1, 311

Tosefta

Kippurim
    1:6, 34
    2:1, 65
    2:14, 201
    2:15, 12

Palestinian Talmud

Berakhot 4:1 (7a), 5
Erubin 5:1 (22c), 272
Yoma
    1:1 (38c), 311
    1:7 (39b), 314
    3:6 (40c), 262
    5:1 (42b), 278
    5:3 (42c), 64, 65, 279
    5:6 (42b), 10
    1:3 (39a), 34
Ḥagigah 2:1 (77a), 106
Sotah 7:4 (21d), 320

Babylonian Talmud

Shabbat
    99a, 105
    104a, 12
Eruvin 18b, 200
Pesaḥim 118a, 307
Yoma
    4a, 311
    36b, 16, 53
    53b, 65
    54a, 278
    56b, 16, 53
Megillah 31b, 5
Taanit 2a, 5
Sotah 48b, 320
Bava Batra
    60b, 4
    74b, 33
Sanhedrin 19b, 197
Menaḥot 110a, 5
Ḥullin 138a, 321
Niddah 13b, 262

Midrash

Gen Rabbah
    1:1, [27], 30, 224, 311
    3:7, 225
    8:10, 135
    9:2, 225
    5:4, 114
    19:3, 28
    31:7, 156
    31:12, 155
    32:5, 154
    32:7, 155
    38:13, 306
    38:28, 27

42:15, 28
84:8, 262
98:12, 182
98:20, 185
99:10, 182
Exod Rabbah
   15:22, 296
Lev Rabbah
   1:2, 33
   20:4, 279
Num Rabbah 21:18, 33
Sifra
   Aḥare Mot 2, 58
   Aḥare Mot 3:6, 276
   Aḥare Mot 3:12, 280
   Aḥare Mot 6:7, 285
   Ṣav 2:1, 262
Sifre Num 119, 194
Sifre Deut
   Eqev 43:16, 45
Tanḥuma
   Bereshit 1, 26
   Bereshit 9, 149
   Ḥaye Sarah 3, 107
   Ṣav 14 , 5
   Shemini 7, 33
   Suqqat 12, 301
Seride Tanḥuma-Yelamdenu, p. 34
Pesiqta de-Rav Kahana
   13, 202
   13:11, 4
   24, 5
Midrash Ekhah
   Petiḥta 25, 4
Avot de-Rabbi Natan
   A 2, 73
   A 4, 5
   B 8, 5
Midrash Tannaim
   Deut 11:13, 5
Midrash Tehillim
   66, 5
   90:7, 157

Pirqe de-Rabbi Eliezer
   3, 110
   6, 118
   9, 108
   14, 300
   12, 137
   37, 171
   41, 37

Targum

Pseudo-Jonathan
   Gen 1:21, 33

Hekhalot and Related Texts

(cited according to Schäfer, *Synopse zur Hekhalot-Literatur*)

3 Enoch
   °50, °916, 98
Seder Rabbah deBereshit
   °181, 102

Piyyut and liturgy

Atah Barata, 3, 367
Atah Konanta Olam me-Rosh, 367, 367, 369–71
Az be-ʾEn Kol, 3, 221, 230, 368
Az Hayetah (Eleazar ha-Qallir), 350
Azkir Gevurot, 3, 291, 303, 368
Shiʿvat Yamim, 3, 324

Medieval Sources

Ibn Ezra, commentary to Eccl 5:1, 12
Rashi, commentary to b. Yoma 36b, 5
Rashi, commentary to Exod 28:41, 175
Siddur Rav Saʿadiah Gaʾon, 69, 221

SUBJECT INDEX

Aaron, 74, 76, 174, 178, 194, 248, 250, 310, 367, 370–71
Abraham, 44–46, 72, 160–70, 242–46, 304–6, 369
Adam, 28–29, 33, 44, 106, 108, 144, 369
Adam and Eve, 28–29, 132–42, 144–50, 232–35, 298–302, 368
Angels, 36–38, 43, 48, 96, 98, 102, 124, 132, 136, 168, 170, 178, 246, 250, 344
Apocrypha, 28–29, 95, 343. *See also* source index
Avodah
 controversies surrounding, 2, 26
 history of, 15–20, 367–68
 in the liturgy, 1, 19–20, 21–22, 69, 95, 291
 literary techniques in, 20–24
 significance of, 1–3
 sources used in, 24–30
 themes in, 30–39
 use of ideal figures in, 369–71
Azazel, 60, 62, 82, 206, 274

Behemoth, 31–32, 124

Cairo Genizah, 2
Cain and Abel, 144–50, 156, 236–38, 302
Confession, 16–17, 21–22, 39, 58, 60–62, 66, 80, 82, 88, 204–6, 208, 214, 274–75, 282, 324, 326, 332–34
Creation, 18, 21, 26–27, 30–34, 44, 102–28, 224–30, 292–98, 367, 369
 of humanity, 124–28, 132–136, 296–98

David, 302, 356
Dead Sea Scrolls, 2. *See also* source index

Eschatology, 31, 33
Eden, 29, 70, 136–38, 228, 234, 298
Eleazar ben Qallir, 11–12, 15, 19, 95, 368
Elijah, 114, 230, 298
Eve, 29, 126, 134–35, 138–40, 142, 234, 298, 300–302

Flood, 152–60, 240, 304, 369

Gehenna, 226, 244–45
God
 created humankind to praise Him, 33–34
 presence of, 3, 5,118, 170, 222–24. *See also* Shekhinah
 praise of, 21, 96, 126, 222–24

Ḥataʾat, 208
Ḥazan, 7, 9–10
High priest, 3, 4, 24–25, 34–39, 69, 176–92, 200, 260–88, 310–39, 343, 344–46, 350, 362, 369
 glorification of, 34–39, 367
 wife of, 196, 254

Isaac, 6, 168–70, 224–46, 370
Ishmael, 168
Israel, 43, 72, 114, 130, 176, 188, 224, 286, 306, 338, 356, 358, 362, 364,

Jacob, 46, 72, 170, 180, 246–48, 298, 308, 368
Jerusalem, 56, 314, 362
"Jeweled style," 11, 12
Jonah, 108, 114, 228
Joseph, 176, 316
Joshua, 114, 118, 228, 298,

Kinnui. *See* Metonymy

Levi, 21, 48, 74, 182, 246, 308, 370
Leviathan, 31–32, 108, 122, 291

Messiah, 196
Metonymy, 11, 40, 95
Midrash, 2, 12, 26–30, 33–34, 96, 176, 256, 312
Minḥah, 146, 254, 353
Mishnah, 16, 24–26, 53, 69, 282, 370
Moses, 12, 36, 114, 116, 174, 194, 226, 248, 250, 252, 298, 308, 344, 367, 370

Noah, 44, 70, 152, 156, 240, 304, 369

Piyyut, 1–2, 10, 11–15, 19, 176
 meter and rhythm in, 39–40
Priests, priesthood, 9, 10, 14–15, 38, 72, 310, 314. See also High priest
Poets, 10, 11–15
Payetan. *See* Poets
Pharisees, 24–25

Rabbis, 2, 3, 5, 7, 9, 10. *See also* Sages

Sacrifice, 1, 3, 4, 5, 30, 39, 146, 158, 312, 350, 368, 371
Sabbath, 29, 128-32, 254
Sages, 9, 21, 24-25, 198, 256. *See also* Rabbis
Sarah, 168
Scapegoat, 206, 214-16, 274 282, 286, 326, 322-34, 338-40
Sepphoris, 6-7, 14
Shekhinah, 4, 118, 178, 212. *See also* God, presence of
Snake, 138, 142, 234, 300
Synagogue, 5-10, 13, 14, 371

Tamid, 17, 56-58, 200, 270, 284, 338
Temple, 1, 2, 3, 4-5, 6, 12, 30, 224, 352, 354, 360, 364, 371

Torah, 3, 26-27, 95, 102-4, 110, 158, 224, 256, 310, 368
Tower of Babel, 156-60, 304
Translation, 39-40, 349
Twelve tribes, 82-86

Urim and Thummim, 192, 260, 322, 350

Vestments, 35-36, 48, 74, 78-80, 90, 92, 176-92, 200, 260-70, 316-22, 334, 336

Yom Kippur, 1, 15, 16, 18, 48, 54, 89, 169, 196, 214, 282, 316, 336, 349
Yose ben Yose, 3, 11, 12, 15, 18-19, 31, 34, 35, 95, 221, 291, 349

Zion, 200, 362

www.ingramcontent.com/pod-product-compliance
Lightning Source LLC
Chambersburg PA
CBHW021929290426
44108CB00012B/777